/

The
Blue Sea
Cookbook

The Blue Sea Cookbook

by

SARAH D. ALBERSON

Edited by Eleanor Porter
Illustrated by Sidnee Neale

HASTINGS HOUSE, PUBLISHERS
New York

ACKNOWLEDGMENTS

To: Eleanor Porter, who did a magnificent job of editing; the United States Department of the Interior, Bureau of Commercial Fisheries, Fish and Wildlife Service, for the use of charts, technical and other information; Ball Brothers Company, Inc., Muncie, Indiana, for canning information in the *Ball Blue Book;* Charm-glow Gas Outdoor Grill Products, Antioch, Ill. for use of information in their *Wonderful World of Outdoor Cooking.*

Copyright © 1968 by Sarah D. Alberson

Published simultaneously in Canada
by Saunders, of Toronto, Ltd., Don Mills, Ontario

Printed in the United States of America

Contents

*To my husband, Haynes Christopher Alberson,
without whose love, understanding and help
my task would have been much harder.*

Introduction

WHY YOU SHOULD EAT SEAFOODS

ALMOST EVERYONE enjoys fish and shellfish because of their varied flavors. They can be prepared in many different ways, pleasing the most delicate appetite. Besides taste appeal, aquatic foods are good natural sources of calcium, phosphorus, iron and copper, and they provide protein of unexcelled quality. Some species also furnish vitamins. Sea fish are rich in iodine.

PROTEINS—Seafoods are an important source of proteins, which must be included in the diet to provide the elements needed for growth and the repair of body tissues. Protein is the basis of all diets for man and animals. It is necessary for normal growth and maintenance of life. Proteins are really little building blocks known as amino acids. The food value of different proteins depends on the variety and content of these amino acids. Some proteins are incomplete and must be supplemented with other protein foods if the body is to remain in normal health. Fish proteins are complete in that they contain *all* of the amino acids required for the upkeep and growth of the body. Fish proteins are easily digested and they are superior to most vegetable proteins and equal to most meat proteins.

MINERALS—Seafoods are also an excellent source of most of the minerals needed for proper development and for the body to perform its functions. Calcium and phosphorus for the proper development of bones and teeth oc-

11

cur in fish in about the same quantities as in beef. Marine fishes are especially rich sources of iodine, required for the proper functioning of the thyroid gland, containing fifty to 200 times as much of this essential element as any other food. Oysters, shrimp, and crabmeat provide half as much calcium, five times as much magnesium and slightly more phosphorus than milk. Iron and copper, which build up the hemoglobin content of the blood and prevent or remedy nutritional anemia, are easily obtained by eating more fish. Oysters and shrimp are the best known sources of these two minerals. Sulphur, as a constituent of cystine, one of the essential amino acids in proteins, is important for body growth.

VITAMINS—Although fish-liver oils have long been recognized as first-class sources of vitamins A and D, it is less widely known that the flesh of fish is also a source of several other vitamins. The absence of any one of the vitamins results in a so-called "deficiency disease." A deficiency of vitamin A causes an eye disease, a lack of vitamin B is evidenced in beriberi, scurvy is caused by the absence of vitamin C, insufficient vitamin D brings about rickets, and pellagra results from the absence of vitamin G.

On the average, daily vitamin requirements can be obtained from ordinary serving portions of fish as follows: vitamin A, 10 percent; vitamin D, more than adequate amounts; thiamine (vitamin B_1), 15 percent; riboflavin (vitamin B_2), and nicotinic acid, niacin (another element of the vitamin B complex), 70 percent.

FATS—The body needs fats for heat and energy. The fat content of fish varies from 1 to 20 percent by weight, depending on the species of fish and the season of the year. The fat content of most fish and shellfish compared with the fat content of most meat, eggs and milk—other complete-protein foods—is low. Fish fats are relatively rich sources of the polyunsaturated fatty acids, making fish and shellfish especially adaptable and useful in your diet (See FISH OILS AND FATS).

Research conducted by the Hormel Institute of the University of Minnesota under contract with the Bureau of Commercial Fisheries proved conclusively that the "unsaturated" or soft fats found in fish will reduce blood serum cholesterol levels when they are included in the diet. A "saturated" or hard fat congeals at low temperature while an "unsaturated" fat does not congeal readily. It is this property which permits oil-laden fish to move freely in water of low temperatures. The generous use, then, of fish in the diet will provide not only the vital protein and energy needed by the body, but will also encourage better health for the family by diminishing the possibility of circulatory diseases such as arteriosclerosis.

COMPOSITION AND VITAMIN CONTENT
IN EDIBLE PORTION OF A POUND OF
SALMON, BEEF, OR CHICKEN (approximate)

Component		Fresh			Canned		
		SALMON	BEEF, ROAST	CHICKEN, ROASTER	SALMON	BEEF, ROAST	CHICKEN, BONED
Calories		990	874	882	766	985	796
Protein	gm.	79	86	92	94	114	99
Fat	gm.	75	59	57	44	59	44
Carbohydrate	gm.	0	0	0	0	0	0
Calcium	gm.	59	50	73	304	41	145
Phosphorus	gm.	1,099	926	990	1,298	745	990
Iron	gm.	4.5	12.7	8.6	5.9	10.0	8.6
Vitamin A	I.U.	370[1]	0	(Trace)	370[1]	0	(Trace)
Thiamine (Vitamin B$_1$)	mg.	0.93	0.53	0.50	0.15	0.07	0.05
Riboflavin	mg.	0.64	0.68	0.80	0.80	1.08	0.69
Niacin (nicotinic acid)	mg.	33.7	23.2	39.9	29.6	20.4	16.8
Ascorbic acid (Vitamin C)	mg.	41	—	—	—	—	11

[1] Pink salmon; canned red salmon may have a value several times higher.
(*From National Research Council*)

NUTRITIVE VALUE OF ONE SERVING OF FISH

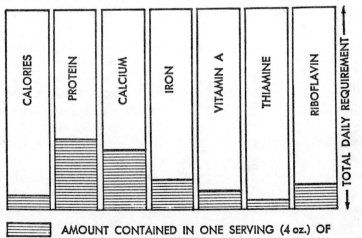

AMOUNT CONTAINED IN ONE SERVING (4 oz.) OF
CANNED SALMON

This chart shows examples of a few important fish and shellfish and their content of vitamins, protein, fat and mineral nutrients. The absence of a specific vitamin or other nutritional factor from the chart does not always indicate that the fish in question does not contain this factor, but may simply indicate that this fish has not been tested for it.

COMMODITY	VITAMINS	PROTEIN	FAT	MINERAL NUTRIENTS
Blue fish	A,B	19%	0.5%	Calcium, phosphorus, copper, sulphur, iodine
Butterfish	A,B	18%	11%	Calcium, phosphorus, copper, sulphur, iodine
Catfish and Bullheads	A,B	14%	21%	Calcium, phosphorus, copper, sulphur, iodine
Clams	A,B,D,G	9%	1%	Calcium, iron, phosphorus, copper, sulphur, iodine
Crabs	A,B,G	17%	2%	Calcium, phosphorus, copper, sulphur, iodine
Croaker	A,B	18%	3%	Calcium, phosphorus, copper, sulphur, iodine
Flounder	A,B	14%	0.6%	Calcium, phosphorus, copper, sulphur, iodine
Lobsters	A,B	16%	2%	Calcium, phosphorus, copper, sulphur, iodine
Mackerel	A,B	19%	7%	Calcium, phosphorus, copper, sulphur, iodine
Mullet	A,B	19%	5%	Calcium, phosphorus, copper, sulphur, iodine
Oysters	A,B,D,G	6%	1%	Calcium, iron, phosphorus, copper, sulphur, iodine
Sardine (pilchard)	A,B,D	25%	13%	Calcium, phosphorus, copper, sulphur, iodine
Shad	A,B	19%	9%	Calcium, phosphorus, copper, sulphur, iodine
Sheepshead	A,B,D	20%	4%	Calcium, phosphorus, copper, sulphur, iodine
Shrimp	A,B,D	25%	1%	Calcium, phosphorus, copper, sulphur, iodine
Squeteague or "sea trout"	A,B	19%	2%	Calcium, phosphorus, copper, sulphur, iodine

(*From tables compiled by U. S. Fish and Wildlife Service, Washington, D.C.*)

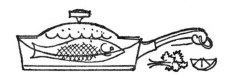

FISH OILS AND FATS

POLYUNSATURATION OF FISH OILS

Science has shown that certain unsaturated fatty acids found in fish are essential for normal growth and the maintenance of normal healthy skin, liver and kidney functioning.

Fats serve other functions beyond being just a concentrated source of energy. Science has shown that certain unsaturated fatty acids found in fish influence the cholesterol level and its dispersion in the blood, so intimately associated with heart disease.

It is believed that vegetable oils such as cottonseed, corn, peanut, safflower, etc., have a high content of polyunsaturation. Research indicates that this is of great value in lowering blood cholesterol. And fish oils possess even greater polyunsaturation than do vegetable oils.

USE OF OILY FISH IN THE DIET

A pleasant way of assuring the desired amount of polyunsaturated oils in the diet is to eat generous servings of fish several times a week. Some species contain high quantities of oil in the edible flesh, so that eating them provides considerable fish oil. Some fish average 15 percent oil. A 160-gram serving would furnish 24 grams or nearly an ounce of fish oil rich in polyunsaturated acids. This neutralizes any harmful effects of other saturated fatty acids that might be consumed at the same meal, and probably contributes somewhat to reduction in blood cholesterol level. Thus, eating fatty fish as a main course permits consumption of such foods as dairy and meat products by reducing the possibility of harmful effects resulting from the lack of unsaturation in their fat.

The fish oil in different species of fish ranges from only a few tenths of a percent up to 20 percent or more. The oilier species are obviously especially well adapted to lowering of blood cholesterol or to counteracting any harmful effect of saturated fatty acids in other parts of the diet.

USE OF NON-OILY FISH IN THE DIET

Non-oily species of fish can form the main entree of a meal, providing the protein requirements yet not introducing any undesirable saturated fats. Many meats contain 20 percent or more of fat, almost all of the undesirable saturated type. Use of lean fish as the main dish may eliminate 35 or more grams of saturated fat.

FAT AND LEAN FISH

It is good to know before preparing a fresh fish whether it is fat or lean. The chart called *Guide for Buying Fish* tells you. However, this is not absolutely necessary. Fat fish are those containing more than 5 percent fat. Lean fish are those containing less than 5 percent fat. Since fish fats are polyunsaturated, they are not in the least harmful to persons on low-fat diets.

Fat fish are especially suitable for baking and may also be broiled, while lean fish are best adapted to steaming, boiling and frying. Lean fish may be cooked by any recipe calling for medium-fat or fat fish if more fat or oil is added during cooking. Most varieties of fish and some shellfish are also good sautéed or fried.

COOKING METHODS AND FUEL VALUE OF FISH

SALT-WATER FISH	BROIL	BAKE	BOIL	FRY	CHOWDER	FUEL VALUE OF EDIBLE PORTION IN CALORIES PER POUND.
Alewife	Yes	No	Yes	Yes	No	550
Barracuda	Yes	No	Yes	No	No	510
Bluefish	Yes	Yes	No	Yes	No	535
Blue Runner	Yes	Yes	No	Yes	No	445
Butterfish	Yes	No	No	Yes	No	745
Cod	Yes	Yes	Yes	No	Yes	315
Croaker	Yes	Yes	Yes	Yes	Yes	415
Cusk	Yes	Yes	Yes	Yes	Yes	315
Drum, Red	No	Yes	Yes	No	Yes	345
Eel, Common	Yes	No	Yes	Yes	No	710
Flounders:						
Blackback (winter)	Yes	Yes	Yes	Yes	Yes	290
Fluke (summer)	Yes	Yes	Yes	Yes	Yes	290
"Sole" (Pacific)	Yes	Yes	Yes	Yes	Yes	345
Southern	Yes	Yes	Yes	Yes	Yes	395
"California Halibut"	Yes	Yes	Yes	Yes	Yes	415
Groupers	Yes	Yes	Yes	No	Yes	370–395
Haddock	Yes	Yes	Yes	No	Yes	325
Hake	Yes	Yes	Yes	No	Yes	340
Halibut	No	Yes	Yes	No	Yes	550
Herring, Sea (AC & PC)	Yes	Yes	No	No	No	620–825

17

SALT-WATER FISH	BROIL	BAKE	BOIL	FRY	CHOWDER	FUEL VALUE OF EDIBLE PORTION IN CALORIES PER POUND.
Horse Mackerel (PC)	Yes	No	Yes	No	No	620
Kingfish (PC)	Yes	Yes	No	Yes	Yes	360
Kingfish (King Mackerel)	Yes	Yes	No	No	Yes	900
King Whiting (Kingfish)	Yes	No	Yes	Yes	No	455
Lingcod"	Yes	Yes	Yes	No	Yes	355
Mackerel (AC & PC)	Yes	Yes	No	No	No	715–900
Mullet	Yes	Yes	Yes	Yes	Yes	530
Pollock	Yes	Yes	Yes	Yes	Yes	425
Pompano	Yes	Yes	Yes	No	No	730
Rockfish (PC)	Yes	Yes	No	No	No	375
Rosefish	Yes	Yes	No	Yes	No	455
Sablefish	Yes	Yes	Yes	Yes	No	900
Salmon: Atlantic	Yes	Yes	Yes	No	No	955
Chinook (King)	Yes	Yes	Yes	No	No	990
Chum (fall)	Yes	Yes	Yes	No	No	600
Pink	Yes	Yes	Yes	No	No	625
Silver	Yes	Yes	Yes	No	No	725
Scup (Porgy)	Yes	Yes	No	Yes	No	520
Sea Bass: Black (AC)	Yes	Yes	Yes	Yes	Yes	395
White (PC)	Yes	Yes	No	Yes	No	410

SALT-WATER FISH	BROIL	BAKE	BOIL	FRY	CHOWDER	FUEL VALUE OF EDIBLE PORTION IN CALORIES PER POUND.
Sea Trout						
Gray	Yes	Yes	No	Yes	No	390
Spotted	Yes	Yes	Yes	Yes	Yes	455
Shad	Yes	Yes	Yes	No	No	740
Sheepshead (AC)	Yes	Yes	No	Yes	No	490
Smelt:						
Atlantic	Yes	No	No	Yes	No	395
Pacific	Yes	No	No	Yes	No	900
Snapper, Red	Yes	Yes	Yes	Yes	Yes	395
Spanish Mackerel	Yes	Yes	No	Yes	No	900
Spot	Yes	No	No	Yes	No	455
Striped Bass	Yes	Yes	No	Yes	No	455
Sturgeon	Yes	Yes	No	No	No	405
Swordfish	Yes	Yes	No	No	No	520
Tautog	Yes	Yes	No	Yes	No	380
Tilefish	Yes	Yes	Yes	No	No	340
Tomcod (AC)	Yes	Yes	Yes	Yes	No	330
Tuna (all species)	Yes	Yes	Yes	No	No	570–770
White Perch (AC)	Yes	Yes	No	Yes	No	515
Whiting	Yes	Yes	No	Yes	No	340
Wolffish	Yes	Yes	Yes	Yes	Yes	455
Yellowtail (PC)	Yes	Yes	No	Yes	No	600

Note: AC = Atlantic Coast
      PC = Pacific Coast

FRESH-WATER FISH	BROIL	BAKE	BOIL	FRY	CHOWDER	FUEL VALUE OF EDIBLE PORTION IN CALORIES PER POUND.
Blue Pike	Yes	Yes	No	Yes	No	360
Buffalo Fish	Yes	Yes	No	Yes	No	430
Carp	Yes	Yes	Yes	Yes	No	420
Catfish	No	No	Yes	Yes	Yes	445
Lake Herring	Yes	Yes	No	Yes	No	615
Lake Trout	Yes	Yes	Yes	Yes	No	745
Pickerel (Jacks)	Yes	Yes	No	Yes	Yes	360
Sauger	Yes	Yes	No	Yes	No	355
Sheepshead	Yes	Yes	Yes	Yes	No	445
Smelt	Yes	Yes	No	Yes	No	395
Suckers	Yes	Yes	No	Yes	No	420
Whitefish	Yes	Yes	No	Yes	No	680
Yellow Perch	Yes	Yes	No	Yes	No	370
Yellow Pike	Yes	Yes	No	Yes	No	360

SHELLFISH
See the *Shellfish* section.

BUYING FISH

FRESH FISH

HOW TO SELECT FISH—Insist upon freshness. A fresh fish has firm and elastic flesh, scales that cling to the skin (in most species), pink-red gills, bright bulging eyes, and a pleasant deep-sea fragrance.

WHEN TO BUY—Fish of any species are of the highest quality and cheapest when most abundant, for commercial fishermen are bringing in their catches more often, and these are shipped immediately.

FROZEN FISH AND SHELLFISH

Frozen fish and shellfish are available all the year around in all sections of the United States. The frozen products compare favorably in appearance, food value and flavor with fresh fish.

HOW MUCH TO BUY—Use the same scale as for fresh fish and shellfish. That is, for fresh fish you may wish to start with ⅓ pound per person. If your family really goes for fish, ½ pound would be about right, if the fish is to be cooked without added sauces, vegetables, fruits, etc.

On most packages and cans of fish and shellfish you will find the weight given and sometimes the number of persons it will serve.

STORING FROZEN FISH—Frozen fish should be put in your freezer while still frozen, and it should never be thawed and then re-frozen. The reason for this is that between the time the product is thawed and re-frozen, bacteria may have had time to form. Anyway, it is always a good rule not to re-freeze. This also applies to shellfish.

THAWING FROZEN FISH AND SHELLFISH—Dressed frozen fish, fillets and steaks may be started cooking before thawing, but additional cooking time must be allowed. When fish are to be breaded and fried, or stuffed, it is suggested that you thaw them first. You will find this more convenient in handling. Whole or drawn fish should be thawed before cooking. Some shellfish may begin cooking while frozen, such as shrimp, but frozen crabmeat, lobster meat and oysters are better if thawed before cooking.

TIP: If you like a special recipe and have an extra supply of seafood, double the recipe and freeze extra servings for future meals.

HOW MUCH TO BUY—A QUICK TABLE

			Number served
Fish fillet, steak, or sticks	⅓ lb.	for	1
	30 lb.	"	100
Dressed fish	½ lb.	"	1
	45 lb.	"	100
Whole fish	1 lb.	"	1
	90 lb.	"	100
Oysters (shucked)	1 qt.	"	6
Scallops (shucked)	3½ gal.	"	100
Crabs, cooked meat	1 lb.	"	6
	15 lbs.	"	100
Lobster, cooked meat	¾ lb.	"	6
	12 lbs.	"	100
Shrimp, headless	1½ lb.	"	6
	24–30 lbs.	"	100
Shrimp, cooked and shucked	¾ lb.	"	6
	12–15 lbs.	"	100

NOTE: *Many species of edible seafoods, such as deep-sea sports fish and fresh-water game fish, are not listed as they are not sold in the markets in many states. Deep-sea game fish such as dolphin, amberjack and snook are smoked and sometimes sold in restaurants. The sale of fresh-water sports fish such as large- and small-mouth bass, is prohibited in Florida and many other states.*

GUIDE FOR BUYING FISH

SALT-WATER FISH	FAT OR LEAN	USUAL MARKET RANGE OF ROUND FISH	USUAL MARKET FORMS
Bluefish	Lean	1 to 7 pounds	Whole and drawn
Butterfish	Fat	¼ to 1 pound	Whole and dressed
Cod	Lean	3 to 20 pounds	Drawn, dressed, steaks, fillets
Crevalle	Lean	1 to 7 pounds	Whole, dressed, and fillets
Croaker	Lean	½ to 2½ pounds	Whole, dressed, and fillets
Drum	Fat	3 to 30 pounds	Drawn, dressed, steaks, fillets
Flounder	Lean	¼ to 5 pounds	Whole, dressed, and fillets
Grouper	Lean	5 to 15 pounds	Whole, drawn, dressed, steaks, fillets
Haddock	Lean	1½ to 7 pounds	Drawn and fillets
Hake	Lean	2 to 5 pounds	Whole, drawn, dressed, fillets
Halibut	Lean	8 to 75 pounds	Dressed and steaks
Herring, Sea	Fat	¼ to 1 pound	Whole
Lingcod	Lean	5 to 20 pounds	Dressed, steaks, and fillets
Mackerel	Fat	¾ to 3 pounds	Whole, drawn, and fillets
Mullet	Fat	½ to 3 pounds	Whole, dressed, drawn, fillets
Pollock	Lean	3 to 14 pounds	Drawn, dressed, steaks, and fillets
Rockfish	Lean	2 to 5 pounds	Dressed and fillets
Rosefish	Lean	½ to 1¼ pounds	Fillets
Salmon	Fat	3 to 20 pounds	Drawn, dressed, steaks, and fillets
Scup (Porgy)	Lean	½ to 2 pounds	Whole and dressed
Sea Bass	Lean	¼ to 4 pounds	Whole, dressed, steaks, and fillets
Sea Trout	Lean	1 to 6 pounds	Whole, drawn, dressed and fillets
Shad	Fat	1½ to 6 pounds	Whole, drawn, and fillets
Snapper, Red	Lean	1½ to 15 pounds	Whole, drawn, dressed, steaks, fillets
Spanish Mackerel	Fat	1 to 5 pounds	Whole, drawn, dressed, and fillets
Spot	Lean	¼ to 1¼ pounds	Whole and dressed
Whiting	Lean	½ to 1½ pounds	Whole, drawn, dressed, and fillets
FRESH-WATER FISH			
Buffalo Fish	Lean	5 to 15 pounds	Whole, drawn, dressed, and steaks
Carp	Lean	2 to 8 pounds	Whole and fillets
Catfish	Fat	1 to 10 pounds	Whole, dressed, and skinned
Lake Herring	Lean	½ to 1 pound	Whole, drawn, and fillets
Lake Trout	Fat	1½ to 10 pounds	Drawn, dressed, and fillets
Sheepshead	Lean	½ to 3 pounds	Whole, drawn, dressed, and fillets
Suckers	Lean	½ to 4 pounds	Whole, drawn, dressed, and fillets
Whitefish	Fat	2 to 6 pounds	Whole, drawn, dressed, and fillets
Yellow Perch	Lean	½ to 1 pound	Whole and fillets
Yellow Pike	Lean	1½ to 10 pounds	Whole, dressed, and fillets

Shellfish
See that section.

PRODUCTION AND MARKET AREAS

North Atlantic = Coastal states from Maine to Connecticut
Middle Atlantic = New York to Virginia
South Atlantic = North Carolina to Florida
Gulf = Alabama to Texas
Pacific = Washington to California
North Pacific = Washington, Oregon and Alaska
Midwest = Central and inland states
South Atlantic and Gulf = Around the Florida keys

MAIN PRODUCTION AREAS	MAIN MARKET AREAS
Middle and South Atlantic	Middle and South Atlantic
North and Middle Atlantic	North and Middle Atlantic
North Atlantic; North Pacific	Entire United States
Middle and South Atlantic	Middle and South Atlantic
Middle and South Atlantic	Middle and South Atlantic
Middle and South Atlantic	Middle and South Atlantic
All Coastal Areas	Entire United States
South Atlantic; Gulf	South Atlantic; Gulf
North Atlantic	Entire United States
North and Middle Atlantic	North and Middle Atlantic; Midwest
Pacific	Entire United States
North Atlantic; North Pacific	North Atlantic; North Pacific
Pacific	Pacific
North and Middle Atlantic; California	North and Middle Atlantic; California
South Atlantic; Gulf	Middle and South Atlantic; Gulf; Midwest
North Atlantic	Entire United States, except Pacific
Pacific	Pacific and Midwest; Gulf
North Atlantic	Entire United States
Pacific	Entire United States
North and Middle Atlantic	Middle and South Atlantic
Middle and South Atlantic; California	Middle and South Atlantic; Pacific
Middle and South Atlantic; Gulf	Middle and South Atlantic; Gulf
Middle and South Atlantic; Pacific	North, Middle and South Atlantic; Pacific
South Atlantic; Gulf	Middle and South Atlantic; Gulf
South Atlantic; Gulf	Middle and South Atlantic; Gulf
Middle and South Atlantic	Middle and South Atlantic
North and Middle Atlantic	Entire United States, except Pacific
FRESH-WATER FISH	
Mississippi Valley	Midwest
Lakes and Rivers	Midwest; Middle Atlantic
Lakes and Rivers	Middle and South Atlantic; Midwest; Gulf
Great Lakes	Midwest
Great Lakes and Lakes	Midwest
Lakes and Rivers	Midwest
Lakes and Rivers	Midwest
Great Lakes	Midwest
Great Lakes, Lakes and Rivers	Midwest
Great Lakes and Lakes	Midwest

COMMON MARKET FORMS

WHOLE (*sometimes called "round"*) **FISH** are those marketed in the form in which they come from the water, and fall into three classifications: fish that keep as well or better when not dressed; small fishes; and small sizes of larger species. Before cooking, whole or round fish are eviscerated and in all but very small sizes, heads, scales and sometimes fins are removed.

DRAWN FISH are those marketed with only the viscera removed. To prepare these fish for cooking, the heads, scales, and the fins are removed, and the fish may be split or cut into serving-size pieces if too large to be cooked whole.

DRESSED or **PAN-DRESSED FISH** have had the head and viscera removed and the tails and fins may be cut off. If dressed fish are large, they may be cut into pieces before cooking. Very large dressed fish are usually marketed in pieces or steaks.

STEAKS are pieces or slices about half an inch thick which are cut crosswise from a large dressed fish.

FILLETS are meaty slices cut lengthwise from the sides of the fish. Fillets contain no bones or other waste. The weight varies with the size of the fish.

STICKS are pieces of fish cut lengthwise or crosswise from fillets or steaks into equal-size portions.

BUTTERFLY FILLETS are the two sides of the fish—that is, two single fillets—held together by uncut flesh and skin.

Common Market Forms of Shellfish—See that section.

SOME DO'S AND DON'T'S IN
SEAFOOD COOKING

DO

- Avoid overcooking seafoods. Fish is done when it loses its transparent look, turns white, and the flesh flakes easily when lifted with a toothpick or fork.
- Sprinkle fish with salt, freshly ground black pepper, and a generous amount of lemon, lime or grapefruit juice before cooking. The longer this marinade is used before cooking, the better the fish will be. Then drain off any surplus and cook by almost any recipe, including frying.
- Use all left-over fish. Flake cooked fish from bones and skin and use it in recipes calling for canned or flaked fish. Good and easy to use in salads, casserole dishes, chowders and many other recipes. Freeze surplus cooked fish for future use.
- Where there are fishermen in the home, a good tip is to poach surplus supplies of fish and freeze. Place dressed fish in enough boiling salted water to cover. Turn heat to simmer and when fish turns white, drain off the water, cool and flake. Freeze in packages in one-meal amounts.
- Always cover fish tightly when storing it in the refrigerator. Rinse and dry, place in a covered dish or roll in waxed paper. Store in the coldest part of the refrigerator.
- Line pan with foil when baking or broiling fish. When ready to serve, remove foil and all. Helps with the dishwashing, too.
- Dry fish thoroughly before frying to keep the fat from spattering when fish is placed in it. Place fish with the flesh side down to prevent curling. Have the fat hot but never smoking. Turn to brown on other side. When broiling, do just the opposite, place in pan with skin side down. When broiling thin fillets no turning is necessary.
- Rub lemon juice over fingers before handling fish to prevent any odor from clinging to them. When Pop dresses his "catch" suggest to him that he put salt on his fingers for a tight grip.
- Remember that fresh fish has bright bulging eyes, firm flesh, pink gills and a sweet deep-sea aroma.
- Keep frozen fish frozen until you use it. Cooking may begin before or after thawing, but fish requires longer cooking time if cooked frozen. When in a hurry you can thaw fish under cool water, but the best way is to let it thaw in the refrigerator.
- Slice a lime or lemon into water when poaching or boiling fish and shell-fish. This prevents the fish from falling apart and improves the flavor.

DON'T

- Don't leave fish, except the salted kind, soaking in water, as this makes it flabby and takes away much of the delicate flavor.
- Don't heat smoked fish too much. It is already cooked and too long under fire tends to dry it out and make it tough.
- Don't overcook shellfish. Shrimp turn pink with cooking and should be boiled only until tender. Give them the old taste-test.

Oysters and clams curl around the edges when cooked enough. Clams that are unusually large are very hard to cook tender. It is best to grind them and use in recipes including other foods.

Crabs and lobsters are either alive or precooked. If alive, plunge them into boiling water until they turn pink. Canned fresh or frozen crab and lobster meats require only thorough heating.

A WORD ABOUT SAUCES AND GARNISHES

The attractiveness of almost any fish or shellfish dish will be increased greatly by the use of sauces that subtly enhance or complement the flavor. You do not want to overwhelm the delicate flavor of fish and shellfish with too many added spices and condiments, however. Adding the right amount becomes a habit with experience.

Fresh and colorful garnishes also add much attractiveness to seafood dishes. They can also please the palate themselves and tempt the appetite of finicky eaters and children. Many fruits and almost all vegetables go well with fish and shellfish, but the following is a list of suggested garnishes:

Beets, cooked whole, or sliced
Celery, tops, hearts, sticks
Carrots, tops, hearts, sticks or curls
Green pepper, strips or rings
Grapes, bunches or scattered singly
Hard-cooked eggs, slices or wedges
Parsley, chopped or sprigs
Limes, lemons, grapefruit-orange sections
   (Limes and lemons are usually sliced or in wedges)
Paprika, sprinkled
Radishes, whole, slices, or roses
Tomatoes, slices or wedges
Watercress, sprigs or chopped
Mixed salad greens, chopped

A WORD ABOUT RANGES WITH THERMOSTATICALLY CONTROLLED TOP BURNER

Since many of the new ranges have thermostatically controlled top burners, these temperature settings may be helpful. Always read manufacturer's direction book carefully.

RECOMMENDED TEMPERATURE SETTING FOR AUTOMATIC BURNER

To Keep Warm

Cooked fish and other foods	175°
Coffee	175°

For Cooking

Sauces	200°
Covered vegetables	225°
Eggs (fried)	225°
Potatoes (fried)	300°
Fish (fried)	325°
Shellfish (fried)	325°
Fish (boiled)	225°
Shellfish (boiled)	225°
Hamburger	325°
Bacon	325°
Other meats (brown, sear, fry)	350°
Pancakes	375°
Deep fat frying	400°

SOME GENERAL COOKING TIPS

- Soft bread crumbs—Pull bread (stale is best) with fork into crumbs.
- Dry bread crumbs—Remove crusts from old bread. Dry in a very slow oven. Watch carefully to prevent browning. Bread should be dry but not brown. Crush bread with a rolling pin or put through blender or food grinder.
- Use kitchen scissors to trim crusts from bread; two or three slices can be trimmed at the same time.

- Drawn butter—Place butter in a small saucepan or skillet. Melt over low heat. Skim off the foam on top as it forms; then pour the clear liquid from the whitish substance which has settled on the bottom. The clear liquid is called "drawn butter."
- Boiling foods—After water or other liquid comes to a boil, turn down the heat to low. Food will cook as fast at low-medium boil as at high temperature, and will break apart less.
- Always lift the lid of a steaming saucepan from the back so the escaping steam won't burn you.
- If peeled apples are soaked for about 15 minutes in cold water to which a little lemon juice is added they will retain their color during cooking.
- When slicing boiled eggs dip the knife in water to keep yolks from breaking.
- When spaghetti has to wait, coat with several tablespoons of butter; place in a colander over small amount of boiling water. Cover colander with a towel.
- Peeling tomatoes—Hold one at a time on a fork and rotate over low gas flame or dip in boiling water for one minute. The skins then slip off easily.
- For a pudding with a satinlike texture, put clear plastic wrap or waxed paper directly on top after cooking. Smooth it out clear to the sides of the bowl and let it touch the surface. Chill and at serving time just pull off the paper.
- To retain the snowy whiteness of cauliflower do not lift the cover of saucepan while it cooks.
- Measuring orange or lemon rind is much easier if you grate it over paper toweling. Pat the toweling over the rind several times to remove excess oil, then scrape the rind off the paper and measure it.
- If you like muffins crisp on the sides, grease the whole cup; for softer ones grease only the bottom.
- For a gloss on baked cookies, brush them lightly with cream or evaporated milk just before putting them in the oven.
- Make your own croutons for soups and salads—Cut bread into small cubes and place in an oven at lowest temperature until cubes are very dry and toasted, or fry cubes of bread in hot oil until brown. Drain on absorbent paper.
- A fork or wire whip used to mash potatoes makes them whiter and fluffier than a spoon.
- You can get more juice from a lemon if you drop it into hot water for a few minutes before squeezing.
- Put rice in a large strainer and place over hot water in a saucepan when you have to reheat it. Cover and steam 15 minutes.

SOME MEASUREMENTS AND SUBSTITUTIONS

- 4 slices bread yield 2 cups bread crumbs
- 2 egg whites measure ¼ cup
- 18 crackers yield 1 cup crumbs
- ⅛ teaspoon garlic powder equals 1 clove garlic
- 1 tablespoon cornstarch equals 2 tablespoons flour for thickening
- 4 to 6 lemons equals 1 cup juice
- 6 limes equals 1 cup juice
- 1 cup milk, or half evaporated milk and half water, plus 1 tablespoon lemon juice or vinegar, equals 1 cup sour milk or buttermilk. Note: This is *not* sour cream, usually prepared commercially.
- ¼ teaspoon baking soda plus 1 teaspoon cream of tartar equals approximately 1 teaspoon of baking powder.

- Butter Measurements
   1 pound = 4 sticks = 2 cups
   ½ pound = 2 sticks = 1 cup
   ¼ pound = 1 stick = ½ cup
   ⅛ pound = ½ stick = ¼ cup or 4 tablespoons

- Canned Foods
   6-ounce can of liquid   = ⅔ cup
   4½-ounce can packed solid = ½ cup

(All recipes referred to in this book can be found in the Index)

Oven-Cooked Fish

Broiling, Baking, Planking and Barbecuing

ALL VARIETIES OF fish both fresh and frozen may be cooked by any of the following basic recipes for broiling, baking and planking, if allowance is made for the fat content. That doesn't mean that it is necessary to know whether each fish is fat or lean, but that during the cooking period very lean fish, such as halibut, ocean perch, and buffalofish, will need basting with more melted butter, margarine, or oil. Fish classed as fat—bluefish, mackerel, salmon, mullet and shad, to name a few out of hundreds—require less added fat.

It is so easy to cook fish, there is really no trick to it at all. Any variety and all cuts, such as steaks and fillets, and whole small fish are delicious broiled. It takes only a few minutes to cook fish this way, as you must not overcook. Fish needs no long cooking period to break down tough connective tissue, as do meats, because fish is already tender and the less cooking the better. When the flesh loses its translucent appearance, turns white and can be flaked easily with a fork, it is ready. Be sure it is hot and moist, never cold and dried out.

BROILING

- Have the broiling pan and oven hot.
- Oil the broiling pan or oven dish. To help with the dishwashing, line the pan with aluminum foil, then oil the foil.
- Sprinkle fish with salt, pepper and paprika (optional) before broiling for a delicately browned fish.
- If fish is thin, ¼ to ½ inch, no turning is necessary. Place thin fillets in pan with skin side down. Broil 4 to 7 minutes.
- For thick fillets, ½ to 1 inch, the broiling time is 8 to 10 minutes.
- Even thicker fish, over 1 inch, broil skin side first 8 to 10 minutes. Turn and broil other side 5 to 8 minutes more.
- Do not overcook. Remove from oven when fish loses its transparent look, turns white, flakes easily when tested with a fork and the surface is light brown.
- Fruit and vegetable garnishes may be added to the pan the last 3 or 4 minutes of cooking. Canned or cooked vegetables should be used. They are only to be heated with the fish, not cooked.
- Frozen fish should always be allowed to thaw in the bottom of the refrigerator before cooking. Never soak frozen fish in water to thaw.

PLAIN BROILED FILLETS

*

Broiled Fillets or Steaks

Basic Recipe

*2 pounds any fish fillets or steaks,
    fresh-water, deep-sea, commercial
    or game*
1 teaspoon salt
⅛ teaspoon pepper
*4 tablespoons butter or other fat,
    melted*
⅛ teaspoon paprika (optional)

Preheat and grease a broiler pan. Sprinkle both sides of the fillets or steaks with salt and pepper. Lay the fish in the pan and brush with the melted butter. Sprinkle top of fish with paprika, if it is used. For thin fish, ¼ to ½ inch, place broiler 2 to 3 inches from heat. Thicker fish, ½ to 1 inch, should be about 4 to 5 inches away from heat, and still thicker fillets or steaks are better broiled for a slightly longer period on the bottom rack, or about 6 inches from source of heat. Thin fish requires 4 to 7 minutes; thick fish 8 to 10 minutes. If fish is over an inch thick broil, after turning, 5 to 8 minutes more, or until it flakes easily when tested with a fork. Remove the broiled fish carefully to a platter. Garnish with parsley or lemon slices, if desired. Serves 6.

With wine: Omit the paprika. After brushing with butter, pour ½ cup sauterne slowly over the fillets or steaks. Baste often, adding more wine if needed. When fish is almost done, place close to source of heat to brown quickly.

TIPS: Fillets or steaks may be marinated in French dressing before cooking. Use about ½ cup dressing for 2 pounds fish. Place fish in greased broiler pan, sprinkle with salt and pepper and pour over the dressing. Set aside to marinate for 15 to 45 minutes. Before broiling, drain off the excess dressing. Omit the butter and brush during broiling with the dressing used for marinade.
• Taste French dressing before preparing fish and if it is salty, do not sprinkle fish with salt.

French Lemon Dressing

½ cup salad or olive oil
¼ cup lemon juice
3 tablespoons wine vinegar
1 teaspoon salt
⅛ teaspoon pepper
Clove of garlic, crushed
2 tablespoons sugar

Mix all ingredients and shake well. Pour over fish as marinade. Drain before broiling fish and use the marinade to baste it occasionally. Makes about ⅔ cup of dressing.

Pepper-Broiled Fish Steaks

2 pounds any fish steaks
½ teaspoon salt
2 tablespoons lemon juice
Butter
Freshly ground black pepper

Several hours before cooking time sprinkle the fish steaks with salt and spoon the lemon juice over them. Let stand at room temperature. When ready to broil, place fish in greased broiler pan and dot with butter. Broil 4 to 5 inches from heat 8 to 10 minutes, or until fish flakes easily when tested with a fork. Before serving grind fresh peppercorns over the broiled fish. Serves 6.

Blue Sea Lemon Broil

2 pounds any fish fillets or steaks
1 teaspoon salt
¼ teaspoon pepper
3 tablespoons Spanish olive oil
1 lemon, sliced
Paprika

Wash and dry the fish and sprinkle with salt and pepper. Grease the pan with 2 tablespoons olive oil. Place the lemon slices on the bottom of pan. Arrange fillets or steaks on them, skin side down. Spoon over the fish another tablespoon of oil and sprinkle generously with paprika. Broil until the flesh will flake when tested with a fork. Serves 6.

TIP: Two tablespoons lime juice may be substituted for the sliced lemon, and butter or other fat for the olive oil.

Mixed Seafood Broil

Mixed seafoods may be broiled. Prepare as for *Mixed Seafood Bake*. Broil about 7 to 8 minutes, 5 inches from the heat. Turn the shellfish and fish fillets if they are thick and broil on other side until tender. Allow ⅓ pound fish and 4 to 6 shellfish per person.

FILLETS BASTED WITH SAUCE

Broiled Fillets Pinky

2 pounds any thin fish fillets
1 teaspoon salt
Dash pepper
1 teaspoon paprika
2 tablespoons lemon juice
1 teaspoon grated onion
¼ cup butter or other fat, melted

Sprinkle the fillets with the salt and pepper. Preheat and grease broiler

pan and place fillets skin side down. Combine the other ingredients and spoon the sauce over the fish. Broil about 5 inches from heat for 4 to 7 minutes, or until fish flakes easily when tested with a fork. Serves 6.

TIP: When lemon juice or sauces are used over fish in broiling, it is a good idea to place the rack an inch or more farther away from the heat.

Sweet-Sour Fish Broil

2 pounds fish portions
3 tablespoons butter or other fat,
   melted
1 small onion, grated
2 tablespoons lemon juice
2 teaspoons dry mustard
¼ cup light brown sugar
½ teaspoon salt
⅛ teaspoon pepper

Wash and dry the fish. Combine the remaining ingredients. Place fish in a baking pan and cover with the sauce. Broil 4 to 5 inches from heat for 8 to 10 minutes. Turn and broil other side 5 to 8 minutes more, according to thickness of fish. Stir the sauce and baste with it during broiling. Serves 6. Serve with fluffy cooked rice.

Broiled Steaks Chinatown

2 pounds fish steaks
¼ cup soy sauce
¼ cup orange juice
2 tablespoons catsup
2 tablespoons salad oil
1 tablespoon lemon juice
½ teaspoon oregano
½ teaspoon pepper
1 clove garlic, finely chopped.

Place fish in a single layer in baking pan. Combine the remaining ingredients into a marinade. Pour it over the fish and let stand for an hour or more. Drain off marinade. Broil fish 3 inches from heat for 4 to 8 minutes, or until brown. Baste during the broiling with the marinade. Turn and repeat on other side. Serves 6.

Herbed Broiled Fillets

2 pounds any fish fillets
¼ cup butter or margarine
2 tablespoons chopped parsley
2 tablespoons chopped chives
1 teaspoon tarragon
½ teaspoon thyme
1 teaspoon salt
⅛ teaspoon pepper
⅛ teaspoon paprika

Place fillets in greased broiling pan without rack, skin side down. Blend together the butter and other ingredients. Spread the herb butter over the fillets. Broil 5 inches from heat 8 to 10 minutes according to the thickness of the fish. Baste occasionally with butter mixture. No turning is necessary. Remove when flesh flakes easily. Serves 6.

Broiled Fillets
with Mild Barbecue Sauce

2 pounds any fish fillets
2 tablespoons butter or margarine,
   melted
2 tablespoons vinegar
2 tablespoons catsup
1 tablespoon Worcestershire sauce

Cut fillets in several pieces if they are large. Sprinkle with salt and pepper. Place in a greased baking or broiling pan. Mix the melted butter with the remaining ingredients. Pour over the fish and broil 4 to 5 inches from heat for 7 to 8 minutes, or until fish flakes when tested and sauce is bubbly. Serves 6.

Broiled Fish with Soy-Tomato Sauce

2 pounds any fish fillets or steaks
2 tablespoons butter or margarine,
melted
2 tablespoons lemon or lime juice
4 tablespoons catsup
2 tablespoons soy sauce

Place prepared fish fillets or steaks on ovenproof platter. Combine butter, juice, catsup and soy sauce and spoon over fish. Broil 8 to 10 minutes, or until fish flakes easily. Brush with the sauce frequently while broiling. Garnish with lemon slices and celery sprigs. Serves 6.

Broiled Fillets with Olive-Oregano Sauce

2 pounds thin fish fillets, such as
flounder
1 teaspoon salt
⅛ teaspoon pepper
¾ cup olive oil
6 tablespoons lime juice
⅛ teaspoon oregano
2 tablespoons fresh minced parsley or
1 tablespoon dried parsley flakes

Sprinkle the fish on both sides with salt and pepper. Place on broiler pan greased with some of the olive oil. Brush with mixture of 2 tablespoons lime juice and about ½ cup olive oil.

Broil 3 to 5 inches from heat for 8 minutes. Blend ¼ cup olive oil with 4 tablespoons lime juice. Heat and pour over the cooked fish. Sprinkle with oregano and minced parsley. Serves 6.

TIP: If dried parsley flakes are used soak them a few minutes in small amount of water or lime juice. Drain off water if it is used.

Puffy Fish Steaks or Fillets

2 pounds fish fillets or steaks
1 teaspoon salt
⅛ teaspoon pepper
¼ cup butter or other fat, melted
½ cup mayonnaise
1 teaspoon Worcestershire sauce
½ cup grated American cheese
1 teaspoon prepared mustard
1 egg white, beaten

Wash and dry fillets or steaks. Place on a preheated, greased broiler pan. Brush with butter. Broil 5 to 8 minutes about 3 inches from heat, or until light brown. Baste with butter. Turn carefully once if steaks are used or fillets are thick. Repeat on other side.

While fish is broiling, combine mayonnaise, Worcestershire sauce, grated cheese, and mustard. Beat the egg white and fold in the mayonnaise mixture. Spread mixture on fish and brown in broiler about 1 minute longer. Serves 6.

BROILED FILLETS WITH SEPARATE SAUCE

*

Broiled Fillets with Almond Sauce

2 pounds fillets of flounder or other fish
¼ cup flour
1½ teaspoons salt
1 teaspoon paprika
2 tablespoons melted butter
2 tablespoons salad oil

Wash and dry the fish. Mix the flour, salt, and paprika. Roll the fillets in flour mixture. Grease the broiler pan with the butter and salad oil mixed. This gives the fish a golden-brown color when broiled. Place fish under broiler and baste with the fat as needed. Broil 4 to 5 minutes or until surface is crusted. Remove fish to a hot platter and pour *Almond Sauce* over them. Serves 6.

ALMOND SAUCE

Heat in a saucepan 3 tablespoons butter; add ½ cup slivered blanched almonds. Brown lightly. Skim up almonds and scatter on the fillets. Add 2 tablespoons lime or lemon juice and several dashes of hot pepper sauce to the pan. Heat and pour over all.

TIP: Watch the almonds carefully while browning, as they burn easily.

Broiled Steaks Anchovy

2 pounds fish steaks: halibut, haddock, grouper, snapper, or other fish
1 teaspoon salt
⅛ teaspoon pepper
3 tablespoons butter, margarine, or other fat, melted

Cut steaks into serving portions. Wash and dry. Sprinkle with salt and pepper. Preheat and grease a broiler pan. Arrange fish in pan. Brush with butter and broil 5 inches from heat 8 to 10 minutes or until lightly browned. Baste the fish with butter and turn carefully. Broil 5 to 8 minutes longer. Remove · from broiler and pour *Anchovy Butter* over fish. Serves 6.

ANCHOVY BUTTER

1 teaspoon anchovy paste
2 tablespoons lemon juice
3 tablespoons butter or other fat, melted
⅛ teaspoon paprika
1 tablespoon fresh chopped parsley or ½ tablespoon dried parsley flakes

Combine all ingredients thoroughly. Serve over broiled fish.

Ripe Olive Butter

¼ cup butter or margarine, melted
¼ cup pitted ripe olives, sliced
2 teaspoons lemon juice
1 tablespoon fresh chopped parsley
  or 1 teaspoon dried parsley flakes

Combine all ingredients thoroughly. Heat and serve hot over broiled fish. Enough for 6.

Broiled Fish with Pineapple and Lemon-Butter Sauce

2 pounds any fish fillets
¼ cup melted butter or margarine
1 teaspoon salt
¼ teaspoon pepper
1 #2 can sliced pineapple or chunks

Place fillets in foil-lined broiler pan or glass oven-dish. Brush with melted butter and season with salt and pepper. Broil 2 to 3 inches from heat for 5 minutes. Baste again with melted butter. Remove from oven and place the drained pineapple around fish and return to oven for 3 minutes longer. Serve with *Lemon-Butter Sauce* or plain. Serves 6.

TIP: Other fruits may be used such as drained grapefruit and orange sections, or peach halves, canned or fresh.

LEMON BUTTER SAUCE

½ cup butter, melted
¼ cup lemon juice
1 tablespoon chopped parsley

Combine ingredients, heat and serve.

Broiled Mullet with Tarragon Sauce

Serve broiled mullet or any other fish with the following sauce for a real taste-tempter:

TARRAGON SAUCE

2 egg yolks
¼ teaspoon dried tarragon or 2 tablespoons tarragon vinegar
1 cup commercial sour cream
¼ teaspoon minced garlic
½ teaspoon salt
1 bay leaf, crumbled
1 tablespoon capers, drained well

Place egg yolks in a bowl and beat with the tarragon until thick. Heat the sour cream over low heat with the garlic, salt and bay leaf added. Do not boil. When bubbles form around edges of pan, strain and discard the garlic and bay leaf.

Pour a little of the hot sour cream into the egg mixture, stirring constantly, then pour the rest in slowly. Over low heat bring the sauce to boiling point. Add capers. Makes 1 cup.

Broiled Fish with Tomato Halves

2 pounds fish fillets or steaks
1 teaspoon salt
⅛ teaspoon pepper
3 tablespoons butter or margarine, melted
3 medium-size tomatoes
1½ teaspoons dried basil

Place fish in greased broiler pan, not on a rack. Sprinkle fish with salt and pepper. Spoon over it the melted butter. Broil 2 to 3 inches from heat for 5 minutes.

Remove from heat and arrange halved tomatoes around the fish. Sprinkle tomatoes with salt and the dried basil, crumbled. Dot with butter and return pan to broiler until fish flakes easily and the tomatoes are light brown. Serves 6.

TIP: For a change place fish over a bed of sliced lemon and celery tops. Baste and broil as above. For a complete dinner in one dish arrange cooked or canned vegetables, such as potatoes, green beans, beets and so on, around partly cooked fish. Return platter to oven until vegetables are heated and serve in same oven platter.

BROILED WHOLE FISH

*

Broiled Whole Small Fish

6 to 8 small panfish
1 teaspoon salt
¼ teaspoon pepper
2 tablespoons lemon or lime juice
Flour
Salad or cooking oil

Clean small fish but leave them whole. Wash and dry. Cut 2-inch slashes on both sides of fish to prevent curling. Sprinkle with salt, pepper, and lemon juice. Set aside for as long as possible before cooking, at least 15 minutes to an hour.

Roll fish in flour, then in salad oil. Grease a shallow pan and heat in oven. Place fish in pan and broil 6 inches from heat for 10 minutes, or until fish is brown; turn and broil other side for 10 minutes, placing 2 to 3 inches from heat last minute or two if necessary to brown. Watch closely to prevent burning. Remove fish to a hot platter and garnish with sliced tomatoes and celery-sprigs. Serves 6 to 8.

Aromatic Broiled Fish

2-pound fish, whole
½ cup butter or margarine, melted
1 teaspoon salt
⅛ teaspoon pepper
¼ teaspoon ground cardamom
1 tablespoon coriander
1 teaspoon paprika
2 tablespoons lemon or lime juice
1 cup yoghurt
1 bunch dill or fennel

Wash and dry fish. Combine all the ingredients except dill or fennel. Brush fish inside and out with this mixture. Cook in preheated broiler until brown on both sides. Baste while cooking several times. This requires about 25 minutes. Remove fish to a heated platter. Place several sprigs of dill or fennel on broiler. Arrange fish on top of herbs and broil for 5 more minutes. Remove fish to a platter and discard herbs. Serves 6.

Broiled Salt Fish

2 pounds salt fish, such as mackerel
¼ cup melted butter
1 tablespoon chopped parsley
Lemon or lime wedges

Place fish in a flat pan or ovenproof dish, skin side down. Cover with cold water and let soak 12 hours. Drain and dry on a paper towel.

Brush fish with melted butter and place on hot broiler pan, skin side up. Broil 5 to 6 minutes, or until skin is browned, basting with butter as needed. Turn and baste flesh side with butter; broil to desired brownness. Serve plain or garnished with parsley and wedges of lemon or lime. Serves 6.

Broiled Fish and Roe

3-pound fish, such as mullet or shad
1 pair roe

½ pound small fresh mushrooms or
  1 3-ounce can, drained
Salt and pepper
¼ cup melted butter or margarine
1 tablespoon lemon juice
2 tablespoons white wine
1 tablespoon minced parsley

Dress and bone the fish, as described elsewhere, and cut into serving pieces. Preheat broiler. Arrange fish, skin side down, on an ovenproof glass or metal platter and place the roe and cleaned mushrooms around it. Sprinkle with salt and pepper. Mix the lemon juice and butter and spoon over all. Broil 2 to 3 inches from heat 8 to 10 minutes, basting as needed. Turn the fish, roe, and mushrooms and broil on other side about 5 minutes, or until fish flakes easily when tested with a fork.

Spoon the wine over fish and sprinkle with sparsley just before serving. Serves 6 to 8 persons.

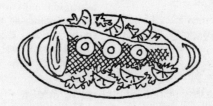

BAKING

Baking fish is as easy as broiling and the results are as satisfactory. Even brand-new cooks are enthusiastic after they try it just once. It is the simplest thing in the world. As in broiling, any fish, whether fat or lean, small or large, turns out deliciously without fail.

Fish may be baked perfectly plain, with only a bit of seasoning and butter or oil, as needed. People on fat- and salt-free diets can eat fish broiled or baked with just citrus juices as basting, and even this simple preparation is pleasing. The nice part about baked fish is that it can be plain or fancy: stuffed with numerous easy ingredients, served with sauces or with vegetables and fruits. Again this method requires only a very short time.

Dressing fish for stuffing and baking

Dress fish for baking just as for other methods of cooking. The head and tail may be kept intact if desired. The fish is slit down the belly and sometimes the head and tail cut off. For baked stuffed fish, the stuffing is spooned into the slit cavity. However, the slit should not be all the way to the tail section, but from the vent (anal opening) to the head. This leaves enough connective flesh to hold in the stuffing.

41

The following tips should help you turn out a really beautiful baked fish:
- Have oven hot and bake fish 10 minutes per pound.
- When baking, fish need not be turned, for heat is all around it.
- Fillets and steaks, as well as whole fish, may be baked.
- Any fish, frozen or fresh—whole, fillets, and steaks—is good baked simply with salt and pepper, basted with melted butter, margarine, olive, or other vegetable oil.
- Frozen fish should be thawed before placing in the oven. If time does not permit this, lengthen cooking period.

BAKED WHOLE FISH

Plain Baked Fish

3- or 4-pound fish, dressed
1½ teaspoons salt
4 tablespoons butter or other fat,
  melted
3 slices bacon (optional)

Clean, wash, and dry fish. Sprinkle inside and out with salt and place in a greased baking pan. Brush with melted butter and lay slices of bacon over the top. Bake in oven at 400 F for 30 to 40 minutes. Serve plain or garnished with slices of citrus fruits or with salad greens. Serves 6.

Lemon-Pepper Baked Fish

3 to 4 pound fish
Salt
Lemon
½ teaspoon pepper
Melted butter

Wash fish, dry and sprinkle with salt inside and out. Pour ¼ cup lemon juice over fish. Sprinkle with freshly ground black pepper. Let stand in refrigerator 2 hours or at room temperature 30 minutes.

Bake in a hot oven 400 F 30 to 40 minutes or 10 minutes per pound, basting with melted butter as needed. Serves 6.

Serve with this delicious fish creamed potatoes, fried eggplant and tomatoes, tossed green salad and caramel custard.

Citrus Roasted Fish

This is delicious for people on diets.

2- to 4-pound whole fish, fillets or
  steaks
1 lemon or lime, sliced, or ½ cup
  grapefruit or orange juice
¼ cup lemon or lime juice
Paprika

Ask the dealer to dress and remove head of fish if whole. Rinse, dry and sprinkle fish with salt and pepper. Line the center of the pan with slices of lemon or lime and lay fish on top. Sprinkle fish with lemon juice and roast in oven at 350 F for 20 to 40 minutes. Baste often with the citrus juice. Sprinkle cooked fish with paprika. Serves 6 to 8.

TIP: If a lemon or lime is not available, use fresh fruit juices such as grapefruit and orange. Unthawed concentrate may be substituted but is not as successful as the fresh juices.

Baked Bass

2- to 3-pound black bass (large or
* small mouthed)*
½ teaspoon salt
¼ teaspoon pepper
4 tomatoes, sliced thin
½ to 1 cup bread stuffing (prepared
* stuffing is fine)*
4 strips bacon or salt pork
1 cup hot water
2 tablespoons grated cheese

Grease baking dish or pan. Rinse fish and drain. Split down the underside then season inside and out with salt and pepper. Inside the fish arrange a layer of sliced tomatoes and place a spoonful of the stuffing on each slice. Repeat layer of tomatoes and stuffing until filled, saving a few slices of the tomato. Sew or close with skewers. Place in baking dish and arrange the bacon over the fish. Pour the hot water in pan. Bake for 30 minutes in a 350 F oven. Remove from oven and lay rest of the tomato slices on fish; sprinkle with the cheese. Bake an additional 20 minutes, or until fish flakes easily when tested with a fork. Serves 6 to 8.

Baked Fish à la Florida

3- to 4-pound red snapper or other
* fish, cleaned and dressed*
1 can frozen orange concentrate
* (do not thaw)*
1 cup light brown sugar
2 tablespoons melted butter or
* margarine*
¼ cup prepared mustard
2 teaspoons curry powder

Rub fish inside and out with salt and pepper. Place fish in pan lined with aluminum foil. Mix the other ingredients, mashing the concentrate to blend, and pour over fish.

Bake at 400 F for 30 to 40 minutes, basting occasionally with the glaze. Serve with rice and chutney.

Baked Red Snapper Italian Style

3-pound red snapper or other fish
2 tablespoons chopped parsley
3 medium onions, sliced
4 medium potatoes, quartered
2 stalks celery, cut in 1-inch pieces
* (2 cups)*
1 No. 2 can tomatoes
1 lemon, sliced
1 cup olive oil
½ teaspoon oregano
Salt and pepper

Wash fish and remove dark inside skin. Place in baking dish, lightly oiled with some of the olive oil. Cover fish with vegetables and lemon slices. Pour remaining olive oil over top and sprinkle with seasonings. Bake at 350 F for 1 hour. Serves 6.

Baked Flounder
with Vegetables

2- to 3-pound flounder or other fish
⅛ teaspoon pepper
2 tablespoons thin bottled French
*   dressing, in which a garlic clove*
*   has steeped*
Canned or cooked fresh vegetables
Salt and pepper
2 tablespoons butter or other fat,
*   melted*

Wash fish and dry. Line pan with foil and grease with oil. Sprinkle fish with pepper. Arrange fish in pan and spoon over the French dressing (the thin garlic kind). Bake in hot oven at 450 F for 20 to 25 minutes, according to thickness of fish. Remove from oven and arrange around the fish a combination of canned or cooked vegetables such as shoe-peg corn, beets or carrots, and tiny green peas. Sprinkle vegetables with salt and pepper and spoon melted butter over them. Return dish to oven for 5 minutes to heat vegetables. Serves 6.

Olive Baked Fish
with Grapefruit

3- to 4-pound whole fish
Salt and pepper
Spanish olive oil
1 No. 2 can or 2 cups grapefruit
*   sections*
3 slices lemon
Parsley or celery sprigs

Have the fish dressed with head and fins removed. Wash and dry fish; sprinkle with salt and pepper inside and out. Line baking pan with foil and grease with 2 tablespoons olive oil. Place fish in center and bake in hot oven (400 F) for 25 minutes, basting with more olive oil if needed. Remove pan from oven and place grapefruit sections around fish. Place lemon slices on top (this is optional). Use ¼ cup grapefruit juice instead if you prefer. Return fish to oven for 5 more minutes. Garnish with parsley or celery sprigs. Serves 6 to 8.

Easy Baked Fish
with Stewed Tomatoes

3- to 4-pound whole fish
1 No. 2 can stewed tomatoes (2 cups)
2 tablespoons melted butter or
*   margarine*
2 tablespoons lemon juice
1 tablespoon flour
2 tablespoons tomato juice
2 tablespoons chopped parsley

Wash and dry the fish. Rub with salt and pepper. Place in a greased baking pan.

Mix tomatoes, melted butter, and lemon juice and heat. Mix the flour and tomato juice (using some of the juice from the stewed tomatoes) and stir it into the tomatoes. Pour over the fish and bake at 425 F for 30 to 40 minutes, according to size of fish. Serve with chopped parsley sprinkled over the fish if desired. Serves 6.

BAKED SHAD

*

Shad is now an important commercial fish. People used to think it had to be netted but they have found that this game fish can be caught with fishing tackle. Trolling or casting for shad is a very popular sport. It is now caught commercially also.

Shad is a most delicious fish, though very bony. The average weight is 3 pounds, but the fish grow as large as 10 pounds. The eggs, called roe, are a delicacy. When the trick of boning shad is accomplished, a delightfully flavorful fish is the result.

BONING SHAD

Scale the fish and wash it. Leave the head and tail intact. Cut down the belly with scissors. Remove the insides and wash the fish out again.

With a good sharp knife (a large pocket knife is fine for this job) cut the length of the fish, from head to tail, close to the backbone on each side. This cut should be about half an inch deep and go through the ribs. Turn the head toward you and press the meat downward from the bones. Cut through the backbone just behind the head and pull! The entire bone should come out easily.

With your hand, flatten out the thick meat at the center of the back. Wipe away any blood with a damp cloth.

With knife or pliers, pull out the long ribs. Place the point of the knife at the middle of the rib and give a firm pull. Remove all large bones the same way. Cut out the rows of bones holding each fin. Fish may be cut into fillets, or held together by skin at tail.

Use the same procedure for boning trout, Spanish mackerel, mullet and other fish.

TIP: If shad is boiled a few minutes before boning, the job is easier. Just boil a very short time so bones come out more easily.

Shad with Madeira Sauce

Bake boned shad in a greased pan at
400 F. All it needs is salt and pepper
with perhaps a dash or two of paprika.
Bake for 10 minutes per pound. Serve
plain or with a wine sauce such as
Madeira Sauce.

Madeira Sauce

1 tablespoon catsup
1 tablespoon flour
1 tablespoon water
Juice of 1 lemon
¾ cup Madeira wine

Mix the flour and water. Then stir
all ingredients into the drippings
where shad was baked. Heat a little.
Serve separately in a sauce bowl.
Makes approximately 1 cup.

TIP: Sherry may be substituted for
the Madeira.

Boneless Baked Shad

2- to 3-pound shad
2 cups water
1 cup white vinegar
1 medium onion, sliced
2 tablespoons lemon juice
1 tablespoon grated lemon rind
1 bay leaf
2 teaspoons salt
½ teaspoon pepper

In this recipe the shad is not boned
first.

Place the dressed whole shad in a
roaster on a rack. Combine the other
ingredients and pour into roaster.
Cover and cook on top of stove over
moderate heat, until the water boils.
Turn heat to low and cook 40 minutes.

Lift fish out on rack and drain the
liquid from the pan. Return the fish
to roaster, cover it and bake in low
oven, 200 F, for 4 hours. The fish
will be soft, and so will the bones,
and may be eaten as canned salmon
is. Serves 6 to 8.

MIXED SEAFOOD BAKE

Any combination of seafoods may be baked. Have the oven hot and line
the pan with foil. Grease it and arrange several slices of lemon or lime on the
bottom, if desired. Over the lemon place as many different varieties of seafoods as you wish: fish fillets, steaks, or small whole fish with scallops, shrimp,
and drained oysters, for instance. Sprinkle generously with salt and pepper.
Bake in a hot oven at 425 F for 15 to 20 minutes, basting with melted butter
or other fat. Remove from pan and sprinkle with paprika or garnish with
salad greens.

BAKED STUFFED FISH

Baked Fish with Savory Green Pepper Stuffing

3- or 4-pound whole fish, dressed
1½ teaspoons salt
2 tablespoons melted butter or other
    fat

Clean, wash, and dry the fish. Sprinkle inside and out with salt. Stuff fish loosely with *Savory Green Pepper Stuffing* and sew the opening with needle and string, or close with skewers. Place fish in a greased baking pan. Brush lightly with melted fat. Bake in a moderate oven, 375 F, for 30 to 40 minutes. Serves 6.

SAVORY GREEN PEPPER STUFFING

2 cups soft bread crumbs or coarsely
    rolled cracker crumbs
¼ cup melted butter or margarine
¼ teaspoon salt
⅛ teaspoon pepper
¼ cup chopped onion
¼ cup chopped green pepper

Place the bread crumbs in a mixing bowl. Stir in the melted fat and other ingredients and stuff fish. Serves 6.

Baked Fish with Rice-Olive Stuffing

6-pound fish, dressed
Salt and pepper
2 tablespoons melted butter or other
    fat

Sprinkle fish inside and out with salt and pepper and stuff with *Rice-Olive Stuffing.* No trussing is necessary. Baste with butter. Bake in preheated oven at 500 F for 10 minutes, then lower the heat to moderate, or 375 F, and continue baking for 50 minutes longer, or until fish flakes easily.

RICE-OLIVE STUFFING

½ cup butter, margarine or salad oil
1 large onion, minced
2 cups minced celery
2¼ cups cooked rice
2 cups chopped stuffed olives
½ teaspoon salt
½ teaspoon pepper
½ teaspoon thyme

Sauté the onion and celery in the butter until soft, about 3 minutes. Add the other ingredients and mix well. Stuff fish. Any extra stuffing may be heated thoroughly and served separately. Serves 6 to 8.

Baked Pompano Surprise

2- to 3-pound pompano, dressed

STUFFING

1 cup croutons
1 cup cooked peas
1 egg, beaten
2 tablespoons butter
1 small onion, chopped
1 cup minced celery
½ teaspoon salt
¼ teaspoon pepper

Wash and dry fish. Combine all the ingredients for the stuffing and stir lightly. Fill fish with stuffing. No trussing is necessary. Bake in greased pan for 20 to 30 minutes in moderate oven, 350 F. Then turn up heat to 400 F, if fish is not lightly browned, and bake another 5 minutes. Serve garnished with parsley, vegetables or citrus fruits. Serves 6.

Sour Cream Stuffing

¼ cup salad oil or other fat
¾ cup chopped celery
½ cup minced onion
4 cups dry bread cubes
½ cup sour cream
¼ cup lemon juice
2 tablespoons grated lemon rind
1 teaspoon salt
1 teaspoon thyme

Heat the salad oil and cook the celery and onion in it until soft. Combine all other ingredients with celery mixture and mix thoroughly. Stuff fish and bake as directed under *Baked Fish with Savory Green Pepper Stuffing.* Enough for a 3- to 4-pound fish. Serves 6.

Vegetable Stuffing

2 pounds fish
2 carrots, shredded
2 green onions, chopped
¼ cup chopped pimento
1 cup pitted ripe olives, chopped
2 cups bread cubes
¼ cup butter or other fat
Salt and pepper

This stuffing is for coiled fillets, steaks or whole fish. Prepare the fish. Shred carrots and mix with chopped green onions, pimento, and ripe olives. Mix melted butter into the bread cubes. Mix with vegetables and add salt and pepper to taste. Stuff a whole fish, spoon into centers of coiled fillets, or use between two large fish steaks. Bake in oven 10 minutes to pound of fish at 375 F, or moderate. Serves 6.

Shrimp Stuffing

½ pound shrimp
¼ cup chopped onion
¼ cup butter or other fat, melted
1 egg, beaten
2 tablespoons milk
2 cups soft bread cubes
½ teaspoon nutmeg
1 teaspoon salt
⅛ teaspoon pepper

Peel the shrimp and remove the veins. Wash and cut into small pieces. Cook the onion in the butter until soft and add shrimp. Stir until shrimp is heated. Combine the beaten egg and remaining ingredients. Mix all together until well moistened. Enough for a 4-pound fish.

TIP: By increasing the bread cubes

to 3 cups, this stuffing can be used with a 4- to 5-pound bird, and is delicious.

Oyster Stuffing

1 pint oysters
½ cup chopped celery
½ cup chopped onion
¼ cup butter, melted
4 cups day-old bread, torn into pieces
1 tablespoon chopped parsley
1 teaspoon salt

⅛ teaspoon savory seasoning, mace or thyme
⅛ teaspoon pepper

Drain the oysters, saving any liquor, and chop them. Cook the chopped celery and onion in the butter until tender. Combine the oysters with the celery-onion mixture, add bread pieces and seasonings and mix thoroughly. Moisten with oyster liquor or warm water if stuffing seems too dry. Enough for a 4-pound fish.

WHOLE FISH IN WRAPPER

✳

Fish Dinner in Foil

3- or 4-pound fish
1 lemon, sliced
½ cup butter or margarine, melted
Salt and pepper
Paprika
1 cup each cooked sliced potatoes, peas, beets or other vegetable combinations

Place dressed fish in the center of a large piece of aluminum foil in a broiler pan or square oven dish. Turn down the sides of the foil to fit pan. Season fish. Spoon half of the melted butter over fish and place slices of lemon on top. Bake in hot oven, 450 F, for 20 to 30 minutes. Remove from oven, place vegetables around fish and heat in oven.

If you wish, wrap the foil around fish and vegetables until serving time. Package can then be placed in the oven again and heated. Serves 6.

TIP: This is a fine way to prepare fish in advance for an outdoor dinner at the grill. Simply take the package to the grill and heat there. Individual fish and vegetable packages can be fixed in the same manner.

Small Fish Baked in Foil with Bacon

2 to 3 pounds whole small fish, such as smelt
2 teaspoons salt
⅛ teaspoon pepper
Paprika
⅓ cup chopped onion
⅓ cup chopped parsley (optional)
Strips of bacon cut in half

Dress, wash, and dry fish. Divide into 6 portions. Cut heavy foil in squares large enough to wrap fish. Place each in the center of a square of greased foil. Sprinkle each serving with salt, pepper, paprika, onion and parsley. Place a half strip of bacon on top. Wrap servings in the foil, pressing edges to seal tightly. Place packages of fish in a hot oven, 400 F, and cook 15 minutes. Remove fish and open foil. Place opened packages under broiler and heat 3 minutes to brown before serving. Serves 6.

TIP: The sealed packages of fish may be placed in a bed of hot coals and cooked 15 minutes. Turn packages during cooking several times.

Fish en Papillotes

6 small fish fillets or whole fish
Salt and pepper
¼ cup soft butter or margarine
2 tablespoons minced green onion
2 tablespoons prepared mustard
¼ cup chili sauce

Sprinkle fish with salt and pepper. Cut foil or brown paper in squares large enough to completely wrap fish servings. Grease each piece of paper and place a fish fillet in center. Mix butter, onion, mustard and chili sauce and spread equally over fish. Wrap packages. Tie with string if brown paper is used. Bake on a cooky sheet in oven at 375 F for 30 minutes, or until fish flakes easily when tested with a fork. Serve in wrapping. These are good with baked potato, mixed green salad and lemon pie. Serves 6.

Fillets with Easy Caper Sauce

2 pounds fish fillets
¼ cup lemon juice
2 tablespoons capers and juice
½ teaspoon salt
⅛ teaspoon pepper

Place fish fillets in center of foil pieces large enough to cover, or if in a hurry, place fish in lightly greased oven pan. Combine the lemon juice and capers. Sprinkle fish with the salt and pepper. Spoon caper sauce over fish. Bake in a moderate oven, 350 F, for 20 minutes. Or wrap fish securely in foil and bake, turning several times, opening a package carefully after 20 minutes to test for doneness. Brown under broiler before serving. Serves 6.

TIP: Prepare fish as above and cook under broiler instead of baking or wrapping in foil, if you prefer.

BAKED FILLETS

*

This recipe and the following demonstrate again that there is nothing better on fish than lemon and lime juices with spices.

Lime-Ginger Baked Fish I

2 pounds fish fillets or steaks
Salt and pepper
½ cup lime juice
2 tablespoons grated onion
1 teaspoon powdered ginger
1 bay leaf, crushed
¼ cup butter, melted
Sliced lime

Arrange fish in shallow oven dish or broiler pan, and salt and pepper it. Mix the lime juice with the onion, ginger and bay leaf and pour the marinade over the fish. Let marinate 1 to 2 hours.

When ready to cook, pour melted butter or other fat over fish and place a slice of lime on each piece. Bake in a moderate oven, 350 F, for 20 minutes. Serves 6.

Lime-Ginger Baked Fish II

2 pounds fish fillets or steaks
¼ cup lime juice
1 tablespoon onion flakes
1 teaspoon ground ginger
⅛ teaspoon black pepper
½ teaspoon salt
Butter

Wash and dry fish. Place in greased pan or baking dish. Mix the lime juice, onion and spices. Dot the fish with butter and spoon the lime mixture over it. Bake in a moderate oven, 350 F, for 20 minutes. Serve fish on hot platter or in the same baking utensil. Garnish with tiny whole potatoes, mushrooms or other vegetables. Serves 6.

Tangy Baked Fillets

2 pounds fish fillets or steaks
2 tablespoons lemon juice
1 teaspoon dehydrated onion flakes
1 teaspoon salt
1 teaspoon ground mustard
¼ cup oil
1 teaspoon paprika
Dash cayenne pepper

Place fillets in greased baking pan, skin side down. Mix other ingredients and spoon over fish. Bake in a moderate oven, 350 F, for 20 minutes. Serves 6.

Lemon-Baked Fish Steaks and Roe

6 small fish steaks, any variety
2 pairs roe
Salt
Pepper
Paprika
2 tablespoons salad oil
1 lemon, thinly sliced

Wash and dry the fish and the roe. Sprinkle with salt, pepper, and paprika. Line baking pan with foil and spoon over it the salad oil. Arrange slices of lemon in the pan. Place fish and roe on top. Bake in hot oven, 400 F, for 20 minutes. Baste occasionally with the oil in pan. Serves 6.

Baked Fish with Garlic Butter

2 pounds fish fillets or steaks
Salt
Pepper
1 lemon, thinly sliced
2 tablespoons melted butter
1 clove garlic, minced

Line baking pan with foil. Grease it lightly with butter. Arrange slices of lemon on foil. Sprinkle fish with salt and pepper. Place on top of lemon slices. Combine garlic and butter and pour garlic-butter over fish. Bake in moderate oven, 400 F for 20 minutes. Serves 6.

These recipes are easy because the almonds come prepared in packages.

Baked Fish Amandine I

2 pounds snapper, mackerel, or other
* fish steaks*
Salt and pepper
2 tablespoons lime or lemon juice
¼ cup melted butter or salad oil
½ cup blanched slivered almonds
2 tablespoons butter
¼ cup lemon or lime juice

Line baking pan with foil. Grease lightly with some of the butter. Place steaks on foil and sprinkle with salt, pepper and lime juice. Spoon rest of fat over steaks. Bake in hot oven, 425 F, for 20 minutes.

Before serving, melt 2 tablespoons butter in a skillet and in it brown the almonds over low heat. Watch carefully as they burn quickly. Toss until evenly browned. Remove almonds. If more sauce is desired, add ¼ cup lemon or lime juice to the butter in the pan and stir until heated.

Spread the almonds over the cooked fish and pour the butter or lemon-butter over all. Serves 6.

Baked Fish Amandine II

2 pounds fish fillets or steaks
1 cup evaporated milk
1 teaspoon salt
Dry bread crumbs or cracker meal
½ cup melted butter or margarine
1 cup blanched slivered almonds
2 tablespoons lemon juice

Have fillets cut into serving pieces. Wash fish and dry. Combine milk and salt. Dip fish in milk, then roll in the bread crumbs. Place in a well-greased baking dish and spoon ¼ cup butter over fish. Bake in a hot oven, 400 F, for 15 to 20 minutes. The fish will be crusted but not too brown.

Before serving melt butter or margarine in a skillet and brown the almonds over low heat. Watch carefully as they burn quickly. Toss until evenly browned. Remove almonds. Add 2 tablespoons lemon juice and ⅛ teaspoon salt to butter in the pan. Stir until heated. Spread almonds over fish when ready to serve and pour the lemon-butter sauce over all. Serves 6.

Oven-Poached Fish Steaks with Grapes

3 tablespoons butter or margarine
2 pounds fish steaks, such as haddock,
   whitefish or grouper
1 teaspoon salt
1 cup water
1 cup evaporated milk
1 cup seedless grapes (optional)

Melt the butter in a baking pan. Arrange fish in pan and sprinkle with salt. Add water and milk. Place pan in a moderate oven, 350 F, and let fish poach until tender, about 45 minutes.

Plump grapes in simmering water to cover for about 3 minutes. Drain grapes and cut in half if you wish. Before serving, sprinkle over fish. Serves 6.

Ask your dealer to fillet your fish and cut in even-sized strips. Take scraps for fish flakes.

Fish Sticks Cornie

6 to 9 fish sticks (fillets cut in even
   strips about 1 by 4 inches)
1½ cups corn meal, sifted
¾ teaspoon soda
1 teaspoon salt
Small onion, chopped
2 eggs
1⅓ cups buttermilk
¼ cup melted shortening
Chili sauce or butter and mustard

Mix sifted corn meal, soda and salt. Add chopped onion. Beat eggs, add buttermilk and stir into corn meal. Add hot melted shortening and beat well. Turn the batter into greased square pan or baking dish. Now place fish sticks in batter in rows about 2 inches apart, leaving room to cut between. Push fish down into batter.

Spread each fish stick with chili sauce or an equal amount of mustard and melted butter mixed well. Bake in a hot oven, 450 F, 25 to 30 minutes. When corn bread cooks it will rise around the fish. Cut in squares to resemble hot dogs in buns. Serve with relish and cole slaw. Serves 6 to 8.

FILLETS BAKED WITH SAUCE

*

Company Baked Fish

2 pounds fillets of large fish, like
    snapper, grouper, salmon or kingfish
3 tablespoons lemon juice
½ teaspoon Worcestershire sauce
2 teaspoons prepared mustard
1½ teaspoons salt
¼ teaspoon pepper
2 medium onions, chopped
1½ cups cream
Paprika
Celery sprigs

Rinse fish and dry. Place in greased baking dish. Combine the juice, Worcestershire sauce, mustard, salt and pepper. Pour over fish. Add chopped onions and pour in cream. Bake in a hot oven, 400 F, for 30 minutes. Sprinkle with paprika and garnish with leaf sprigs from celery. Serves 6.

With this dish try serving canned small potatoes, buttered and browned in the oven, Brussels sprouts, pear and cream cheese salad and, for dessert, baked custards. (Most of the dinner can be prepared in advance and then cooked in the oven.)

Baked Flounder De Luxe

2 pounds flounder or other fish fillets
1 teaspoon salt
⅛ teaspoon pepper
1 4-ounce can mushrooms (stems and
    pieces)

2 tablespoons butter or other fat,
    melted
1½ tablespoons lime juice
1 teaspoon dried onion flakes

Sprinkle flounder on both sides with salt and pepper. Place, skin side down, in a greased baking pan or dish. Combine mushrooms, butter, lime juice and onion flakes. Pour over flounder. Bake in a moderate oven, 350 F, for 35 minutes or until fish flakes easily when tested with a fork. Serve garnished with celery sprigs and cherry tomatoes. Serves 6.

Baked Fillets with Green Pepper Sauce

2 pounds any fish fillets
Salt and pepper
½ cup chopped onion
1 small clove garlic, finely minced
½ cup thinly sliced green pepper
2 tablespoons butter
⅓ cup water
½ teaspoon powdered ginger
3 tablespoons vinegar
1 tablespoon brown sugar
¼ teaspoon salt

Place fish in greased baking dish. Sprinkle with salt and pepper.

Sauté onion, garlic, and green pepper in melted butter until tender, 5 to 10 minutes. Add water, ginger, vinegar, brown sugar and salt. Simmer for 5 minutes. Pour the sauce over the fish fillets. Bake in a hot oven, 400 F, 20 minutes. Serves 6.

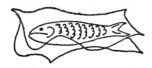

Baked Fillets with Creamy Sauce

2 pounds fillets of trout, mullet,
    mackerel or other fish
1 cup commerial sour cream
2 teaspoons lime juice
1 teaspoon salt
½ teaspoon sugar
4 tablespoons cracker meal
½ teaspoon paprika

Sprinkle fish with salt and pepper.
Arrange in a baking dish. Mix the next
five ingredients and spread over fish.
Sprinkle with paprika. Bake in a
moderate oven, 375 F, for 30 minutes.
Garnish with cooked vegetables or
tomato halves. Serves 6.

Swiss Baked Fish

2 pounds fish fillets or steaks
1 cup sour cream
½ cup chopped green onions and
    tops
⅓ cup grated Swiss cheese
2 teaspoons salt
Paprika

Cut large fillets or steaks into serving-
size portions. Place fish in a greased
baking pan. Combine the other ingredients and spread over the top of
fish. Bake in a moderate oven, 350 F,
for 20 to 30 minutes. Serves 6.

Baked Fillets with Easy Shrimp Sauce

1 can frozen cream of shrimp soup
1 pound fish fillets
Salt and pepper
2 tablespoons butter or margarine
¼ cup grated Parmesan cheese
Paprika

Thaw the soup. Place fish fillets in
buttered baking dish. Sprinkle with
salt and pepper. Dot with butter.
Spread the soup over fillets and
sprinkle cheese over the top. Bake in
a hot oven 400 F, 20 minutes. Serve
with baked potato, asparagus tips and
tossed salad and serve lemon pie for
dessert. Serves 4.

Baked Fillets or Steaks with Surprise Clam Topping

6 small fish fillets or steaks
1½ teaspoons salt
1½ teaspoons white pepper
3 tablespoons butter
1 cup peeled, thinly sliced white onion
1 can clam chowder
½ cup sherry
¼ cup dry bread crumbs
¼ cup grated American cheese

Wash fillets or steaks and sprinkle
with the salt and pepper. In a large
iron skillet, or one with detachable
handle, melt the butter and sauté the
onion until lightly browned. Place
fish in the skillet. Mix together the
clam chowder and sherry. Pour over
fish and bake in a moderate oven,
375 F, for 20 minutes. Remove from
oven and sprinkle with the bread
crumbs and cheese. Return to oven
and bake 5 minutes longer. Serves 6.

Baked Fish Savannah

2 pounds fillets or steaks
¼ cup chopped onion
¼ cup chopped green pepper
3 tablespoons butter or other fat,
    melted
2 tablespoons flour
2 cups canned tomatoes
1 teaspoon salt
½ teaspoon pepper
1 bay leaf
1 garlic clove, minced

Place fish in a greased baking pan. Cook the chopped onion and green pepper in butter until tender. Blend in the flour and cook a minute. Add tomatoes and seasonings and cook the sauce until thick, stirring constantly. Remove the bay leaf. Cover fish with the sauce and bake in a moderate oven, 350 F, for 35 to 40 minutes. Serves 6.

Baked Fish-Mushrooms Imperial

2 pounds fish steaks or fillets
½ cup melted butter or other fat
1 pound fresh mushrooms or ¼ ounce
    can whole mushrooms or pieces,
    drained
2 tablespoons lemon juice or 1
    tablespoon lime juice
1 teaspoon salt
1 teaspoon grated onion
⅛ teaspoon pepper
Paprika

If fresh mushrooms are used, they should be pared, washed and sliced, then sautéed in butter until soft before adding to the sauce.

Wash and dry fish. Place in a greased baking pan. Combine all ingredients (including the butter but not the paprika) and pour over fish. Bake in a moderate oven, 350 F, for 30 minutes. Sprinkle paprika over top. Serves 6.

Baked Fish Steaks with Orange Sauce

2 pounds any fish steaks
1 teaspoon salt
⅛ teaspoon pepper
4 tablespoons frozen orange
    concentrate (unthawed)
3 tablespoons butter or margarine,
    melted
½ teaspoon nutmeg

Grease a baking pan and arrange steaks in a single layer in it. Combine the remaining ingredients, mashing the concentrate to blend, and pour over the fish. Bake in a moderate oven, 350 F, for 20 minutes. Serves 6.

Cheese-Baked Fillets

2 pounds fish fillets
Salt and pepper
2 tablespoons butter
1 can cheese soup
2 tablespoons Sherry
Paprika

Place fillets in a buttered baking pan. Sprinkle lightly with salt and pepper. Melt butter and spoon over the fish. Bake in a hot oven, 450 F, for 10 minutes. Remove pan from oven. Blend undiluted soup with the Sherry (if Sherry is omitted, use ¼ cup of water). Pour over fish and sprinkle with paprika. Place fish under broiler heat until light brown and bubbly—from 5 to 7 minutes. Serves 6.

Fish Fromage

2 pounds fish fillets
1 medium onion, chopped
2 cups grated American cheese
1½ teaspoons Worcestershire sauce
1 teaspoon prepared mustard
1 teaspoon salt
¼ teaspoon pepper
1 cup cream or milk

Wash and dry fillets. Spread the chopped onion and 1 cup cheese in a greased baking dish. Place fish on top and cover with remaining cheese. Combine other ingredients well and pour the mixture over fish. Bake in a hot oven, 425 F, for 20 to 25 minutes. Serves 6.

Fillets Marguery

6 small fish fillets
Salt
Paprika
⅓ cup white wine
2 cups fish stock (see Poaching Fish)
18 cooked clams
    or
18 small cooked shrimp, shelled
1 boiled lobster, shelled and sliced
2 tablespoons butter
2 tablespoons flour
⅛ teaspoon pepper
¼ cup grated Parmesan cheese

Butter a baking dish and arrange the fish in it. Sprinkle with salt and paprika. Add the wine. Cut a piece of brown paper the size of the dish, butter it, and lay it lightly over the dish to edges. Bake the fish in a moderate oven, 350 F, for 15 minutes.

Combine the fish stock, the shell of the lobster, and 6 of the cooked clams. Simmer until the liquid measures about 1 cup and strain it. Melt butter in a skillet, blend in the flour and cook a minute. Gradually add the strained fish stock and any liquid drained from the cooked fillets. Cook until consistency of thin pudding. Season with salt and pepper.

Arrange the fish on a heatproof serving platter and pour the sauce over it. Garnish with the sliced lobster meat and the remaining clams or the shelled cooked shrimp. Sprinkle the dish with cheese and bake in a moderate oven, 350 F, until cheese is melted and fish is hot. Serves 6 to 8.

TIP: Lemon or lime juice and water may be substituted for the wine. Garnish also with parsley, watercress or celery sprigs.

Shrimp Sauce

Try this delicious sauce over any plain cooked fish—fried, baked or broiled.

½ pound cooked shrimp
2 tablespoons butter or other fat, melted
2 tablespoons flour
1 cup milk
½ teaspoon salt
2 hard-cooked eggs, chopped
2 tablespoons chopped parsley
    (optional)

Cut the shrimp into small pieces and brown in butter 3 to 4 minutes. Blend in flour, cook a minute and add milk gradually, stirring. Add salt. Cook sauce until thick, stirring constantly. Add the egg and parsley. Serve over cooked fish. Serves 6.

BAKED STUFFED FILLETS

*

Stuffed fillets are always skinned. If small fish are used, lap the small end over larger after spooning the stuffing in center. If fillets are large, cut lengthwise. Stand in greased baking pan or dish. They may also be placed in greased muffin tins or custard cups, leaving room in center for stuffing. Baste as they cook with melted butter or other fat.

Fish-Shrimp Roll-Arounds

3 pounds small fish, filleted and
    skinned
3 tablespoons butter
1 small onion, minced
2 cups soft bread crumbs
1 teaspoon salt
½ teaspoon pepper
3 tablespoons water
¼ cup chopped dill pickles
1 cup chopped shrimp
½ cup sour cream
½ cup milk
Paprika

Melt the butter in a large skillet and cook the minced onion until soft. Add the bread crumbs, salt, pepper and water, toss to mix. Add pickles and shrimp. Place equal amount of stuffing in center of each fillet and roll around, fastening with toothpicks. Stand stuffed fillets in a greased shallow baking dish. Mix the sour cream and milk, pour around fillets. Bake at 350 F for 20 to 25 minutes or until brown. Baste with the sour cream-milk mixture as the fish cooks. Sprinkle with paprika before removing from oven. Serves 6 to 8.

Fillets Stuffed with Crab and Shrimp

2 pounds fish fillets, skinned
Salt and pepper
2 tablespoons butter
2 tablespoons flour
1 cup milk
½ cup cooked crabmeat, flaked and
    boned
½ cup cooked shrimp, chopped
¼ cup chopped celery
¼ cup chopped green onion
2 tablespoons butter, melted
1 tablespoon chopped parsley
1 teaspoon salt

Place fillets in baking pan and sprinkle with salt and pepper. Then prepare the filling:

Melt the butter in a saucepan and stir in the flour. Cook a minute, stirring. Gradually add the milk, cooking and stirring until thickened. Remove from heat and stir in the crabmeat and shrimp.

Cook the celery and green onion in melted butter. Add parsley and salt. Stir this mixture into the crab-shrimp sauce. Divide the filling equally among fillets, roll from small end and secure with toothpicks. Place in a greased baking dish and bake in hot oven, 400 F, for 30 minutes. Baste with melted butter. Serve with additional cream sauce if desired. Serves 6.

Luau Crab-Stuffed Fish Rolls

2 pounds small fish fillets, skinned
Salt and pepper
1 cup flaked cooked or canned
  crabmeat
1 cup pineapple tidbits, drained
½ cup cubed sharp Cheddar cheese
⅓ cup prepared barbecue sauce
1 tablespoon celery flakes, or ⅓ cup
  fresh chopped celery
4 tablespoons stuffed olives, sliced

Wash and dry the fillets; sprinkle lightly with salt and pepper, then set aside. Combine crabmeat, pineapple, cheese, barbecue sauce, celery flakes or fresh celery and olives. Mix lightly. Spoon the crab stuffing in center of each fillet, roll and fasten with toothpicks. Stand in well-greased baking pan and bake in oven at 350 F, for 15 to 20 minutes or until fish flakes easily when tested with a fork. Baste if needed with melted butter as fish cooks. Serves 6.

Fillets with Dill

2 pounds small fish fillets, skinned
4 tablespoons butter
1 small onion, minced
2 cups soft bread crumbs
2 tablespoons capers, drained and
  chopped
½ teaspoon salt
¼ teaspoon pepper
1 teaspoon dried crushed dill or ¼
  cup chopped dill pickles
2 or 3 slices bacon

Sprinkle fillets with salt and pepper

to taste. Set aside. Melt butter in skillet and sauté onion until soft. Add bread crumbs, capers and seasonings. Toss together. Roll fillets loosely inside greased custard or muffin cups. Spoon the stuffing into the center of each. Top each roll with ¼ slice bacon. Bake in moderate oven, 350 F, 15 to 20 minutes, or until bacon and stuffing are browned. Serves 6.

Cheesy Baked Fillets

3 pounds fish fillets, skinned
½ cup prepared Italian dressing
1½ cups finely crushed cheese
  crackers
2 tablespoons melted butter or other
  fat
Dash cayenne

Cut fillets into serving-size pieces. Dip fish in dressing, then roll in crumbs of the cheese crackers. Roll fillets and fasten with toothpicks. Place in a well-greased shallow baking pan. Spoon melted butter or other fat over fish. Sprinkle lightly with cayenne. Bake in hot oven, 450 F, for 15 minutes or until fish flakes when tested with a fork. Serve with browned potatoes and broiled tomato halves. Serves 6 to 8.

Fish-Crab Rolls with Creamy Sauce

6 small fish fillets, skinned
1 6-ounce package crabmeat, fresh
  or frozen
¼ cup melted butter, or other fat
2 cups (6 slices) bread, cubed
2 tablespoons chopped parsley
2 pimentos, minced
2 green onions, chopped
Salt and pepper
1 package frozen tiny peas, cooked
1 4-ounce can mushrooms
Paprika

Thaw crabmeat, if frozen. Wash and dry fillets. Melt butter and mix with bread cubes, parsley, pimentos, onions and crabmeat. Season lightly with salt and pepper. Spoon filling onto fillets and coil from small end. Secure with toothpicks. Place fillets in greased baking dish and spoon some melted butter over top. Bake in moderate oven, 375 F, 20 minutes. Remove from oven and pour off some of the liquid in the dish. Arrange mushrooms and peas around the fish rolls and garnish with pimento. Sprinkle fish with paprika. Serve with *Creamy Sauce.* Serves 6.

Creamy Sauce

2 tablespoons butter
1 tablespoon flour
1 cup milk
⅓ cup dry white wine or lemon juice
¾ teaspoon salt
Dash pepper
2 slightly beaten egg yolks

Melt the butter in top part of a double boiler over hot water. Stir in flour. Add milk gradually, stirring until thick and smooth. Add the wine or lemon juice, salt and pepper and heat. Stir a little of the hot liquid into the egg yolks. and add them. Cook 2 minutes, stirring. Serve the sauce in a separate bowl. Makes 1½ cups sauce.

Fish Fillets with Corn-Bread Stuffing

6 fish fillets, skinned
1 teaspoon salt
⅛ teaspoon pepper
½ cup butter or margarine, melted

Sprinkle fish with salt and pepper. Line greased muffin tins or custard cups with fillets, leaving space in center for stuffing, but overlapping ends. Spoon *Corn-Bread Stuffing* into center of fish and brush generously with melted butter. Bake in a moderate oven, 350 F, for 25 to 30 minutes. Serves 6.

CORN-BREAD STUFFING

2 tablespoons chopped onion
½ cup chopped celery
¼ cup butter or margarine, melted
¼ cup water or fish stock
1 teaspoon salt
⅛ teaspoon pepper
1 teaspoon thyme or savory seasoning
1 cup cooked crumbled corn bread
1 cup lightly toasted bread, moistened

Sauté onion and celery in butter until tender. Combine other ingredients with water or fish stock. Combine onion mixture.

TIP: For an all-bread stuffing, omit the corn bread and increase bread crumbs to 2 cups. In this case do not use toasted bread but use day-old bread for crumbs.

Fillets with Parmesan-Cheese Stuffing

4 to 6 small fish fillets, skinned
Salt and pepper
Melted butter

Sprinkle the fillets lightly with salt and pepper. Coil around, lapping small end over larger end. Leave space in the middle for stuffing. Place fillets in muffin tins or custard cups or stand in greased baking pan. Spoon *Parmesan-Cheese Stuffing* into center of fish. Baste top with melted butter, and bake in moderate oven, 350 F, for 20 to 25 minutes, or until stuffing is lightly browned. Serves 4 to 6.

PARMESAN-CHEESE STUFFING

1 hard-boiled egg, chopped
2 tablespoons butter
½ cup chopped onion
½ cup chopped celery
2 cups fresh bread crumbs
¼ cup grated Parmesan cheese
½ teaspoon salt
¼ teaspoon pepper
½ teaspoon mace
½ teaspoon dried basil, crumbled

Chop egg. Heat butter in skillet and cook chopped onion and celery until soft. Combine all ingredients and mix thoroughly.

Fish Steaks Curry

2 large fish steaks (about ¾ pound each)
1 teaspoon salt
1 cup cooked rice
1 cup soft bread cubes
2½ tablespoons lemon juice
1 cup drained crushed pineapple
¾ teaspoon curry powder
½ teaspoon salt
2 tablespoons butter or other fat, melted

Sprinkle fish steaks with salt. Place one steak in greased baking pan. Combine the rice with the next 5 ingredients. Spoon the rice mixture over the steak and cover with the other one. Fasten together with skewers or toothpicks. Brush with the melted butter. Bake in a moderate oven, 350 F, for 35 minutes. Serves 4. Serve with small cups of chopped peanuts and flaked cocoanut.

Planked Fish

Planked fish is simply fish baked on a hardwood plank. A bake-and-serve platter answers the same purpose, but many years ago, before such utensils were available, the hardwood plank with grooves for fat was used. Fish, such as mackerel, bluefish, lake trout and so on, are sometimes planked. Here is a basic recipe:

2- to 4-pound fish
Salt, pepper
Paprika
Butter or margarine
Vegetables such as small tomatoes and canned potatoes

Split fish and remove backbone, leaving skin along back. Wash and dry. Sprinkle with salt, pepper and paprika.

Heat wooden plank in oven or broiler and grease with butter, margarine or other fat. Place fish, skin side down, on plank. Dot with butter. Bake in a hot oven, 425 F, for 20 minutes. Remove from oven. Spoon vegetables around fish and return to oven to heat. Serves 6.

When broiling, to prevent exposed parts of plank from burning, cover with a damp cloth.

TIP: Any variety of vegetables may be used. Lightly whipped potatoes, tomato halves and marinated cucumber slices are often used. Use thin French dressing for the cucumber marinade. Potatoes should brown lightly.

OVEN-BARBECUED AND DEVILED FISH

Almost any variety of fish, fresh, frozen or canned, fillets, steaks and whole, may be oven-barbecued or deviled. The sauce is the thing and may be plain basic barbecue sauce or elaborate with added spices and vinegars. Bottled prepared barbecue sauce is good spread over fish before broiling or baking, or served separately with the plain broiled or baked fish.

You will find many additional recipes in the chapter on outdoor cookery, but in case it rains just pop the fish in the oven, with or without sauces, and everyone will be happy.

Oven-Barbecued Fish

2 pounds fish fillets or steaks
¾ cup tomato catsup
2 tablespoons vinegar
¼ cup lemon or lime juice
1 tablespoon onion flakes or chopped
 onion
2 tablespoons brown sugar

½ teaspoon salt
⅛ teaspoon pepper

Wash and dry fish. Arrange in broiler pan or baking dish. Combine all the other ingredients and pour over fish. Bake in hot oven, 425 F, for 20 to 25 minutes, or until fish flakes easily when tested, and sauce is bubbly. Serves 6.

Barbecued Fish—Indoor or Outdoor

2 pounds fish fillets or steaks
⅓ cup salad oil or other fat
¾ cup catsup
1 tablespoon prepared mustard
4 tablespoons vinegar (tarragon is good)
1 tablespoon Worcestershire sauce
2 tablespoons hickory liquid smoke
Dash Tabasco
Dash paprika
1 large onion, sliced thin

Grease shallow pan with part of fat and place the fish in it. Mix remainder of fat with other ingredients except the onion. Peel and slice onion and spread on top of fish. Pour the barbecue sauce over all. Place on lower rack of a hot oven, 450 F, for 20 minutes, basting. Add a little water if necessary. Place under broiler last few minutes of cooking time. Serves 6.

For outdoor barbecue, place fish on top of grill and baste with sauce as above.

For barbecuing fish in the oven, here is a "dilly" of a recipe.

Dill Barbecued Fish

2 pounds fish fillets or steaks
¼ cup bottled cocktail sauce
1 teaspoon lime juice
3 tablespoons melted butter or other fat
1 teaspoon prepared mustard
½ teaspoon salt
¼ teaspoon pepper
1 tablespoon onion flakes or grated fresh onion

2 tablespoons chopped dill pickles or 1 teaspoon dried dill flakes, crumbled
½ cup water

Wash fish and dry thoroughly. Place in oven pan or dish. Combine all the other ingredients and spread over fish. Bake in hot oven, 450 F for 20 minutes, or until sauce is light brown. Serves 6.

For outdoor barbecue, omit the water for a thicker sauce and brush fish occasionally with the sauce as it cooks.

Pepper-Chili Sauce Deviled Fish

2 pounds fish fillets or steaks
2 tablespoons salad oil or other fat
1 tablespoon steak sauce
2 tablespoons prepared mustard
½ cup chili sauce
¼ teaspoon freshly ground black pepper
½ teaspoon salt

Wash and dry fish. Place in greased pan. Mix all the other ingredients and spread evenly over the fish. Place under broiler heat for 5 to 7 minutes, or until lightly browned and fish flakes easily when tested with a fork. Serves 6.

Oven Deviled Fillets

2 pounds fish fillets
½ cup hot catsup or chili sauce
2 tablespoons salad oil
2 tablespoons prepared mustard
2 tablespoons prepared horseradish
1 tablespoon Worcestershire sauce
½ teaspoon salt
¼ teaspoon pepper

Wash and dry the fish. Place in greased broiler pan. Mix together all the other ingredients and spread evenly over the fish fillets. Broil about 4 inches from heat for 5 minutes, or until the fish flakes easily when tested with a fork. Garnish with slices of lemon and parsley sprigs. Serves 6.

Mustard Shad

After boning, slice 2 pounds shad fillets into sticks or pieces. Place in greased broiler pan and sprinkle with thin French dressing. Broil or roll in corn meal and fry. Make this sauce in advance.

MUSTARD SAUCE

5 tablespoons boiling water
2 tablespoons dry mustard
2 teaspoons horseradish
1 cup salad oil
1 teaspoon salt
1 teaspoon sugar
½ teaspoon black pepper
½ teaspoon lemon or lime juice
1 tablespoon tarragon vinegar

Pour boiling water over dry mustard. Set aside. Combine horseradish, salad oil, salt and sugar, black pepper, lemon or lime juice and tarragon vinegar. Blend the boiling water and mustard with electric mixer or rotary beater. Slowly beat in the oil mixture. If too thick, thin with small amount of cold water. Serve sauce in a bowl, surrounded by the shad fingers. Serves 6.

Frying Fish

Pan-, Deep-Fat- and Oven-Fried Fish

IN PAN-FRYING, the trick is quick cooking. Cook the fish last after the rest of the meal is prepared, so that the fat can be quickly heated, the fish fried, fat drained and skillet washed immediately. This method prevents any odors from escaping and remaining in the house. Here is how to pan-fry: Heat enough fat in the bottom of the skillet to come up about ⅛ inch on the fish. Have the fat hot but not smoking. If you have more than enough fish to fry in one skillet, use two, so all the fish will be ready at the same time. After the fat gets hot, turn heat to moderate to avoid burning fish. Quickly fry over moderate heat until the fish is brown on one side, turn and brown the other. Lift fish out of skillet onto a heated platter and serve plain or garnished.

Deep-fat frying of fish used to be done almost exclusively in restaurants, but with the advent of electrical appliances, such as skillets, Dutch ovens, and deep-fat fryers, this method is now being used in the home. It is easy and fast, and since so many kinds of fats may now be used over and over, it is economical too. For the average serving of fish the fat should be heated in advance to 370 F. Test the temperature with a cooking thermometer or with a 1-inch cube of bread dropped into the fat: the temperature is right when the bread browns in 1 minute. If the fish is thick it requires lower heat (350 F) so the center will cook. Deep-fried fish is done when it is evenly browned. Remember not to overcook. Drain the fish on absorbent paper. Hush puppies may be cooked in the same fat, and then it is saved for the next fish fry.

Oven-frying of fish is really baking. Fish is breaded and salad oil or other fat poured over it and it is fried in the heat of the oven. This is an ideal way to fry fish. The breading is done by dipping the prepared cuts of fish in milk, evaporated milk, beaten egg, wine, French dressing or water, then coating with corn meal, flour, bread or cracker crumbs, crushed corn or wheat flakes, biscuit mix, pancake mix or crushed potato chips. Heat the pan and preheat the oven to hot, 400 F. Pour a small amount of melted fat into the pan. Arrange fish in one layer, spoon some of the fat over the breaded fish. Bake according to size, about 10 minutes per pound of fish or until fish has a crusted covering and is light brown.

Serve all fried fish as soon as possible so it will be hot and moist.

Here are some fish that are especially good fried:

Whole, dressed	Fillets or Steaks
Bass	Cod
Butterfish	Flounder
Flounder	Haddock
Lake herring	Halibut
Mackerel	Mullet and roe
Perch	Ocean perch
Pike	Pickerel
Pompano	Pollack
Smelts	Red snapper
Trout	Rockfish
Whitefish	Shad (boned) and roe
Whiting	Sole
	Swordfish

Indoor or Outdoor Fried Fillets

4 or 5 small ocean fish
Lemon juice
Salt
Pepper
Flour
½ cup bacon fat

SAUCE

1 can stewed tomatoes
1 clove garlic, minced (or garlic juice is fine)
1 tablespoon dehydrated onion flakes
2 tablespoons lime juice
5 drops Tobasco sauce

Dress fish by cutting off the heads and split down the back, cutting down each side of the backbone. Remove bone and wash fish in water with juice of a lemon added. Dry fillets with paper towel. Roll lightly in seasoned flour. Heat bacon fat in heavy frying pan and brown fish on both sides. Remove to a platter. In the pan where fish was fried, pour the stewed tomatoes and add other ingredients. Simmer for 3 minutes. Season with salt and pepper to taste and pour over fried fish. Serves 4 to 5.

Browned Fillets Parsley

2 pounds fish fillets
1 teaspoon salt
½ teaspoon pepper
1 cup flour
1 cup dry bread crumbs
½ cup butter or other fat
1 tablespoon lemon or lime juice
1 tablespoon snipped parsley

Cut fish into serving-size pieces. Wash and dry. Sprinkle both sides with salt and pepper. Combine the flour and bread crumbs. Roll fish in the mixture. Heat butter, watching carefully so it doesn't burn. Fry fish until brown on both sides. Remove fish. Add the lemon or lime juice to the butter where fish was fried and heat. Pour over fillets. Garnish with the snipped parsley. Serves 6.

Rainbow Trout, Pan Fried

6 small rainbow trout or other small
    fish
½ cup evaporated milk
2 teaspoons salt
¼ teaspoon pepper

1 cup flour
¼ cup corn meal
1 teaspoon paprika
Lemon slices

Clean, wash, and dry fish. Combine milk, salt, and pepper. Mix together the flour, corn meal, and paprika. Dip fish first in milk mixture, then in flour mixture. Heat ⅛ inch of fat hot in heavy frying pan but not smoking. Fry fish at moderate heat for 5 minutes on each side. Drain on absorbent paper. Serve garnished with lemon slices. Serves 6.

TIP: Add several slices of lemon to the hot fat while frying fish and turn lemon with fish.

Fried Fillets Sesame

2 pounds fish fillets
1 cup flour
2 eggs
2 tablespoons lemon juice
2 cups white corn meal (or cracker
    meal)
1 tablespoon salt
½ teaspoon pepper
½ teaspoon paprika
¾ cup sesame seeds
4 tablespoons salad oil
4 tablespoons butter

Cut fillets into serving-size pieces. Wash and dry. Roll in flour. Beat eggs with the lemon juice. Mix together the corn meal and other dry ingredients. Dip fish first in the egg mixture, then roll in corn meal.

In a heavy skillet heat the salad oil and butter (the combination makes fish nice and brown) or use shortening. Fry until brown on both sides. Drain. Serves 6.

Trout with Almonds

4 to 6 skinned fillets
2 eggs, beaten
½ teaspoon salt
¼ teaspoon pepper
1 cup flour
1 cup cooking oil or other fat
½ cup blanched slivered almonds

Wash and dry fillets. Mix eggs, salt
and pepper. Dip fillets in egg mixture,
then roll in flour. In a skillet heat the
oil. Brown fillets on both sides. Remove from oil and place on a hot
platter.

In a small frying pan sauté the
almonds in 2 tablespoons of butter
or oil until evenly browned. Watch
closely and toss constantly, as they
burn easily. Remove almonds from
fat and scatter on top of cooked fillets.
Serves 6. Serve with this sauce:

SAUCE

¼ pound butter
¼ teaspoon salt
¼ teaspoon pepper
1 small clove, minced
1 tablespoon minced parsley

Melt the butter and mix in the other
ingredients.

Fried Crispies
with Louis Dressing

2 pounds snapper steak or other fish
1 egg
2 tablespoons Worcestershire sauce
Dash of Tabasco
2 cups cracker meal
1 teaspoon salt
½ teaspoon pepper
2 tablespoons dried celery flakes or
    tarragon

Cut fish in pieces about 2 inches
square or into thin sticks. Beat egg
and add Worcestershire sauce and
Tabasco. Mix salt, pepper and celery
flakes (or tarragon) with cracker meal.
Dip fish first in egg mixture, then roll
in meal. Fry until brown on both sides.
Serve with wooden picks and a bowl of
Louis Dressing. Serves 6.

LOUIS DRESSING FOR
FRIED CRISPIES

1 cup mayonnaise or salad dressing
3 tablespoons catsup
1 tablespoon chopped onion
2 tablespoons pickle relish

Combine all ingredients and chill.
Serves 6.

Fish Kabobs

2 pounds red snapper, trout or other
    fish fillets
Flour
Cooked potatoes
Tomato wedges
Stuffed olives
Cooking oil
Lime wedges

Wash, dry and cut fish in bite-size pieces. Roll lightly in flour. Arrange pieces on skewers alternately with potatoes, tomatoes and olives. In a heavy frying pan heat ⅛ inch of oil until it is hot but not smoking. Put in kabobs and cook, turning the skewers to brown on all sides. Serve with lime wedges. Serves 6.

Country Panfish and Oyster Fry

PANFISH
Small fish or fillets
Salt and pepper
Buttermilk
Water-ground white meal
Cooking oil

Cut fish in serving-size pieces. Season with salt and pepper. Dip in buttermilk, then in white meal. Pat on well and let dry. Heat oil or fat hot but not smoking. Fry until brown, about 3 to 5 minutes.

OYSTERS
1 pint large oysters
1 egg, beaten
3 tablespoons flour
1 teaspoon salt
Dash pepper
½ cup salad oil

Combine egg, flour, salt and pepper. Add the oysters and stir to coat them.

Heat oil in large skillet and fry oysters, turning once to brown both sides, about 5 minutes total cooking time.

Serve fish and oysters on a large platter garnished with parsley. Serve *Tartare Dill Sauce* separately.

TARTARE DILL SAUCE

½ cup salad dressing
1 tablespoon lemon juice
2 tablespoons dill pickle, chopped fine
1 tablespoon minced onion

Combine all ingredients.

Snapper Escabèche

2 pounds snapper fillets or steaks, or other fish
6 tablespoons lemon juice
Flour
Butter
1 clove garlic, crushed
⅓ cup orange juice
⅓ cup olive oil
½ cup minced green onions
⅓ teaspoon hot pepper sauce, such as Tabasco
Salt

Have the fish skinned and remove bones. Place 3 tablespoons of the lemon juice in a bowl. Dip fish in juice, then rub with a little flour. Brown in hot butter, cooking 3 to 5 minutes on each side. Remove fish to a shallow bowl. Combine the crushed garlic with the remaining lemon juice, orange juice, olive oil and minced green onions. Add pepper sauce and salt to taste. Pour over the fish and marinate in the refrigerator overnight or longer. Serves 6.

Cheese-Fried Fish with Hush Puppies

2 pounds fish fillets
1½ cups white corn meal
¼ cup grated Parmesan cheese

Wash and dry fillets. Mix corn meal with cheese and roll fillets in it. Fry in deep fat fryer at 375 F, or in a skillet in ½ inch of fat for 3 to 5 minutes or until golden brown. Serve with hush puppies. Serves 6.

HUSH PUPPIES

1 cup corn meal
1 medium-sized onion, minced
2 teaspoons baking powder
½ teaspoon salt
1 egg
¼ cup milk or water

Mix corn meal with minced onion, add baking powder and salt. Break in egg and mix well. Add liquid. Shape into patties or drop by teaspoonful into fat heated to 375 F. They rise to the top of fat. Turn if needed until brown. Remove from fat and drain on paper towel. May also be cooked in a heavy skillet in about 1 inch of fat. Hush puppies may be cooked in the same fat the fish was cooked in.

Deep-Fried Fish

2 pounds fish steaks or fillets
Salt and pepper
¼ cup flour
2 eggs, beaten
2 tablespoons lemon juice
1 cup fine dry bread crumbs
Cooking oil or shortening
Cucumbers
Tomatoes

Cut steaks or fillets into serving-size pieces. Sprinkle with salt and pepper. Roll lightly in flour. Rolling in flour first prevents fish and breading from separating.

Combine beaten eggs and lemon juice. Dip fish in egg, then in crumbs. Fry in deep fat at 375 F about 3 to 5 minutes, or until golden brown. Drain on absorbent paper. Garnish with sliced cucumber and tomato quarters. Serves 6.

Baking Powder Batter-Fried Fish

2 pounds fish fillets or small whole
* fish*
1 teaspoon salt
1 cup flour
½ teaspoon double-action baking
* powder*
½ teaspoon salt
⅛ teaspoon onion salt
1 egg, beaten
1 cup water

Wash and dry fish and sprinkle with salt. Sift together the flour, baking powder, salt, and onion salt. Combine beaten egg and water. Blend into flour mixture. Dip fish in this batter and fry in deep fat, 350 F, for 2 or 3 minutes, or until fish is brown on one side. Turn and fry 2 or 3 minutes on other side, or until brown. Drain on paper. Serves 6.

Fish 'n' Chips, English Style

FISH
3 pounds fish fillets
1 teaspoon salt
¼ teaspoon pepper
1 cup flour

3 slightly beaten eggs
1 cup milk
1 cup flour
⅛ teaspoon salt

Wash fish and sprinkle with the salt and pepper. Roll it in flour. Rolling fish in flour before dipping in batter prevents breading from separating from fish.

Mix beaten eggs and remaining ingredients into a batter. Dip floured fish in batter. Fry in deep fat at 375 F, 3 to 5 minutes, or until brown. Have oil hot but not smoking. Drain on absorbent paper. Serves 6 to 8.

ENGLISH CHIPS
4 potatoes
Salt

Peel potatoes and cut into 1-inch cubes. Let stand in ice water for 1 hour or longer. Drain and dry thoroughly. Sprinkle with salt. Allow to stand 5 minutes, then dry again. Cover the bottom of fry basket with one layer of potatoes (do not use more than one layer). Fry in deep hot fat, 350 F, for 6 minutes. Continue until all are used. Set aside.

Raise heat of oil to 400 F. Return all potatoes at once to fry basket and let down into hot fat. Cook until brown. Drain and sprinkle fish and

chips with salt and vinegar lightly if desired. Serves 6 to 8.

In England each serving of fish and chips is placed in a square of waxed paper and the whole thing wrapped in a cone-shaped newspaper.

While the salt-water variety of catfish is seldom eaten, the fresh-water variety is relished as a delicacy. It is most often fried and river-bank restaurants advertise it as river or channel catfish and serve it fried with hush puppies. This fish is always skinned by cutting around the head and stripping the skin off. Pliers are used for this purpose. Catfish are sold fresh or frozen, and often packaged already breaded for frying.

Fried Catfish

6 small catfish, skinned and whole
1 teaspoon salt
¼ teaspoon pepper
2 cups white corn meal

Wash dressed catfish and dry. Sprinkle with salt and pepper. Roll in corn meal and fry in deep fat without a basket for about 3 to 5 minutes, according to size, on each side. Drain on absorbent paper and serve with hush puppies, corn pones, or rye bread. Garnish with lemon slices if desired. Serves 6.

Boiling and

BOILING and poaching mean cooking in liquid.

The only difference between them is in the amount of liquid used. For boiling, completely immerse large fish in water. In poaching barely cover with water. Fine-grained, firm type of fish are more successful poached than the coarse-grained type, which tend to break apart more easily.

Whole fish as well as cuts of fish may be boiled, but the latter are usually poached. Fish steaks are often boiled satisfactorily.

With the recipes used by gourmet chefs and published in various cookbooks, some home cooks can turn out beautiful dishes, but the average homemaker is afraid to tackle tying fish between two plates or placing on a board and wrapping in cheesecloth before lowering it into a kettle of court bouillon. We are therefore not emphasizing these suggestions but giving you our own simpler method for boiling and poaching fish:

Poaching Fish

BASIC POACHING RECIPE

Place enough water in a large skillet to cover the fish, adding for flavor what you have in the kitchen in the way of spices and vegetables, such as celery tops and parsley sprigs, pickling spices (packaged), bay leaf, and perhaps a small amount of vinegar. When water boils, reduce the heat and place the fish in the spiced water. Gently simmer until the fish loses its transparent look and flakes easily. With slotted spatula remove fish carefully to a platter and serve with any one of the many sauces given in this section.

A more complicated way is to make a fish stock first, then add the fish.

Poach fish in same pan or baking dish in which it is to be served. Drain off liquid and add sauce if desired. Helps with the dishwashing and keeps fish from breaking into pieces when removed to serving dish.

Fish Stock

Bones, skin, and scraps from 2 pounds
  fish, dressed and filleted
3 cups water
1 cup white wine
Lemon, sliced
2 slices onion
2 tablespoons pickling spices
½ bay leaf
2 teaspoons salt

Combine all and boil until the liquid is reduced to one third. Strain the stock and discard the solid ingredients. Should give about 1⅓ cups stock.

Fish Rolls
with Lemon Cream Sauce

2 pounds fish fillets
Fish stock

Roll the fillets, broad end first, and fasten with toothpicks. Put in a saucepan and just cover with fish stock. Simmer about 15 minutes. With a slotted spoon remove fish to a hot dish. Save the stock for use in the sauce. Remove toothpicks. Serve with *Lemon Cream Sauce*. Serves 6.

LEMON CREAM SAUCE

1½ tablespoons butter
2½ tablespoons flour
½ cup plus 2 tablespoons light cream
1 cup fish stock (saved from cooking the fillets)
Juice of ½ lemon
½ teaspoon salt
⅛ teaspoon white pepper
1 egg yolk

Melt the butter in a skillet, blend in the flour and cook a minute. Add ½ cup cream slowly, stirring, and then the fish stock. Stir constantly until smooth. Simmer 15 minutes. Remove from heat and continue stirring until smooth. Season and add lemon juice. Beat the egg yolk with the 2 additional tablespoons cream. Add a little hot sauce and return all to the sauce. Serves 6.

Here's a group of recipes that are very typically French—but easy.

Poached Fillets of Fish with Mushrooms
or
Filets de Sole Bonne Femme

6 fillets of sole or other fish
2 tablespoons butter
2 shallots or 1 small onion, chopped
12 mushrooms, cleaned and thinly sliced (canned may be used)
¾ cup white wine
1 teaspoon minced parsley

Melt butter in a large shallow pan and spread in it the chopped shallots and 6 of the sliced mushrooms. Sprinkle fish with salt and pepper. Arrange in pan with the vegetables. Spread 6 more mushrooms over fish. Add the wine and sprinkle with parsley.

Cover the fish with a piece of wax paper cut to fit inside the pan. Make a small hole in the center of the paper to let out some steam. When liquid boils cover the pan and cook 10 to 15 minutes, according to thickness of fish. It's ready when it flakes easily. With a spatula remove fish and vegetables to a warm platter. It may be served plain or with any one of several sauces.

Sauces for Poached Fillets

The cooked fillets are always removed from broth (liquid in which they have been poached) with a spatula and kept warm. The sauce is then made with the liquid and served over the fish.

PLAIN SAUCE: Cook the liquid in the pan until it is about 1 cupful. Blend in *manié* butter—this is 1 tablespoon butter mixed with 1 teaspoon flour. Test and add salt and pepper if needed. Remove sauce from heat and pour over the poached fish.

CREAM SAUCE: Cook the liquid in the pan until it is about 1 cup. Thicken by adding ½ cup cream blended with 1 tablespoon corn starch and 1 beaten egg yolk, after removing pan from heat. Return to burner, season with salt and white pepper. When sauce comes to the boiling point (don't let it boil), remove from heat and pour over cooked fish.

Variations of Fillets of Fish
Bonne Femme

Fillets of Fish Paysanne: Instead of using the shallots and mushrooms in *Filets de Sole Bonne Femme*, use 2 carrots and 2 onions, thinly sliced and cooked first in small amount of water until tender-crisp. Add 1 tablespoon butter to water for added flavor.

Fillets of Fish Dugléré: Substitute 4 tomatoes, peeled, seeded, and chopped for the mushrooms. Add ½ cup tomato juice and 1 clove of garlic. Thicken the sauce with 1 tablespoon butter mixed with 1 teaspoon flour (*manié* butter). Stir to blend the sauce and add 1 tablespoon butter before removing sauce from heat.

Fillets of Fish Véronique—Follow recipe for plain sauce, adding 1 cup white wine. After sauce has thickened add 2 cups fresh or drained canned seedless white grapes. Grapes may also be placed on the platter with the poached fish and sauce poured over all.

Spiced Fish
with Creole Sauce

2 pounds fillets
Enough water to cover fish
1 sliced lemon
¼ cup tarragon or cider vinegar
3 tablespoons salt
Several sprigs parsley
2 stalks celery with tops, cut into large pieces
3 tablespoons packaged pickling spices, loose

Cut fillets into serving-size pieces. In a large skillet add enough cool water to cover fish, but do not add it yet. Add all other ingredients. Bring to boil, turn to simmer, and cook until the celery is tender.

Remove pan from heat and let water cool. Now place fish fillets in the cool, spiced water and return to high heat. When water comes to a boil, reduce to simmer and cook about 10 minutes, or until fish flakes at the touch of a fork. Drain fish and place on a hot platter. Pour *Creole Sauce* or another sauce over fish. Serves 6.

CREOLE SAUCE

2 tablespoons butter
1 onion, chopped
½ green pepper, chopped
1 No. 2 can stewed tomatoes
1 teaspoon Worcestershire sauce
Salt and pepper
1 tablespoon flour
2 tablespoons tomato juice

Melt the butter in a skillet and sauté the chopped onion and green pepper. When tender pour in the stewed tomatoes. Add the Worcestershire sauce and salt and pepper. Cook 10 minutes. Thicken with 1 tablespoon flour and 3 tablespoons of water blended together if sauce is thin.

Golden Sauce

2 tablespoons butter or margarine
2 tablespoons flour
1 cup milk
1 egg yolk
2 tablespoons cream
¼ teaspoon salt

In a skillet melt butter and stir in the flour. Cook until it starts to brown.

Add milk gradually, stirring constantly. Cook until thickened. Beat the egg yolk with the cream. Add a little of the hot sauce to the egg yolk mixture, then pour all back into the pan. Bring to boiling point but do not allow to boil. Add salt.

Serve over poached fish. Sprinkle top with chopped parsley and slices of pimento. Serves 6.

TIP: Canned soups, undiluted, with onion flakes, make quick sauces. Add a dash of mace or thyme for a change in taste.

Red Snapper with Tomato Sauce

2 pounds red snapper fillets
Salt
1 lemon

Place 2 pounds red snapper fillets in a wire basket or wrap in a piece of cheesecloth. Lower fish into 2 quarts boiling water with salt and a sliced lemon added. Turn heat down (do not actually boil fish) and simmer for 10 minutes, or until fish flakes when tested with a fork. Remove to a platter and garnish with mashed potatoes and tomato sauce.

TOMATO SAUCE

1½ cups stewed tomatoes (canned are excellent)
½ cup sliced mushrooms
1 tablespoon margarine
1 tablespoon flour
1 beef bouillon cube
1 cup hot water

Simmer stewed tomatoes and mushrooms together about 5 minutes. Melt margarine in saucepan, gradually stir in flour. Cook, stirring over low heat until blended. Dissolve bouillon cube in hot water and stir into blended flour. When mixed thoroughly, add to tomato mixture and cook 2 minutes. Makes 2 cups sauce.

In this recipe, the fish is not actually in the water at all, but steamed above it.

Steamed Fillets and Sauce

2 pounds fish fillets
1½ teaspoons salt

Wash fillets. Sprinkle on both sides with salt. Place fish in a greased steamer pan. Cook over boiling water for 12 to 15 minutes or until fish flakes easily when tested with a fork. Remove fish with a slotted pancake turner, draining well. Serve with a *Creole Sauce* or any richly colored sauce. Serves 6.

Cooking with Fish Flakes

MANY RECIPES call for "fish flakes" or "flaked cooked fish." These are the same, and are prepared from boiled or poached fish, with the flesh flaked from the bone and skin.

Where there is a surplus supply of fish on hand, it is economical and easy to prepare it in this form for freezing and use later. Fish flakes or flaked cooked fish can be used in most recipes calling for canned fish. They are good in salads, casserole dishes and in combination with sauces, fruits and vegetables.

Fish Flakes
or Flaked Cooked Fish

2 pounds fish fillets or whole fish
2 cups water
1 tablespoon salt

When salted water comes to a boil
turn heat to simmer and place the fish
fillets in water. Cook gently for about
12 minutes, or until fish flakes easily.
Remove fish from the water carefully,
draining well. With a fork, flake flesh
from the bones and skin. Makes 2
cups flaked fish. Serves 6.

When flakes are cool, if freezing
is desired, wrap in freezer paper or
foil in packets containing enough for
one meal. Mark the packages and
freeze. They will thaw quickly when
ready to use.

Fish Flake-Vegetable
Casseroles

2 cups flaked fish, cooked or canned
3 tablespoons butter or other fat
3 tablespoons flour
2 cups milk
½ teaspoon salt
1 tablespoon grated onion or 1
*   teaspoon onion juice*
½ teaspoon celery salt
¼ teaspoon grated lemon rind
1 tablespoon chopped parsley
1 tablespoon chopped green pepper
¼ cup chopped pimento
3 drops hot pepper sauce
1 egg, beaten
2 tablespoons sherry
2 tablespoons butter or other fat,
*   melted*
½ cup dry bread-crumbs

Melt butter, blend in flour and cook
a minute. Add milk gradually and
add salt. Cook until thick and smooth,
stirring constantly. Add the next 7
ingredients. Stir a little of the hot
sauce into the beaten egg and add
to remaining sauce, stirring constantly.
Add sherry and fish. Spoon mixture
into 6 buttered, individual, 10-ounce
casseroles. Combine butter and crumbs
and sprinkle over top of each casserole.
Bake in a hot oven, 400 F, for 10 to
15 minutes or until brown. Serves 6.

Fish Flakes
and Spanish Corn

2 cups fish flakes, cooked or canned
3 tablespoons butter
1 3-ounce can drained mushrooms
1½ cups canned whole-kernel corn,
*   with peppers and pimentos*
½ teaspoon onion salt
⅛ teaspoon pepper
¼ cup light cream

Prepare fish flakes (cooked lobster,
crabmeat or shrimp may be substituted). Melt butter in a skillet. Add
drained mushrooms and sauté until
soft. Add corn, onion salt, pepper, and
cream. Add fish flakes. Heat thoroughly. Serves 6.

Flaked Fish Roll-Ups

2 cups flaked cooked or canned fish
1 can condensed cream of celery soup
1 tablespoon dehydrated onion flakes
1 tablespoon water
¾ cup grated Cheddar cheese
1 tablespoon lemon juice
2 cups biscuit mix

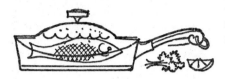

Add onion flakes to water and let stand a few minutes. Heat soup and add onion, cheese and flaked fish. When heated through remove from stove and add lemon juice.

Prepare biscuit mix and roll out into a rectangle about ¼ inch thick and 18 by 8 inches. Spread with fish and roll like a jelly roll, beginning at wide side. Seal ends. Cut top in several places to allow steam to escape. Place on greased baking sheet. Bake at 400 F for 20 to 25 minutes or until brown. Serves 6.

Fish Custard
with Caper Sauce

3 eggs, slightly beaten
¼ teaspoon salt
2 cups milk, scalded
2 tablespoons grated lemon rind
¼ teaspoon freshly grated pepper
2 cups flaked cooked fish
1 package frozen spinach

Lightly beat eggs and add salt. Slowly stir in scalded and lightly cooled milk. Mix in lemon rind and pepper. Poach skinned fish fillets in enough water to cover until fish flakes easily when tested.

Cook spinach just a bit. In a baking dish alternate layers of fish flakes, slightly cooked spinach, and custard, ending with custard. Place in pan with about 1 inch of water in it and bake in slow oven, 325 F, 50 minutes or until a knife inserted off center comes out clean. Serve with caper sauce made by puréeing 2 bottles capers and juice in blender. Serves 6.

Cool Night Supper

1 cup cooked or canned flaked fish or
*   crabmeat*
2 tablespoons butter or margarine
2 tablespoons minced onion
2 stalks chopped celery
1 small package (1⅓ cups) minute
*   rice*
½ teaspoon salt
⅛ teaspoon pepper
1 10½-ounce can condensed
*   mushroom soup*
1¾ cups hot water
2 teaspoons lemon juice

Melt butter in a large skillet. Add onion, celery and rice. Sauté until rice is golden brown. Add remaining ingredients, including fish. Bring mixture to a boil, turn heat down and simmer, uncovered, 5 minutes. Serves 4.

With this quick, good dish serve a mixed vegetable salad, hot rolls and lemon pie.

Baked Fish Flake Loaf

2 cups fish flakes, cooked or canned
2 cups mashed potatoes
1 can condensed cream of celery soup
*   diluted with ¼ cup milk*
Salt and pepper to taste
1 tablespoon prepared mustard
2 tablespoons onion flakes softened
*   in 1 tablespoon water or 2*
*   tablespoons grated onion*
½ cup dry bread crumbs

Mix all together lightly with a fork. Place in buttered baking dish. Sprinkle top with a mixture of bread crumbs and 1 tablespoon melted butter. Bake in moderate oven, 350 F, for 20 to 25 minutes or until brown. Serves 6.

Fisherman's Chow Mein

1 cup cooked or canned fish flakes
1 can condensed cream of chicken
   soup
¼ cup water
1 can chow mein vegetables, drained
1 tablespoon soy sauce
¼ teaspoon salt
¼ cup grated onion
Cooked rice
Crisp Chinese noodles

Mix soup with water and heat. Add drained vegetables and seasonings. Simmer 5 minutes. Add fish flakes and heat again. Serve over hot fluffy cooked rice and sprinkle with Chinese noodles. Serves 4 to 6.

Fish Flake
and Potato Pancakes

1 cup fish flakes, cooked or canned
1 cup mashed potatoes
2 eggs, beaten
½ cup plain flour
2 teaspoons baking powder and
½ teaspoon salt
1 cup milk

Mix together fish flakes, potatoes and beaten eggs. Combine flour, baking powder and salt. Beat in well the flour mixture and milk, alternating a little of each, beating after each addition. When well blended form pancakes and bake on hot griddle in 2 table-

spoons fat until brown. Turn and brown other side. Serves 6.

Fish Cakes

2 cups fish flakes, cooked and canned
4 tablespoons butter
1 medium-size onion, chopped
½ cup chopped celery
1 cup soft bread crumbs
2 eggs, beaten slightly
1 teaspoon salt
½ teaspoon pepper
¼ teaspoon ground ginger
¼ cup cream or evaporated milk
Cracker crumbs

Melt butter and cook chopped onion and celery until soft. Add bread crumbs, fish flakes, beaten eggs, seasonings and cream. If mixture will not hold together, add a little more cream. Form small cakes and roll in cracker crumbs. Fry in 1 inch of hot salad oil until brown on one side, turn and brown other side. Serves 6.

Fish Fritters

1 cup fish flakes, cooked or canned
1½ cups flour
2 teaspoons baking powder
½ teaspoon salt
¼ teaspoon pepper
⅔ cup milk
1 egg, beaten
Fat

Mix flour with baking powder, salt and pepper. Sift. Add milk to beaten egg and combine the mixtures. Add flaked fish. Drop by spoonfuls on skillet or griddle which has been lightly greased with fat. When fritters brown on one side, turn and brown other side. Serves 6.

Cooking with Canned Fish

THERE ARE *many varieties of canned fish and shellfish on the market. Besides the familiar canned salmon, tuna, sardines and shrimp, there are canned mackerel, cod, alewives, mullet, herring, shad, sturgeon, whiting, crabmeat, lobstermeat and so on. Most of the canned seafoods are adaptable to recipes calling for the fresh products. In main dishes, salads, appetizers and casserole dishes the canned is just as good as the fresh fish and shellfish. Using canned fish in these, and in such specialties as fish cakes, fish balls and chowders adds variety to your menus and often saves you money.*

Recipes for canned-fish soups, chowders, salads, sandwiches and appetizers will be found elsewhere in the book.

In the recipes in this section, the canned fish used is interchangeable. Other canned fish not specifically named may be used also. Just watch the size of the cans. Two cans of tuna and sardines are given in recipes to serve 6 people and 1 1-pound can of salmon. With experience, new cooks learn how to judge the right amounts to be used for their families. One good thing about fish and shellfish is that you can hardly go wrong. A little too much of this main ingredient only adds to the deliciousness in flavor.

Canned Salmon

*

Canned salmon is an old standby in our kitchen cabinet. It has always been popular for its convenience and delicious flavor. Readily available in nearly every store in every spot in the United States, canned salmon answers the need for quick, easy, yet highly nutritious dishes. The protein in salmon is a complete protein, in the same food group as meat and poultry, cheese and eggs.

Many recipes call for using the whole can of salmon, including the liquid, bones, and skin. These are good sources of iodine and phosphorus, Vitamin A, Vitamin D, and the B-group vitamins. Equal amounts of salmon and lamb chops contain approximately the same amount of protein, but 4 ounces of salmon contain only 150 calories, while 4 ounces of lamb chops contain 450 calories.

Canned salmon can be prepared in really glamorous dishes, fit for the most discriminating person, or it is good eaten plain, as it comes from the can, with only salt and pepper added. A sprinkling of citrus juices adds to the flavor. Canned salmon can be used in most recipes calling for fresh fish, poached, boiled, flaked, etc. It is tasty for the school lunchbox and picnic sandwiches. It is a change in taste for those diet-conscious people who can't have much salt and fat.

Grades of Salmon: On the Pacific Coast canned salmon is available in 5 different grades, canned by name. The differences are in the types of meat, color, texture, and flavor. The higher-priced are deep red and have a higher oil content. The grades are:

Chinook or king salmon (best)	Medium red salmon
Red or sockeye salmon	Pink salmon
Chum salmon	

Remember, tuna or other canned fish may be substituted for the salmon in these recipes.

Salmon Remick in Scallop Shells

1 1-pound can salmon, drained
2 cups mayonnaise or salad dressing
¼ cup chili sauce
1 tablespoon prepared mustard
6 drops Tabasco sauce
½ teaspoon salt
¼ teaspoon pepper
¼ teaspoon paprika
1 tablespoon lemon or lime juice
2 tablespoons butter or other fat, melted
¾ cup dry bread crumbs
Scallop shells or baking shells

Rinse scallop shells in cold water. Baking shells may be used. Break salmon into as even pieces as possible, about 1-inch cubes, and fill shells. Place shells on broiler pan. Combine sauce ingredients from mayonnaise to butter. Spread sauce over each shell of salmon pieces. Combine butter and crumbs and sprinkle over salmon and sauce. Broil 3 inches from heat for 5 minutes, or until sauce is bubbly. Serves 6.

TIP: If scallop or baking shells are not available, use a glass pie plate and serve as it comes from the oven.

Salmon in Patty Shells

1 1-pound can salmon or 2 7-ounce cans tuna
1 half small green pepper, chopped
2 teaspoons onion, grated
¼ cup pimento, chopped
¼ cup butter or other fat, melted
¼ cup flour
1 teaspoon salt
⅛ teaspoon pepper
2 cups milk
2 egg yolks, beaten
1 4-ounce can mushrooms, drained and sliced, or 1 8½-ounce can drained tiny peas
Patty shells, toast or toast cups

Drain and flake salmon. Cook green pepper, onion, and pimento in butter until tender. Blend in flour and seasonings. Add milk and cook until thick, stirring constantly. Stir a little of the hot liquid into the beaten egg yolks then return to sauce in pan and continue cooking. Add salmon and mushrooms or peas; heat again. Serve in patty shells, on toast, or in toast cups made by pressing bread quarters, with edges cut off, around muffin cups and toasting them. Serves 6.

Salmon-Spaghetti Casserole

1 1-pound can salmon
2 tablespoons butter or other fat
2 tablespoons flour
½ teaspoon salt
⅛ teaspoon pepper
⅛ teaspoon nutmeg
2 cups combined salmon liquid and milk
1 tablespoon sherry
2 cups cooked thin spaghetti
1 4-ounce can sliced mushrooms, drained
2 tablespoons grated Parmesan cheese
2 tablespoons dry bread crumbs
Parsley
Ripe olives, sliced

Drain salmon, reserving liquid. Break salmon into large pieces. Melt butter and blend in the flour, salt, pepper and nutmeg. Add salmon liquid and milk gradually. Cook and stir until smooth. Add sherry. Mix half of the sauce with the spaghetti and add mushrooms. Turn into a well-greased, 2-quart casserole. Mix remaining sauce with salmon. Spoon into center of spaghetti. Combine cheese and crumbs and sprinkle over salmon mixture. Bake in a moderate oven, 350 F, for 30 minutes. Serves 6. Garnish with parsley and sliced ripe olives, or serve plain.

Spanish Salmon and Rice

2 cups flaked canned salmon
2 cups cooked or canned tomatoes and juice
2 tablespoons butter or other fat, melted
¼ cup onion, minced
¼ cup green pepper, diced
1½ cups boiling water
2 teaspoons salt
¼ teaspoon pepper
⅓ cup uncooked rice

Drain salmon. Combine tomatoes, fat, onions, green pepper, water, salt and pepper in a large saucepan. Bring to boil. Add rice and simmer until rice is done, about 25 minutes, adding more water if needed. Stir in salmon and cook 2 minutes longer. Serves 6 to 8.

Salmon Indian Curry

1 1-pound can salmon
¼ cup chopped onion
3 tablespoons butter or other fat, melted
3 tablespoons flour
1½ teaspoons curry powder
½ teaspoon salt
¼ teaspoon ginger

⅛ teaspoon pepper
2 cups combined salmon liquid and milk
3 cups cooked rice

Drain salmon, reserving liquid. Break salmon into large pieces. Cook onion in butter until tender. Blend in flour and seasonings. Add salmon liquid and milk gradually and cook until thick, stirring constantly. Add salmon and heat. Serve over cooked rice with any of the curry condiments below. Serves 6.

Curry condiments: Chopped nuts, chopped hard-cooked egg whites, sieved hard-cooked egg yolks, shredded coconut, chopped green pepper, chopped tomatoes, chow-mein noodles.

Salmon Loaf

2 cups canned salmon
3 tablespoons fat
3 tablespoons flour
1 cup combined milk and salmon liquid
Salt and pepper
2 tablespoons minced parsley
2 cups bread crumbs
1 egg, beaten

Drain canned salmon, saving the liquid. Melt butter or other fat and blend in the flour. Add milk and salmon liquid gradually, stirring. Cook and stir until sauce is thickened. Add salt and pepper and minced parsley. Stir in the salmon, bread crumbs and beaten egg. Form the mixture into a loaf. Bake in an uncovered greased pan in moderate oven, 350 F, for 30 minutes or until brown. Serves 6.

Scalloped Salmon

1 1-pound can salmon
2 tablespoons lemon juice or 1
  tablespoon lime juice
2 tablespoons onion, grated
1½ cups coarse cracker crumbs
½ teaspoon salt
⅛ teaspoon pepper
¼ cup butter or other fat, melted
1⅓ cups combined salmon liquid
  and milk

Drain salmon, saving liquid, and flake the fish. Blend lemon juice and grated onion into salmon. Combine next 4 ingredients. Sprinkle one-third of this mixture in a greased casserole, cover with a layer of the salmon mixture. Repeat the layers ending with crumbs. Heat salmon liquid and milk and pour over all. Bake in a moderate oven, 350 F, for 30 minutes or until brown. Serve plain or with a sauce. Serves 6.

TIP: If tuna is substituted, use all milk instead of liquid and milk combination.

Salmon Mousse De Luxe

ASPIC

1 tablespoon unflavored gelatine
2 tablespoons cold water
1 chicken bouillon cube
1 cup boiling water

Soften gelatine in cold water for 5 minutes. Dissolve bouillon cube in boiling water. Add hot bouillon to gelatine and stir until dissolved. Pour into a 1½-quart mold and chill until firm.

MOUSSE

3 cans salmon, 7¾ ounces each
½ cup mayonnaise
2 tablespoons chopped parsley
1 tablespoon lime juice
1 tablespoon grated onion
1 teaspoon horseradish
¼ teaspoon salt
⅛ teaspoon pepper
2 tablespoons unflavored gelatine
½ cup combined salmon liquid and
  water
1 cup whipping cream

Drain salmon, reserving liquid. Add next 7 ingredients to salmon. Mix well. Soften gelatine in salmon liquid for 5 minutes and stir over hot water until dissolved. Add gelatine to salmon mixture and blend thoroughly. Whip the cream and fold into salmon mixture. Spread mousse over congealed aspic and chill until firm. Unmold on salad plate. Garnish with salad greens. Serves 6.

Salmon Guacomole

1 1-pound can salmon
1 ripe avocado
1 tablespoon lemon juice or 2
  teaspoons lime juice
1 tablespoon salad oil
1 clove garlic, minced
2 teaspoons grated onion
½ teaspoon salt
4 drops Tabasco sauce

Drain and flake salmon. Peel avocado and mash with a fork. Combine all ingredients, mixing lightly. Serve with sesame seed crackers, as a spread. Makes 1 pint of spread.

TIP: Tuna would be an especially good substitute here.

Tuna

*

Grade 1—*Fancy or Fancy Whitemeat:* This is choice cuts of cooked white albacore tuna packed as large pieces of solid meat.

Grade 2—*Standard Tuna:* Cooked tuna meat packed in the approximate proportion of 75 percent large pieces and 25 percent flakes, usually from the albacore tuna.

Grade 3—*Grated or Shredded Tuna:* Cooked tuna from one or more of the species of mackerel other than albacore, packed in small uniform pieces.

Grade 4—*Tuna Flakes:* Cooked tuna packed in small pieces.

All grades of tuna are good. The reason for choosing one grade over another quality-wise would be the way the fish is to be served. The white, large chunk albacore tuna is excellent in salads, cocktail and with white sauces. All the other grades are used in casserole dishes, croquettes, and in combination with other ingredients. The reason for a choice other than quality is the price. The flakes, darker meat usually, are priced lowest, but in all cases the fish is good. It is simply the same as choosing pompano for certain occasions and preparation and again preferring mullet, for instance.

All types of canned tuna fish are available in 3½-, 7-, and 13-ounce sizes. Tuna flakes and grated tuna are packed in 3-, 6-, 12-, and 64-ounce cans.

The entire content of a can of tuna is edible and a single 7-ounce can of tuna used in combination with other foods in casseroles, salads, and sandwiches provides servings for 4 to 6 people.

NOTE: The liquid in the can is high in food value and may be used unless recipe indicates that it be drained from tuna.

Tuna Cakes

1 6-ounce can flaked tuna
2 cups cooked rice
2 teaspoons minced parsley
1 egg, separated
2 tablespoons milk
¼ teaspoon salt
⅛ teaspoon prepared mustard
Cracker meal or dry bread crumbs

Separate egg. Beat yolk and mix with milk. Combine tuna, rice, parsley and egg yolk with milk. Add salt and mustard. Beat egg white and fold it in. Shape into cakes or croquettes and roll in cracker meal or bread crumbs. In a skillet have ⅛ inch of salad oil or other fat hot, but not smoking. Fry cakes for about 3 minutes on each side, until brown. Drain on absorbent paper. Arrange on warmed platter and garnish with parsley, celery tops, or sliced tomatoes. Serves 6.

TIP: Rice may be omitted, in which case use an additional whole egg, beaten, and increase milk to 3 tablespoons. If cakes are too mushy, add 1 tablespoon of flour or cracker meal to mixture.

Tuna Pizza

2 7-ounce cans tuna
½ cup chopped onion
3 tablespoons olive or salad oil
1 8-ounce can tomato sauce
1 6-ounce can tomato paste
1 teaspoon mixed mustard and celery seeds
1 teaspoon whole oregano
½ teaspoon salt
¼ teaspoon pepper
2 unbaked pizza crusts, 9 inches each
½ cup sliced stuffed olives
½ pound mozzarella cheese, sliced

Drain tuna. Flake. Cook onion in oil until soft. Add tomato sauce and paste and seasonings. Simmer 10 to 12 minutes. Place pizza crusts on greased baking sheets. Divide the sauce between the crusts and divide tuna and olives. Arrange cheese slices over the top. Bake in hot oven, 425 F, for 20 minutes, or until crust browns and cheese melts. Makes 2 pies. Serves 6.

Canned Sardines

*

Canned sardines, like salmon and tuna, have long been a basic food on the shelves of grocers all over the United States. And like the other canned products, sardines are rich in nutrition and the entire contents of the can may be used in many varied and delicious recipes. The sardine canning industry is one of the most important of the New England states, and Maine sardines have been popular since the early 1870's.

Most sardines are packed in 3¼-ounce cans using soybean, peanut, olive or cottonseed salad oils. Packs of 3¼ and 12 ounces come in tomato and mustard sauces. Sardines eaten as they come from the small can are enough for 2, but combined with other ingredients a can will serve from 4 to 6 people, according to how the dish is prepared.

SARDINE TIPS

• Mash a can of sardines and combine with filling for deviled eggs. This is really good.

• Coarsely broken canned sardines, stirred into eggs to be scrambled, come in handy for quick Sunday-evening snacks.

• Stir a can of mashed sardines into the batter for corn fritters. There will be calls for seconds.

Sardine Croquettes

2 cans sardines, 3¼-ounces each
1 cup thick white sauce (1 can
    undiluted cream of mushroom soup
    may be used)
1½ cups fine bread crumbs
1 teaspoon Worcestershire sauce
2 tablespoons minced parsley
1 egg, beaten
Salt and pepper

Mash sardines. Add white sauce, ½ cup crumbs, Worcestershire sauce and parsley. Season to taste with salt and pepper. Chill. Shape into 12 croquettes. Roll in remaining crumbs, dip in beaten egg, then again in crumbs. Fry in shallow fat, ½ to 1 inch deep, until brown on one side. Turn very carefully, so as not to break, and brown other side. Serves 6.

Sardine-Corn Burger

2 cans sardines, 3¼-ounces each
1 cup corn flakes, crushed
1 teaspoon lemon juice
¼ teaspoon salt

2 tablespoons chopped parsley
    (optional)
2 teaspoons grated onion

Combine all ingredients and shape into cakes. Fry in butter or other fat 4 to 5 minutes on each side or until nicely browned. Serve on toasted hamburger buns. Serves 4.

Sardine-Stuffed Peppers

2 cans sardines, 3¼-ounces each
6 medium-size green peppers
2 cups cooked rice
1 egg, beaten
1 teaspoon salt
½ teaspoon pepper
1 cup canned tomatoes, drained
¼ cup milk
1 small onion, chopped

Cut tops from peppers. Remove seeds and membranes. Break sardines into pieces. Combine with other ingredients. Spoon mixture into peppers. Place in a greased pan or baking dish. Bake in moderate oven, 375 F, 45 minutes, or until peppers are tender. Serves 6.

Smoking and Canning Seafood at Home

Salt and Smoked Fish

TASTY VARIATIONS in the menu are provided by commercial or homemade salt or smoked fish. Salt fish ordinarily requires one-half to several hours of soaking time before further preparation, while smoked fish usually is ready to eat as it comes from the smoker, or after it is cool.

Smoked Fish

5–6 pounds dressed fish
1 cup salt
1 gallon water
¼ cup olive, peanut or salad oil

Cut the head below the collarbone. Split down backbone, leaving tail on. Spread fish out flat in one "butterfly" piece, or cut fish into pieces suitable for individual servings. Make a brine by mixing salt and water. Soak fish in this solution for 30 minutes.

To smoke fish, use a charcoal fire in a portable barbecue with hood or a lid that closes to make a smoker. Soak 1 pound of hickory or other chips in 2 quarts water. When charcoal fire burns down to a low, even heat, place on it ⅓ of the wet chips. Rinse fish in cold water and dry. Place, skin side down, on well-greased barbecue grill over the smoking fire. Cover the grill and smoke for 1½ hours, adding remaining wet chips at 15-minute intervals to keep the fire smoking.

Increase the temperature by adding more charcoal to the fire and opening the draft. Brush fish sparingly with oil. Cover and cook for 15 minutes. Brush again with oil and continue cooking for 10 minutes or until fish is lightly browned. Serves 6.

HOMEMADE SMOKER

If you have an old refrigerator it is easy to make your own smokehouse for small quantities of fish and other meats. It isn't necessary to have any working parts or motor. The shell is what is used.

Move the refrigerator to its permanent spot, preferably outside but under a roof. Have a small hole drilled in the side for an electric cord. Place an electric hotplate on the bottom. Connect the cord and turn the heat to the lowest point. On the hotplate place an old large-size iron skillet. Fill it with hickory or other chips and when they have burned down, add the dampened chips. The fish, shrimp or other meats to be smoked are placed on the racks in the refrigerator and smoked 1½ hours. *Note:* Be sure to have a chain and lock on the door so when not in use there will be no danger of accidents to curious children.

SMOKE BARREL*

Start with a used 40-gallon charred oak whiskey barrel or anything similar. Saw around the barrel about 8 inches from the top. This is then used as the lid and is secured to the rest of the barrel with a heavy hinge. To keep the lid from toppling over backwards when fish is removed, attach a chain stopper.

The two grill-supporting chains lap over the rim of the barrel and prevent a complete closure of the lid, so notch two shallow V's on either side of barrel. Attach hooks or pins at the base of the V's to fasten the chains.

Allow for 4 or 5 inches of sand in which the fire pot will eventually be imbedded, bore 5 or 6 draft holes, one-half inch in diameter, around the sides of the barrel just above the sand level. Make wooden plugs to fit the holes.

The fire pot can be any heavy metal cylinder such as the bottom of a dutch oven. An ideal pot is an old automobile brake drum. However, it should be small enough to allow for 3 or 4 inches of sand insulation between barrel and the pot.

The round grill for the top of the barrel can be purchased at any store that specializes in barbecue equipment.

The grill is supported by two Y-shaped chains. The upper legs of the Y are equipped with snap-ons to fasten the grill. The bottom leg of each Y fastens on the hooks at the base of the notched V's.

To use the barrel the sand at the bottom should first be soaked with water. The fire is started with charcoal briquets and then the smoke-producing wood is added.

While fish is smoking, care must be taken not to let the fire flare up. This is controlled by inserting the wooden plugs in the draft holes until an ideal balance between fire and smoke is achieved.

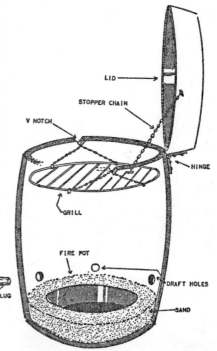

* Courtesy Bureau of Commercial Fisheries, U.S. Fish and Wildlife Service, Washington, D.C.

Wood used for smoking depends upon taste and availability. Any nonresinous hard wood such as alder, apple, maple, oak, birch, or beech can be used.

Wood should be cut into small chunks about 4 inches in length or just long enough so they can be pyramided in the fire pot.

Barrel is now ready for use. Fillet whole fish and remove the backbone. Cut fillets into chunks suitable for individual servings. Soak chunks in saturated brine solution for an hour and a half. (Soaking time can be varied to suit individual tastes.)

Remove the chunks from the solution and arrange a single layer on grill rack, avoiding crowding. Lower grill into smoke barrel about 8 inches. Close and cook for about an hour and a half or until done, making sure fire is smoking and not burning during entire cooking process.

If the barrel is not to be used for some time, it is necessary to remove fire pot, insert draft plug holes, and fill with water to keep barrel from warping.

Most fish are excellent smoked. However the most popular are: buffalofish, butterfish, carp, catfish, chubs, cod, flounder, haddock, halibut, mackerel, mullet, oysters, perch, salmon, shad, shrimp, trout and whitefish.

Smoked Fish and Egg Scramble

½ pound smoked fish, flaked
2 tablespoons butter or margarine
¼ cup chopped onion
½ cup chopped green pepper
½ teaspoon salt
¼ teaspoon cayenne pepper
6 eggs, beaten
¼ cup coffee cream
½ teaspoon Worcestershire sauce

Flake the fish from bones and skin, using a fork. Melt butter and sauté the onion and green pepper until tender. Add seasonings and smoked fish flakes. Combine eggs, cream and Worcestershire sauce. Add to fish mixture and cook and stir until eggs are firm. Serves 6.

Smoked Fish Loaf

2 cups smoked fish flakes (boiled
    or leftover fish can also be used)
1 cup milk
1½ cups soft bread crumbs
4 tablespoons melted butter
3 egg yolks, beaten slightly
2 tablespoons lemon juice
½ cup minced celery
¼ cup chopped onion
½ teaspoon salt
⅛ teaspoon pepper
3 egg whites, beaten

Scald milk. Add bread crumbs and butter, and beat until smooth. Combine with fish flakes, egg yolks, lemon juice, onion, celery, salt and pepper. Fold in stiffly beaten egg whites. Grease loaf pan. Turn in fish mixture and bake at 350 F for 35 minutes. Serve hot with a tomato sauce. Serves 6.

CANNING AND PICKLING SEAFOOD

Use freshly caught fish and shellfish. Use care in dressing and handling so as not to damage these products. Follow instructions in pressure cooker booklet. Containers are usually pint-size glass jars and fittings. Always use a steam-pressure canner. This is a heavy kettle with a cover which can be clamped or locked down to make the kettle steamtight. The cover is fitted with a safety valve, a petcock (vent) and a pressure gauge. All parts of the canner must be clean and in good working order. The pressure gauge should be checked at least once a year; your county home demonstration agent usually can tell you where it can be tested.

We don't recommend processing fish and shellfish in a waterbath canner because a high enough temperature is not reached within a reasonable length of time to destroy all of the bacteria which may cause spoilage.

PREPARATION FOR CANNING

Bleed fish as soon as caught to prevent spoilage and improve the color of the fish. To bleed, cut the throat with a knife and proceed to dress as usual, removing head, tail, dark membrane and insides. Remove all blood along backbone. Wash in cool water, then remove from water immediately. If fish are small, the backbone may be left intact.

Prepare fish and shellfish according to the recipes which follow.

PACKING AND PROCESSING*

Get out all equipment needed. Check jars for nicks, cracks and sharp edges. Wash jars in hot soapy water. Rinse. Cover with hot water. Let jars remain in hot water until ready to use. Wash and rinse fittings. Check manufacturer's instructions for filling and sealing jars. Reread manufacturer's instructions for using the steam-pressure canner.

Prepare and pack meat according to recipe. Wipe top and threads of jar with clean, damp cloth before capping.

Put each jar, as it is filled, on rack in steam-pressure canner containing 2 to 3 inches of hot water. Fasten canner cover on securely, according to manufacturer's instructions. Leave petcock open until steam escapes steadily for 10 minutes. Close petcock and bring pressure to 10 pounds. Start counting processing time. Process for length of time recommended in recipe, keeping the pressure constant.

* Courtesy Ball Blue Book, Ball Brothers Company, Inc., Muncie, Ind.

Remove canner from heat. Let pressure fall to zero. Wait 2 minutes; slowly open petcock. Unfasten cover; tilt the far side up when removing the cover so that the steam escapes away from you. Remove jars. Stand them on cloths or wood, a few inches apart and out of drafts, to cool. About 12 hours later, test jars for seal. Store jars in a dark, dry, reasonably cool place.

If for any reason a jar has failed to seal, repack and process the full length of time or refrigerate and use the food as soon as possible.

NOTE: The majority of these recipes are based upon information supplied by the Division of Fishery Industries, United States Department of the Interior.

Clams

Scrub, steam and open fresh clams. Save juice. Drop clams into weak salt-water. Wash thoroughly, then drop into 1 gallon boiling water containing ½ teaspoon citric acid. Boil 2 minutes. Drain. Pack clams into hot pint Ball jars, leaving 1-inch head space. Pour juice over clams. Add boiling water, if needed, to cover, leaving 1-inch head space. Adjust caps. Process 1 hour and 10 minutes at 10 pounds pressure.

Crabmeat

Add ¼ cup lemon juice, or white vinegar, and 1 cup salt to 1 gallon boiling water. Keep hot. Remove back shell and thoroughly cleanse crabs. Wash bodies through several changes of cool water. Boil 20 minutes in the acid-brine. While crabs are boiling, add 1 cup salt, 2 cups lemon juice or white vinegar, to 1 gallon cool water. Drain cooked crabs. Remove meat from body and claws. Rinse in cool

acid-brine. Squeeze meat to remove some of the liquid. Pack into hot half-pint or pint Ball jars, leaving 1-inch head space. Cover with boiling water, leaving 1-inch head space. Adjust caps. Process half-pints and pints 1 hour and 40 minutes at 5 pounds pressure.

Mackerel, Mullet, Trout, Whitefish, etc.

Dissolve 1 cup salt in 1 gallon cool water to make brine. Cut fish into jar-length pieces. Let stand 1 hour in brine. Drain. Pack into hot pint Ball jars, skin side next to glass, leaving 1-inch head space. Put open jars into kettle. Cover with hot brine (½ cup salt to 1 gallon water). Boil 15 minutes. Remove jars and invert to drain 5 minutes. Adjust caps. Process 1 hour and 40 minutes at 10 pounds pressure.

Salmon and Shad

Dissolve 1 cup salt in 1 gallon water to make brine. Cut fish into jar-length pieces. Let stand 1 hour in brine. Drain 10 minutes. Pack into hot pint Ball jars, skin side next to glass, leaving 1-inch head space. Adjust caps. Process 1 hour and 40 minutes at 10 pounds pressure.

Shrimp

Add 1 cup salt and 1 cup vinegar to each gallon boiling water needed for cooking shrimp. Wash and drain freshly caught shrimp. Drop into boiling brine. Boil 10 minutes. Drop into cold water. Drain and peel. Remove sand vein. Rinse in cool water. Pack into hot pint Ball jars, leaving 1-inch head space. Cover with boiling water, leaving 1-inch head space. Adjust caps. Process 45 minutes at 10 pounds pressure.

Smelt In Tomato Sauce

6 pounds cleaned smelt
2 cups Tomato Sauce
¾ cup oil
¼ cup vinegar
2 teaspoons salt

Pack fish into hot Ball jars, leaving 1-inch head space. Combine remaining ingredients and pour over fish; add water, if necessary, to cover fish, leaving 1-inch head space. Adjust caps. Process pints 50 minutes, quarts 1 hour, at 10 pounds pressure. *Yield: about 7 pints.*

Tuna

Steam tuna until cooked. Chill 6 to 12 hours. Cut into jar-length pieces. Pack into hot pint Ball jars, leaving 1-inch head space. Add 1 teaspoon salt and 2 tablespoons salad oil to each pint. Adjust caps. Process 1 hour and 30 minutes at 10 pounds pressure.

Pickled Fish

Cut fish into serving-size pieces in enough water to cover. When water boils, turn to simmer and cook just until fish loses its transparent look and flakes easily. Remove from heat and drain.

Pack the cooked fish into quart jars or other large containers with one or more raw sliced onions between layers. Pour over all hot *Vinegar Sauce.* Cover and keep in a cool place.

VINEGAR SAUCE

1 quart distilled vinegar
1 pint water
½ tablespoon sugar
2 teaspoons salt
½ teaspoon each of:
  whole black pepper
  cloves
  mustard seed
  celery seed
1 small red pepper pod
1 small clove garlic
1 whole bay leaf (small)

Place vinegar in container. Add water and sugar. Tie spices up loosely in cheesecloth and add to the vinegar mixture. Heat, but do not boil, for 30 minutes. Strain. Enough for 3 to 4 pounds fish.

Pickled shrimp are good appetizers or in a salad

Pickled Shrimp

2½ pounds raw shrimp
½ cup celery tops
¼ cup mixed pickling spices
1 tablespoon salt
2 cups sliced onions
8 bay leaves

Cover shrimp with boiling water. Add celery tops, spices, and salt. Cover and simmer for 5 minutes. Drain, then peel and devein shrimp. Alternate the cleaned shrimp, onions and bay leaves in shallow baking dish. Marinate as follows:

PICKLING MARINADE

1½ cups salad oil
¾ cup white vinegar
3 tablespoons capers and juice
2½ teaspoons celery seed
1½ teaspoons salt
Few drops Tabasco sauce

Combine above ingredients. Mix well and pour over cooked shrimp. Cover. Chill at least 24 hours, spooning marinade over shrimp occasionally. These pickled shrimp will keep at least a week in the refrigerator. Makes about 6–8 servings.

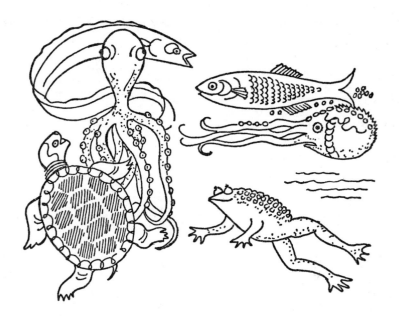

Miscellaneous Recipes

Fish Roe, Frogs' Legs and Others

FISH ROE

*

Broiled Shad Roe

2 pairs shad roe
2 cups boiling water
1 teaspoon salt
1 lemon, sliced
4 tablespoons butter
8 slices crisp bacon

Add salt and sliced lemon to boiling water and drop in cleaned roe. Boil very gently to keep roe from tearing apart, for 15 minutes. Drain carefully. Place in greased preheated broiler pan. Brush with melted butter and broil until golden brown, but soft. Sprinkle with crumbled crisply fried bacon. Serves 2. *Note:* Always use tongs or two spoons to turn and transfer roe to serving dish as it will disintegrate if torn.

Fisherman's Broiled Fish Roe

In a shallow pan place thin slices of lemon (not too many). Place fresh fish roe on top and squeeze on the juice of ¼ lemon. Spoon on top a thin layer of French dressing and a few drops of Worcestershire sauce. Broil 3 inches from heat for 10 minutes, turning with tongs or two forks to broil other side. Add 4 tablespoons water. Cover and steam 3 minutes. Remove cover and brown, basting with juices and melted butter. Pour drippings over roe when ready to serve. Allow 1 pair of roe per person.

Here is a version of fried fish roe that fishermen smack their lips over.

Marinated Fried Fish Roe

Parboil roe or milt (yellow or white) for 15 minutes. Sprinkle generously with tarragon vinegar. Let roe marinate overnight in the refrigerator. Dip the roe in corn meal after forking it out of the marinade. When ready to serve, fry in small amount of bacon fat, serving the crisp bacon crumbled over the roe.

Baked Fish Roe

1 pair shad roe for each person
½ cup butter or other fat
Salt and pepper
Flour
Water

Bring water to a boil in saucepan and simmer roe gently for 15 minutes. Drain. Grease a pie plate. Sprinkle the roe with salt and pepper, roll in the flour. Place in pie plate and dot with butter. Bake in a hot oven at 400 F for 30 minutes, basting occasionally with melted butter and a little water if roe seems to be drying out.

Fish Roe, Skillet Fried

6 soft fish roe
¼ cup flour
½ teaspoon salt
¼ teaspoon pepper
1 beaten egg
1 tablespoon lemon juice
½ cup corn meal
2 tablespoons butter
2 tablespoons salad oil

Wash and dry fish roe. Combine flour, salt, and pepper. Using tongs or two spoons, roll in flour combination, taking care not to break the membrane of roe. Combine beaten egg and lemon juice. Dip roe in it, then roll in corn meal. Have hot in a skillet 2 tablespoons butter, mixed with 2 tablespoons salad oil (this makes a nicely browned food).

Place breaded roe in fat and fry until brown on all sides. Turn carefully with tongs. Serve roe on hot buttered toast. Sprinkle with chopped parsley if desired. Serves 3.

Shad Roe Crispy

Allow 1 pair roe for each person. Wash carefully, so as not to break membrane. Dry and dust with salt, pepper and flour. Fry in moderately hot bacon drippings or butter, turning with tongs or two spoons until brown.

Remove to hot platter and serve with crisp bacon crumbled over top. Garnish with parsley and lemon wedges.

Peanut Shad Roe or Mullet Roe

Allow 1 pair roe for each person. Wash carefully, so as not to break membrane. Dry and dust with salt, pepper, and flour. Brown in moderately hot peanut oil, turning with tongs or two spoons to fry on all sides.

Remove to hot platter and serve with minced parsley sprinkled over top and lemon wedges on side.

Parsley-Fish Roe

Separate 4 pairs roe. Melt ¼ pound butter or margarine in skillet. Roll roe in corn meal seasoned with 1 teaspoon salt and ¼ teaspoon pepper. Fry roe slowly on all sides, giving them time to cook through and to brown. Remove and drain on absorbent paper. Fry bacon crisp. Crumble and spoon over top of roe. Sprinkle with chopped parsley before serving. Serves 4.

Individual Roe Casseroles

2 pairs roe
2 eggs, beaten
½ cup soft bread crumbs
½ teaspoon salt
⅛ teaspoon pepper
⅛ teaspoon paprika
1 tablespoon chopped parsley
1½ cups milk

Two pairs of roe will yield 2 cups broken, according to size if large.

Drop roe in boiling water and cook gently for 20 minutes. Drain, remove membrane, and break up with fork. Grease 6 individual custard cups or timbales with butter or other fat. Combine all ingredients and fill cups ¾ full. Place in a pan of water about 1 inch deep. Bake in oven at 375 F for 30 minutes. Serve with cream sauce or tomato sauce. Serves 6.

Shad Roe Soufflé

1 pair shad roe
3 tablespoons butter
3 tablespoons flour
½ teaspoon salt
1 cup milk
3 eggs

Roll the roe in cracker meal and fry in ⅛ inch mixed salad oil and butter until brown. Fry slowly and turn with tongs or two spoons, to avoid puncturing membrane of roe. Drain on absorbent paper. Cut fried roe in pieces. One pair will yield 1 cup.

Melt butter and blend in flour. Add salt and milk and cook, stirring, until mixture thickens. Separate eggs. Beat yolks. Stir hot sauce slowly into beaten yolks. Fold in shad roe and cool slightly. Beat egg whites until stiff. Fold into roe mixture. Turn into 1½-quart casserole. Bake in a moderately slow oven, 325 F, about 1 hour, or until browned. Serve at once. Serves 6.

FROG LEGS

❋

Frog legs are available in many seafood markets. The hind legs of the frog are the only edible part. These are very delicious. To prepare, cut legs from body, wash in cold water and skin by turning down and ripping skin off like a glove. Cover with boiling water and drain. Legs are now ready to cook.

Smothered Frog Legs

4 frog legs
¼ cup butter or other fat
1 tablespoon flour
2 sprigs parsley
⅛ teaspoon packaged savory
  seasoning
1 bay leaf
1 small onion, sliced
½ teaspoon salt
⅛ teaspoon pepper
1 cup hot water
1 cup cream
2 egg yolks, beaten

Parboil the frog legs in enough water to cover for 3 minutes. Drain. Melt butter in large frying pan. Fry legs until light brown, about 2 minutes. Shake over them the flour and rub in. Add other ingredients and boil gently until legs are tender and gravy thickened. Remove legs. Stir into gravy slowly 2 beaten egg yolks. Place legs in a warm dish and pour the gravy over them. Serves 2.

Fried Frog Legs

Allow 2 frog legs per portion. Salt and pepper them. Dip in dry bread crumbs, in beaten egg, and again in crumbs. Allow to stand 15 minutes. Fry in deep fat, 375 F, for 3 minutes. Serve with lemon-butter sauce.

LEMON-BUTTER SAUCE

½ cup butter
1 teaspoon salt
⅛ teaspoon pepper
1 teaspoon chopped parsley
1½ tablespoons lemon juice

Cream butter until fluffy. Add salt, pepper and parsley. Mix well. Work in lemon juice slowly. Makes ½ cup sauce.

EEL

❋

Eel in Webster's Dictionary is defined as "a voracious snakelike fish having a smooth skin, often without scales and no pelvic fins." Some people would add that it is edible and very good when properly prepared. The eel is skinned by cutting around the neck and peeling off the skin. They run in size from ½ to 10 pounds and are sold in some markets fresh, smoked and pickled. Eel is listed under fat-type fish. They may be broiled, boiled or fried.

Barbecued Eel

2 pounds eels, skinned and cut into
   2- to 3-inch pieces
2 beaten eggs
½ teaspoon salt
¼ teaspoon pepper
Dash of thyme
1½ cups bread crumbs

Combine egg and other ingredients. Dip pieces of eel into egg mixture, then roll in crumbs; back in egg and crumbs again.

Have 2 tablespoons butter and 2 tablespoons salad oil (makes food nice and brown) hot but not smoking. Fry until brown. Serve with this sauce:

BARBECUE SAUCE FOR EEL

5 tablespoons ground mustard
½ teaspoon paprika
8 drops Tabasco sauce
½ teaspoon salt
5 tablespoons boiling water
2 teaspoons olive oil

Mix dry ingredients. Stir in boiling water. Add olive oil. Serves 6.

SQUID AND OCTOPUS

✳

These similar mollusks can only be bought in rare seafood markets. However, if you happen to bring one in from a deep-sea fishing trip, here's how to clean and prepare it:

Wash and cut the body and remove the tooth and translucent pen. Turn body inside out and tear out insides, being very careful not to rupture the ink sac. Skin, wash and French fry.

CONCH

✳

Conches can be boiled in the shell to remove the muscle, or salt can be placed thickly on the snail to cause it to come out of the shell or loosen it so it can be pulled out, or the true "concher" knows the exact place at the top of the shell to cut the muscle loose and pull it out all in a few seconds.

Conches are usually boiled and cut up for salad or ground up or pounded for soups and fritters. The rubbery meat requires a long time to cook.

Boiled conch meat is good chopped in a salad, or oven barbecued. Use sauce in recipe Barbecued Fish Fillets.

Conch Chowder

1 pound conch meat or 6 conches
  in shell
¼ cup fresh lime juice
1 large onion, diced
2 cloves garlic, minced
1 stalk celery, chopped
4 tablespoons fat
2 cans tomato paste
2 quarts water
1 teaspoon salt
½ teaspoon pepper
4 potatoes, diced

If in shells, cook conches in boiling water about 3 minutes or until meat curls. Remove meat and beat with mallet or edge of saucer until meat is in pieces. Pour lime juice over meat and let stand several hours. Sauté onion, garlic and celery in fat until soft and brown. Add tomato paste and simmer 10 minutes. Add water, salt and pepper. Bring to boil and add potatoes. Simmer until about half done. Add conch meat and cook until potatoes are tender. Serves 6.

Substitute rice for potatoes if desired.

TURTLE

*

Barbecued Turtle Steaks

Cut turtle meat into 6 steaks, 2½ to 3 inches thick. Sprinkle generously with salt and pepper. Fry until nice and brown. Cover with the following sauce and simmer for 30 minutes:

BARBECUE SAUCE

3 tablespoons salad oil
1 teaspoon dry mustard
1 teaspoon Worcestershire sauce
2 tablespoons onion flakes
½ teaspoon salt
1 tablespoon lemon juice
¼ cup water
⅛ teaspoon pepper
¼ cup catsup

Simmer together for 5 minutes. Makes 4 to 6 servings.

Fried Turtle Steaks

Have meat dealer slice steaks thin. Allow ¼ pound per person. Ask him to run them through a steak cuber or pound at home with a mallet or the side of a saucer.

Roll steaks in flour to which salt and pepper are added. Fry in hot fat until browned on both sides. Remove from fat and drain. Pour out all except 3 tablespoons fat. Add 2 tablespoons flour. Stir until brown. Add 1 tablespoon salt and ¼ teaspoon pepper. Stir in slowly 1½ cups water. Stir and cook until thickened. Serve over turtle steaks or in a separate bowl.

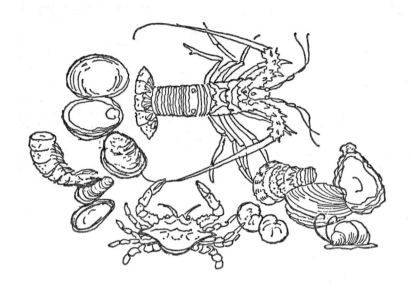

Cooking Shellfish

HOW TO SELECT

IN SELECTING live shellfish such as clams and oysters, be sure all shells are tightly shut, indicating that the animals are still alive. If you prefer, buy the meat in bulk as shucked shellfish. Crabs and lobsters should be bought alive or precooked. If they are to be sold cooked they are placed in boiling water as soon as they are brought ashore, alive and kicking. The shell turns orange-red. They are then sold in the markets in the shell, or the meat is removed in packing houses ready to be packaged or canned for the consumer. Uncooked shrimp can be bought in the shell. Heads are removed soon after they are brought ashore by the shrimpers, and sold as fresh, or green shrimp. The shell should be firm and glossy for freshness. Cooked shrimp, shucked and deveined, is sold also. Scallops are sold in the shell or already shucked like oysters.

MARKET FORMS OF SHELLFISH

LIVE: Shellfish, such as clams, crabs, lobsters and oysters should be alive if purchased in the shell, except for boiled crabs and lobsters.

SHUCKED: This method means that the shellfish have been removed from their shells. Clams, oysters and scallops are marketed in this manner.

HEADLESS: This term applies to shrimp, which are marketed in most areas with the head and thorax removed.

COOKED MEAT: The edible portion of shellfish is often sold cooked, ready to eat. Shrimp, crab, and lobster meat are marketed in this form.

FROZEN: All varieties of shellfish are marketed frozen. It is often packaged, breaded ready to cook and sometimes precooked.

COOKING METHODS AND FUEL VALUE
OF SHELLFISH

	BROIL	BAKE	BOIL	FRY	CHOWDER	FUEL VALUE OF EDIBLE PORTION IN CALORIES PER POUND
Clams (hard and soft)	Yes	Yes	Yes	Yes	Yes	345–355
Crabs	Yes	Yes	Yes	Yes	Yes	370
Lobster—common	Yes	Yes	Yes	No	Yes	380
Oysters	Yes	Yes	Yes	Yes	Yes	365
Scallops	Yes	Yes	Yes	Yes	Yes	335
Shrimp	Yes	Yes	Yes	Yes	Yes	370

A GUIDE FOR BUYING SHELLFISH

	FAT OR LEAN	USUAL MARKET FORMS	MAIN PRODUCTION AREAS*	MAIN MARKET AREAS*
Clams	Lean	In the shell, shucked	All coastal areas	Entire United States
Crabs	Lean	Live, cooked meat	All coastal areas	Entire United States
Lobsters	Lean	Live, cooked meat	North and Middle Atlantic, (South Atlantic)	North and Middle Atlantic; South Atlantic
Oysters	Lean	In the shell, shucked	All coastal areas	Entire United States
Shrimp	Lean	Headless, cooked meat, uncooked, frozen	South Atlantic; Gulf and Pacific	Entire United States
Scallops	Lean	In the shell, shucked	Northern and Middle Atlantic, South Atlantic; Gulf	North and Middle Atlantic; South Atlantic

* North Atlantic—Coastal states from Maine to Connecticut
Middle Atlantic—New York to Virginia
South Atlantic—North Carolina to Florida
Gulf—Alabama to Texas
Pacific—Washington to California
North Pacific—Washington, Oregon and Alaska
Midwest—Central and inland states
South Atlantic and Gulf—Around the Florida keys

QUICK CHART OF AMOUNTS OF SHELLFISH TO BUY

1 pound shelled shrimp	4 servings
1½ pounds shrimp in shell	¾ pound cooked, 6 servings
1 dozen live crabs	4 servings
1 pound can cooked meat	6–8 servings
1 pound live lobster	1 serving
1 pound lobster tails	2 servings
1 dozen live clams or oysters	2 servings
1 pint shucked clams	4 servings
1 pint shucked oysters	4 servings
1 pound scallops	4 servings

SHELLFISH

VARIETY	HOW MUCH EACH PERSON	HOW TO COOK	HOW LONG TO COOK
Shrimp—raw in shell	½ pound	Broil on foil in butter or pan fry	3 minutes for small 4 minutes for large
Shrimp, raw shelled	⅓ pound	Large ones skewered Small, same as raw in shell	2 minutes for small 3 minutes for large
Sea scallops, fresh	⅓ pound	Skewer-broil Sauté in skillet Foil-wrapped in fire Deep-fat fry	8–10 minutes 3–5 minutes 20 minutes 5–8 min. on each side
Bay scallops, fresh	⅓ pound	Skewer-broil Sauté in skillet Foil-wrapped in fire Deep-fat fry	8 minutes 3–4 minutes 20 minutes 5–6 min. on each side
Crabs, soft-shelled, live	1–large 2–small	Broil Broil Pan fry	3–4 minutes each side 2–3 minutes each side 5 minutes on each side
Oysters and clams, shucked	6–8	Can be served raw Skewer broil Roasted, pan Poached in own liquor Fry, pan Fry, deep fat	3 minutes Until edges curl Until edges curl 5 minutes each side 3–5 minutes each side
Oysters, clams, in shell	6	Roasted in shell	Until shells pop open
Lobster—fresh	1 small ½ large	Broil Broil	15 minutes 20 minutes
Lobster tails—fresh or frozen	1 large	Broil	Same as above
Lobster meat, cut up	½ pound	Skewer broil	15–20 minutes

SHRIMPS

This most popular of all shellfish is available in one form or another in almost every section of the United States. Fresh, or green, shrimp are marketed with the heads removed, packed in cracked ice and graded according to size. Although there are various species, ranging from green to brownish red, when cooked there is little or no difference in flavor and texture. All turn pinkish-red when cooked.

The size of shrimp decides the price, the jumbo being most expensive, but of course you use fewer per serving. Consumer-size packages of frozen shrimp are available. Many come already shelled and deveined. Thaw shrimp before using. Also popular with consumers are the packages of breaded and precooked shrimp. Canned shrimp comes in 4½- to 5-ounce cans, either packed in brine or dry. Canned or cooked shrimp may be used in most recipes except those for deep fat batter-frying, broiling, and barbecuing.

The most economical way to buy shrimp is raw in the shell. They number to the pound in grades as follows:

Grade	Number
Jumbo	Under 25
Large	25–30
Medium	30–42
Small	42 and over

Shrimp is boiled either before or after shelling as you prefer.

SHRIMP TIPS

- 1½ pound raw (green) shrimp yields ¾ pound when cooked and shelled, enough to serve 4.
- ¾ pound raw or 7 ounces frozen, shelled shrimp yields 1 cup cleaned, cooked shrimp. Serves 2. In casserole dishes, salads, and where combined with other foods, 1 pound serves 4.
- In selecting fresh shrimp be sure they are grayish green in color and have a fresh, blue-sea fragrance. The shell should fit the body tightly. Shrinkage may be a sign of staleness. There is also available a brownish red and a pink or coral-colored shrimp.
- Cooked shrimp are pinkish-red.
- Shrimp dishes have a special nutritional value, for shrimp, like other fishery products, are rich in calcium, phosphorous, copper and sulphur, all necessary body-building elements.
- Shrimp have a high percentage of high-quality protein and some water-soluble vitamins, plus a high iodine content.

Broiled Shrimp

*

Broiled Shrimp in Shell

2 pounds large raw shrimp
1 cup thin garlic French dressing
Salt and pepper

Cut shrimp shell down the back with scissors. Remove legs but not shells. Wash out the sand veins. Dry with a paper towel. Place shrimp in a large glass dish in a single layer. Cover with French dressing and very lightly with salt and pepper (the dressing probably is salty somewhat). Let shrimp marinate in the dressing overnight or for several hours.

Pour off the marinade (keep for dip) and place shrimp 5 inches from source of heat. Broil 3 to 5 minutes, or until they turn pink and shells are lightly browned. Serve as they are, to be eaten out of the shell. It will take 2 pounds to serve 6, if shrimp is a favorite food.

Peeled Broiled Shrimp

2 pounds raw shrimp, shelled and
    deveined
½ teaspoon salt
¼ teaspoon white pepper
¼ cup melted butter or margarine

Place shrimp in greased broiler pan, not on rack. Sprinkle with salt and pepper. Pour half of the melted butter over the top. Broil 5 minutes, 4–5 inches from source of heat. Turn

shrimp, brush with remaining butter. Return to broil 3 minutes. Serves 6.

TIP: 1 clove of garlic minced and added to the butter is good. Also serve with lemon or lime wedges, if you wish.

Shrimp-Bacon Delights

1 pound large raw shrimp
2 tablespoons lime juice
½ teaspoon salt
⅛ teaspoon pepper
Dash Worcestershire sauce
12 slices bacon

Shell and devein shrimp. Mix together the lime juice, salt, pepper, and Worcestershire sauce. Dip shrimp in this mixture, then wrap each in ½ slice of bacon. Secure with a short toothpick.

Place shrimp in oiled broiler pan and pour sauce over them. Broil 3 inches from heat, turning once, 5 to 6 minutes, or until bacon is crisp and shrimp are tender. Makes about 24 snacks or 4 main dish servings.

Mustard-Honey Broiled Shrimp

2 pounds raw shrimp
½ cup prepared mustard
½ cup honey
2 tablespoons lime juice
1 teaspoon salt

Shell and devein shrimp. Wash and
dry. Mix all other ingredients and
pour over shrimp. Let stand in refrigerator 2 to 3 hours. Drain off sauce
and place shrimp in broiler pan. Broil
5 minutes on each side, basting with
extra sauce. Serves 6.

Broiled Zippy Shrimp

*¾ pound cooked shrimp, peeled and
deveined*
1 cup tarragon vinegar
2 tablespoons water
1 bay leaf
1 teaspoon honey
1 onion, sliced
2 teaspoons salt
¼ teaspoon pepper
3 whole cloves

Place shrimp in a bowl. Mix other
ingredients in a saucepan and bring
to a boil. Pour over shrimp and allow
to cool at room temperature. Place in
refrigerator for 12 hours. Drain shrimp
and serve plain, or broil for 3 minutes
on each side. Serve hot on melba toast.
Serves 6.

Ginger-Sherry Shrimp

1½ pounds raw jumbo shrimp
¼ cup olive oil
¼ cup soy sauce
½ cup sherry
⅛ teaspoon grated garlic
⅛ teaspoon grated ginger

Shell, devein and wash shrimp. Mix
the other ingredients and shake vigorously in a jar until blended. Pour over
shrimp. Allow to marinate several
hours, then broil shrimp until pink
and tender, turning and basting, if
needed. Serve with thick slices of
tomatoes which have been sprinkled

with bread crumbs, salt, pepper and
basil and run under broiler until
crumbs are brown. Serves 6.

Golden Orange Shrimp

*2 pounds raw shrimp, shelled and
deveined*
¼ cup grated orange rind
1 cup orange juice
½ cup grapefruit juice
2 teaspoons salt
1 teaspoon dry mustard
¼ teaspoon black pepper
6 drops Tabasco sauce

Mix all ingredients and pour over
shrimp. Let marinate in the refrigerator several hours or overnight. Drain
off marinade but reserve it for sauce.

Place shrimp in buttered baking
dish or broiler pan. Broil 3 inches
under heat until they turn pink and
are tender, about 4–5 minutes. Turn
and broil other side. Baste with
melted butter if needed.

Remove shrimp and add 3 tablespoons flour to the butter in pan. Pour
in the marinade and add 1 cup water.
Cook on top of the stove until thickened. Serve sauce in a separate bowl.
Serves 6.

Broiled Shrimp
with Barbecue Sauce

2 pounds raw shrimp
¼ cup salad oil
⅓ cup green onions, chopped
1 cup tomato catsup
⅓ cup lemon juice
2 tablespoons brown sugar
2 teaspoons horseradish mustard
2 tablespoons Worcestershire sauce
½ teaspoon salt

Shell and devein shrimp. Set aside. In saucepan heat salad oil, add minced onions, and sauté until tender but not brown. Add other ingredients except shrimp and simmer, covered, 10 minutes. While the sauce is cooking, line broiler pan with foil and arrange shrimp on it. Pour sauce over shrimp and place under broiler about 3 inches from heat. Broil 5–8 minutes, according to size of shrimp. Serves 6.

Shrimp Broiled with Butter Sauce

1½ pounds raw shrimp
¼ cup Spanish olive oil
¼ cup flour

Wash, shell, and remove sand veins from shrimp. Dry with paper towel. Dredge shrimp in flour. Heat oil in a shallow broiler pan. Place shrimp on bottom of pan in the hot oil. Broil 5 inches from heat for 4 minutes. Turn and broil for same length of time on the other side, basting with the following sauce, after turning:

BUTTER SAUCE

4 tablespoons butter
2 tablespoons flour
½ teaspoon white pepper
1 tablespoon lemon juice
1 cup hot water

Melt 2 tablespoons butter, blend in flour to paste consistency; then add pepper, lemon juice, and water. Bring to a boil, stirring constantly. Simmer 5 minutes. Add 2 tablespoons of butter and allow to melt. Add parsley, minced, if desired. Pour this mixture over shrimp before serving. Serves 6.

Baked Shrimp and Casserole Dishes

✳

Easy Crab-Stuffed Shrimp

12 to 15 raw jumbo shrimp
½ pound white crabmeat
1 teaspoon salt
2 tablespoons lemon juice
¼ cup butter
½ teaspoon paprika
¼ cup finely crushed saltines
¼ cup grated Parmesan cheese

Cut shrimp through shell with scissors and remove sand vein without removing shell. Hold shrimp open by inserting a toothpick under the meat and over the shell at both sides. Flake crabmeat; sprinkle with salt and lemon juice. Spoon into cut shrimp. Melt butter and add paprika. Combine with crushed saltines and cheese. Cover shrimp with this mixture. Place shrimp in a shallow baking dish with ¼ cup water in the bottom to prevent drying out. Bake 20 minutes in moderate oven, 350 F, or until brown. Serve 2 or 3 on each plate, according to size of shrimp.

Baked Shrimp Barbecue

1½ pounds raw shrimp, shelled and
   deveined
½ cup butter or other fat, melted
2 tablespoons prepared mustard
6 tablespoons chili sauce
1 teaspoon brown sugar
6 drops Tabasco sauce
1 teaspoon salt
½ teaspoon black pepper
1 tablespoon Worcestershire sauce
Buttered bread crumbs

Boil shrimp with spices of your choice
or commercial mixture added to water. After 5 minutes drain. Cut shrimp
into pieces if large. Arrange in a shallow baking dish. Combine all other
ingredients except buttered crumbs.
Pour over shrimp. Spread the buttered
crumbs over the top. Bake in preheated oven at 350 F for 20 minutes,
or until browned. Serves 6.

Shrimp Pizza

¾ pound cooked shrimp
½ cup olive oil
Small onion, chopped
5 cloves garlic, finely minced
3 cans (6 ounces each) tomato paste
1½ teaspoons oregano
⅓ cup chopped parsley
¼ teaspoon basil leaves, crumbled
3 unbaked pizza crusts, 9 inches each
¾ pound Mozzarella cheese, sliced
   thin

Cut shrimp in pieces, reserving several
whole for garnish. Heat olive oil and
cook onion and garlic until tender.
Add tomato paste and simmer for 5
minutes. Remove from heat and add
oregano, parsley and basil. Place pizza
crusts on greased baking sheets. Cover
each crust with ⅓ of the sauce, layer-
ing with the shrimp over the sauce,
and cover with ⅓ of the cheese. Bake
in a hot oven, 425 F, until crust is
browned and cheese melts, about 20
minutes. Makes 3 pies. Serves 6.

Northern Shrimp
and Acorn Squash

1 pound cooked shrimp, shelled and
   deveined
3 medium-size acorn squash
3 tablespoons butter or other fat,
   melted
¼ teaspoon salt
⅛ teaspoon pepper
½ cup water
2 tablespoons additional fat
2 tablespoons grated onion
6 drops Tabasco sauce
2 tablespoons flour
½ teaspoon salt
½ cup milk
Buttered bread crumbs

Cut shrimp into halves, or pieces if
they are large. Cut squash into halves
lengthwise and remove seeds. Brush
centers with butter and sprinkle with
salt and pepper. Place in casserole
containing water. Cover and bake in
a moderate oven, 350 F, for 1 hour,
or until tender.

Cook onion in additional fat, sprinkle with Tabasco. When onion is
tender blend in the flour and salt.
Gradually add milk and cook, stirring,
until thick. Add shrimp. Fill squash.
Combine ½ cup bread crumbs with
1 tablespoon melted butter or margarine; sprinkle over shrimp mixture.
Return to oven and bake, uncovered,
for 20 minutes or until brown. Serves
6.

Shrimp-Stuffed Eggplant

*1 pound small raw shrimp, shelled
and deveined*
⅓ cup olive oil or other fat
¼ cup chopped onion
1 clove garlic, minced
1 eggplant
1 No. 2 can stewed tomatoes, 2 cups
½ teaspoon salt
¼ teaspoon pepper
1 teaspoon crumbled basil leaves
1 cup dry bread crumbs
4 tablespoons butter, melted

Cook shrimp in salted water to cover. Add nothing else to water. When tender, drain.

Heat oil and cook onion and garlic. Wash and cut eggplant in half, lengthwise. Cut out the pulp and dice. Place the shell in salted water to prevent darkening. Add to the onion and garlic mixture, the pulp, tomatoes, salt, pepper and basil leaves. Cover and cook about 7 minutes, or until eggplant is tender. Add shrimp. Combine bread crumbs with melted butter. Stuff eggplant shells with pulp mixture and top with buttered crumbs. Place in baking pan, adding ¼ cup hot water to prevent sticking. Bake in hot oven, 400 F, for 35 minutes or until brown. Serves 6.

Shrimp-Stuffed Avocados

*1 cup cooked shrimp, shelled and
deveined*
2 avocados
2 tablespoons lemon juice
1 teaspoon salt
1 can condensed cream of celery soup
1 tablespoon onion flakes
½ cup grated cheese

Cut the shrimp in pieces if they are large. Split avocados lengthwise, remove seed, and peel. Sprinkle with lemon juice and ½ teaspoon salt. This prevents discoloring. Heat soup in a saucepan, stirring until smooth. Add remaining salt, onion, and shrimp. Fill avocado halves with shrimp mixture and sprinkle with grated cheese. Place in baking pan and pour in ½ inch of water. Bake in moderate oven, 350 F, for 15 minutes. Serves 4.

TIP: Good with this are macaroni and cheese, cole slaw and apple pie.

Shrimp and Fresh Corn

*1 cup cooked shrimp, shelled and
deveined*
2 cups fresh corn
2 eggs
½ cup light cream
2 tablespoons butter
1 teaspoon salt
⅛ teaspoon mace

Cut shrimp in pieces. Set aside. Cut corn from cob. Beat eggs slightly, add all other ingredients with corn and shrimp. Bake in a greased shallow dish in moderate oven, 350 F, for 20–25 minutes. Serves 4.

TIP: Canned corn may be substituted.

Shrimp Baked in Cream

1½ pounds raw medium-size shrimp
½ teaspoon salt
¼ teaspoon paprika
1½ tablespoons butter, melted
1 cup cream

Shell and devein shrimp. Place in boiling water for 3 minutes. Drain.

Mix salt, paprika, butter and cream. Place shrimp in individual custard cups and spoon cream mixture over them or use a shallow baking dish. Bake in hot oven, 450 F, for 20 minutes. Serves 6.

Shrimp-Cauliflower with Quick Sauce

¾ pound cooked shrimp
1 package frozen cauliflower or 1
  medium head fresh cauliflower
1 can cream of mushroom soup
¼ cup water
1 cup grated American cheese

Cut shrimp into pieces. Cook cauliflower according to instructions on package or in boiled salted water until tender if fresh is used. Drain. Dilute soup with ¼ cup water. Heat and add cheese gradually, blending well. Add cauliflower and shrimp. Spoon mixture into a greased 1-quart casserole. Bake in moderate oven, 350 F, for 20 minutes. Serves 6.

TIP: Broccoli or asparagus may be substituted for cauliflower.

Party Shrimp in Patty Shells

¾ pound cooked shrimp
1 package frozen or bakery patty
  shells

1 can frozen cream of shrimp soup
¼ cup cream
1 tablespoon dehydrated onion flakes
½ cup Cheddar cheese, grated
¼ cup sherry

Preheat oven to 450 F. Bake patty shells. Cut shrimp in half if they are large. Heat soup and cream over low heat. Stir in onion and cheese. When cheese is melted add sherry and the cooked shrimp. Cook and stir 3 minutes but do not boil. Serve the shrimp and sauce in the warm patty shells. Serves 6.

TIP: For a bridge luncheon or small group of guests we suggest you serve also grapefruit-orange salad, shoestring potatoes, mixed pickles, olives and celery, fruit cake and coffee.

Shrimp Golden

2 pounds raw shrimp
¼ pound butter
2 green onions, chopped
2 cloves garlic, minced
2 tablespoons chopped parsley or
  1 tablespoon parsley flakes
1 teaspoon salt
½ teaspoon pepper
⅛ teaspoon nutmeg
⅛ teaspoon ginger
¾ cup dry bread crumbs
½ cup dry sherry

Boil shrimp. Shell, devein, wash and set aside. Melt butter in skillet and sauté until soft the chopped onion and garlic, minced. Toss in shrimp and stir until heated thoroughly.

Mix the parsley, salt, pepper, nutmeg and ginger. Mix thoroughly, then gradually add bread crumbs and sherry. Place shrimp mixture in individual greased custard cups or a shallow casserole. Top with crumb mixture. Bake, uncovered, in hot oven, 450 F, for 5 to 8 minutes or until heated thoroughly. Serves 6.

Shrimp-Rice Casserole

1 pound raw shrimp, shelled and
    deveined
1 cup onions, chopped
1 small green pepper, chopped
4 tablespoons butter
1 No. 2 can stewed tomatoes
½ teaspoon salt
¼ teaspoon pepper
1 tablespoon Worcestershire sauce
2 cups cooked rice
Bacon

Sauté shrimp, onions and green pepper in butter. When shrimp turn pink, add tomatoes. Add seasonings and fluffy rice. Pour into a greased casserole. Lay 4 bacon strips over top. Bake in oven at 350 F until bacon is crisp. Serves 6.

Individual Shrimp Casseroles

¾ pound cooked shrimp, shelled and
    deveined
½ cup sliced mushrooms
¼ cup butter or other fat, melted
¼ cup flour
1 teaspoon salt
½ teaspoon dry mustard
Dash cayenne pepper
2 cups milk
Grated Parmesan cheese
Paprika

Cut large shrimp in half. Cook mushrooms in butter for 5 minutes. Blend in flour and seasonings. Add milk

gradually and cook until thick, stirring constantly. Stir in shrimp. Place in 6 well-greased individual shells or 6-ounce custard cups. Sprinkle with cheese and paprika.

Bake in a hot oven, 400 F, for 10 minutes, or until cheese browns. Serves 6.

This shrimp dish gives any dinner a glamorous and tasty start. Serve in very small individual baking dishes or shells from the seashore. It serves as an appetizer.

Holiday Parsley Shrimp

1 pound small cooked shrimp, shelled
    and deveined
½ cup butter
¼ cup chopped parsley
½ teaspoon paprika
¼ teaspoon white pepper
½ teaspoon ground mace
½ cup cooking sherry
Buttered crumbs

Place shrimp in the dishes or shells. Melt butter and add parsley, paprika, pepper and mace. Mix thoroughly. Add sherry. Spoon sauce over shrimp. Cover with buttered soft bread crumbs. Bake in moderate oven, 325 F, until brown, about 10 minutes. Serves 6 to 8 as appetizer.

TIP: For a festive touch make small wreaths around top of dishes with chopped parsley, dotted with small pieces of pimento.

Shrimp Rockefeller

1 pound cooked, peeled, cleaned
    shrimp
2 packages (12 ounces each) frozen,
    chopped spinach
½ cup butter or margarine
1½ teaspoons Worcestershire sauce
1 teaspoon salt
¼ teaspoon hot pepper sauce, or
    Tabasco sauce
1 teaspoon celery salt
½ cup chopped green onions and tops
½ cup chopped parsley
2 cloves garlic, finely chopped
3 slices white bread, crusts removed
¾ cup water

2 tablespoons butter or other fat,
    melted
½ cup dry bread crumbs
¼ cup grated Parmesan cheese

Thaw frozen shrimp, or prepare as
above, if fresh. Thaw spinach and
drain. Melt butter and blend in seasonings. Add vegetables and sauté for 10
minutes or until tender.

Pour water over bread, add vegetables, and mix well. Place shrimp in
6 well-greased, individual shells or 10-
ounce casseroles, reserving 6 shrimp
for top. Cover with vegetable-bread
mixture. Combine butter and crumbs.
Sprinkle buttered crumbs and cheese
over top of each shell. Place a shrimp
on top. Bake in a hot oven, 400 F, for
15 minutes or until brown. Serves 6.

Batter-Fried Shrimp

Fried Shrimp—Plain

1½ pounds raw shrimp
2 eggs, beaten
1 teaspoon salt
½ cup crumbs (bread crumbs,
    cracker meal, half flour and half
    crumbs, finely rolled cornflakes
    or potato chips)
Fat

Peel shrimp, leaving the last section
of the shell on if desired. Cut almost
through lengthwise and wash out sand
veins. Wash. Combine beaten egg and
salt. Dip shrimp in this mixture, then
in crumbs. Fry in deep fat basket in
fat at 350 F until brown (2 to 3 min-

utes) or heat about an inch of fat in
frying pan and cook until brown on
both sides. Serves 6.

TIP: A commercial breading is available. Do not overcook shrimp. Serve
hot with or without a sauce.

Batter-Fried Shrimp

1½ pounds raw shrimp
½ cup flour
¼ teaspoon baking powder
1 teaspoon salt
½ cup milk
1 egg, beaten

Peel shrimp. Remove sand veins, wash, and dry. Sift flour, baking powder, and salt together. Combine milk and egg; blend into flour mixture. Dip shrimp in the batter and immediately fry in deep fat, 350 F, for 2 to 3 minutes or until brown. Or fry in frying pan with ½ inch fat. Drain on absorbent paper. Serve plain or with a sauce. Serves 6.

TIP: Shrimp are good if marinated in 3 tablespoons lemon juice 15 to 30 minutes before frying. For another change, substitute celery salt for plain salt.

Eastern Fried Shrimp

1½ raw shrimp, shelled and deveined
½ cup lemon juice
1 cup all-purpose flour
3 eggs, beaten
1½ teaspoons salt
Dash mace

Pour lemon juice over shrimp and let stand 15 minutes. Cut shrimp down back to last tail section. Spread out, butterfly style. Place flour in a paper bag and add shrimp. Toss to coat shrimp well with the flour. Combine egg, salt and mace. Dip each shrimp in egg. Heat about ⅛ inch of fat in skillet. When hot drop in enough shrimp to cover bottom. Brown on both sides; then put in more shrimp. Cook about 4 minutes. Drain on absorbent paper. Serves 6.

Fan-Tail Shrimp

1½ pounds large raw shrimp
3 tablespoons white corn meal
3 tablespoons flour

1 teaspoon baking powder
1 teaspoon salt
1 cup milk

Peel shrimp, leaving tails on. Cut down back almost but not all the way through, as for butterfly style. Wash out sand veins. Mix corn meal, flour, baking powder and salt. Beat in milk, making a thin batter. Dip the shrimp in batter and fry in hot fat, 375 F, for 4 to 5 minutes if shrimp are very large. When golden brown they are done. Serves 6.

Serve plain or with the following delicious, easy sauce:

CHINESE SAUCE

¼ cup soy sauce
3 tablespoons sherry
½ teaspoon salt
Dash pepper

Blend all ingredients, heat, and serve with fried shrimp.

Fried Shrimp Parmesan I

1½ pounds raw shrimp
¼ cup flour
1 teaspoon salt
⅛ teaspoon pepper
1 egg, beaten
1 tablespoon lime juice
½ cup cracker meal or dry bread
    crumbs
½ cup grated Parmesan cheese

Wash and dry shrimp. Coat with combined flour, salt and pepper. Combine beaten egg with lime juice and dip in shrimp. Then roll in mixture of crumbs and Parmesan cheese. Fry in 1 inch of cooking oil, heated to 375 F, or test with a cube of bread and when it browns, remove and put in the shrimp. Cook about 3 to 5 minutes or until brown. Drain and serve on hot platter with broiled tomatoes or garnish with parsley. Serves 6.

Fried Shrimp Parmesan II

1½ pounds fresh raw shrimp or 1
* package frozen shrimp*
2 tablespoons tarragon vinegar
1 teaspoon salt
¼ cup flour
1 egg, beaten
1 cup cracker meal
¼ cup Parmesan cheese

Wash shrimp and peel, leaving last section and tail intact. With a sharp knife cut down back almost through but not splitting. Remove sand vein. Spread shrimp open butterfly style. Pour tarragon vinegar over cleaned shrimp and let stand about 10 minutes. Drain shrimp, add salt and place in a paper bag with flour. Shake vigorously to coat shrimp. Remove from sack, dip in beaten egg, then in cracker meal to which Parmesan cheese has been added. Fry in deep fat at 375 F, one or 2 minutes until golden brown. Or fry in ⅛ inch of cooking oil in heavy skillet, browning on both sides. Serves 6. Serve on hot platter with this dip:

ZIPPY BLUE SEA DIP

½ cup catsup
3 tablespoons lime juice
2 tablespoons salad oil
1 teaspoon grated lemon peel
½ teaspoon prepared horseradish
Dash of Tabasco sauce

Mix thoroughly and let stand 30 minutes before serving. Serves 6.

Florida Shrimp

1½ pounds raw shrimp
1 cup sifted flour
½ teaspoon salt
½ teaspoon sugar
1 egg, slightly beaten
2 tablespoons salad oil
1 cup ice water

Peel and devein shrimp. Wash and dry. Mix other ingredients just until blended. Dip shrimp in batter and fry in deep hot fat, 375 F, until brown—not over 3 minutes. Drain. Serves 6. Serve with citrus sections which have been drained and marinated with thin French dressing for several hours.

Lemon-Fried Shrimp

1½ pounds raw shrimp
1 cup sifted flour
1 teaspoon salt
1 egg, slightly beaten
1 cup cold milk
4 tablespoons corn oil
3 slices lemon

Shell and devein shrimp. Wash and dry. Combine all ingredients except shrimp, oil and lemon. Stir and mix well.

Heat oil but do not allow to smoke. Place slices of lemon in fat. Dip shrimp into batter. Fry over lemon until brown on both sides. Drain on absorbent paper. Serve with lemon wedges and cocktail sauce, if desired. Serves 6.

A larger recipe—when guests come to dinner. They will love it.

Citrus-Fried Shrimp

5 pounds raw shrimp, shelled and
    deveined
1½ cups sifted all-purpose flour
4 teaspoons baking powder
1 teaspoon salt
1 egg, beaten
2½ tablespoons hot pepper sauce
½ cup warm water
Salad oil
2 slices fresh lime or lemon

Sift flour, baking powder and salt together. Stir the egg, pepper sauce and
warm water into the dry ingredients
to make a very thick batter. After
washing shrimp, drain and stir into
the batter. Pour oil into a skillet to
1½ inches deep. Heat to 375 F. Place
lime or lemon slices in hot fat. Lift
shrimp out of the batter with a fork
and add a few at a time to hot oil.
Turn heat to moderate and fry shrimp
until golden brown on both sides,
turning once. Serves 12.

Shrimp Nibblers

1½ pounds large raw shrimp
½ cup boiling water
3 tablespoons butter or margarine
½ cup all-purpose flour
1 teaspoon salt
1 teaspoon paprika
⅛ teaspoon ginger

Shell shrimp butterfly or fan-tail style,
leaving last section of shell and tail
on. Cut down back, almost but not all
the way through. Wash out sand vein.
    Combine flour and seasonings. Melt
butter and add water, which should
be boiling. Remove from heat. Add
flour to water and butter all at once,

immediately. Stir well until smooth.
Dip each shrimp in this batter and
lay in 2 inches of fat about 3 minutes.
Turn and brown on other side. Drain
on absorbent paper and serve with
this good sauce:

PAPRIKA-HORSERADISH
SAUCE

½ cup olive oil
¼ cup wet-pack horseradish
¼ cup paprika
1 tablespoon wine vinegar
2 tablespoons celery seeds
½ teaspoon salt
⅛ teaspoon white pepper
2 tablespoons chopped parsley

Mix all together. (Yes, ¼ cup paprika
is correct.) Chill and serve to 6.

Pirate Shrimp
with Guava Sauce

1½ pounds large raw shrimp
¾ cup all-purpose flour
2 tablespoons cornstarch
1 teaspoon baking powder
1 teaspoon salt
2 eggs
½ cup milk
2 teaspoons salad oil

Mix and sift the dry ingredients. Beat
eggs slightly. Add the milk and the
flour mixture. Beat in salad oil until
smooth. Heat in deep fat fryer enough
oil to cover shrimp in fry basket. Dip
shrimp in batter and place one layer
in the basket. Fry until golden brown.
Drain and fry more shrimp. Frying
takes 4 to 5 minutes. Drain.
    Make this sauce in advance:

a few at a time until brown. Serve
with soy sauce to 6.

Sunny Shrimp Balls

2 cups cooked small shrimp
1 cup thick white sauce or canned
    cream soup
¾ teaspoon curry powder
1 teaspoon salt
½ teaspoon ground mustard
6 drops Tabasco sauce
Cracker meal
Flour
1 egg, beaten
¼ cup milk

Grind shrimp with small blade of food
grinder or mince finely. Combine with
the white sauce, curry powder, salt,
mustard and Tabasco. Chill. Shape
into small balls with enough cracker
meal to bind. Roll balls in flour, then
in beaten egg, to which the milk has
been added. Roll again in flour. Fry
in deep fat, 375 F, until sun-gold in
color, about 1 minute on each side.
Makes 25 balls.

WHITE SAUCE

2 tablespoons butter, melted
3 tablespoons flour
1 cup milk
Salt and white pepper to taste

When butter is hot, blend in the flour.
Gradually add milk and cook, stirring
constantly, until thick. Season with
salt and white pepper to taste. Makes
about 1¼ cups white sauce.

TIP: 1 can condensed cream of celery
or mushroom soup, undiluted, may
be used instead of white sauce.

GUAVA SAUCE

½ cup orange juice
3 tablespoons dry mustard
2 tablespoons soy sauce
1 cup guava jam (peach is fine, too)
2 teaspoons grated lemon rind
½ cup crushed pineapple

Heat orange juice in skillet. Pour some
over mustard and stir until dissolved.
Mix back with orange juice and add
other ingredients. Stir until smooth
and hot. Serves 6.

Shrimp Puffs

1½ pounds large raw shrimp, shelled
    and deveined
1½ cups plain flour
2¼ teaspoons double-acting baking
    powder
¾ teaspoon salt
½ teaspoon ground ginger
2 egg yolks
1 egg white
¾ cup milk
1½ tablespoons salad oil
1 teaspoon grated lemon rind

Sift together the flour, baking powder,
salt, and ginger. Beat egg yolks, milk
and salad oil, blending well. Gradually
add flour mixture and beat until
smooth. Then beat egg white and fold
carefully into batter. Add lemon rind.
Heat salad oil or other fat in deep fat
fryer. Dip shrimp in batter and fry

Fried Shrimp Pattycakes

*1 pound raw shrimp, shelled and
    deveined*
3 small stalks celery, chopped
1 small green pepper, chopped
1 medium-size onion, chopped
3 tablespoons flour
4 tablespoons milk
2 eggs, beaten
½ teaspoon salt
*⅛ teaspoon each cayenne and black
    pepper*

Grind shrimp or mince finely. Prepare vegetables and mix with shrimp.

Blend flour and milk to a thin paste. Add beaten eggs to flour mixture. Add ground mixture and seasonings. Heat about 1 inch of fat in frying pan. Drop cakes by spoonfuls into the fat and fry to a golden brown. Serve hot with or without garnishes. Makes about 15 to 17 small cakes.

TIP: To really blend ingredients, grind shrimp, pepper, celery and onion together, using fine blade of chopper. If no chopper is available to grind mixture fine enough, you may have to add a small amount of bread or cracker crumbs to bind the shrimp mixture.

Shrimp—in Skillet and Saucepan
with and without Sauces

SAUTÉED SHRIMP

Shrimp Meunière

1½ pounds raw shrimp
*3 tablespoons butter or margarine,
    melted*
*1 tablespoon lemon juice or
    1½ teaspoons lime juice*
½ teaspoon salt
⅛ teaspoon pepper

Peel and devein shrimp. Wash and

dry. Toss in the hot melted butter for about 10 minutes; watch carefully to prevent burning. Remove shrimp to platter. Add the lemon or lime juice, salt and pepper to the browned butter. Pour over shrimp. Serves 6.

TIP: Suggestion for menu with *Shrimp Meunière:* buttered asparagus tips, broiled tomatoes, cole slaw, lemon pudding-cake.

Shrimp Sauté with Ginger Root

1½ *pounds raw shrimp*
2 *tablespoons butter or margarine*
1 *minced onion*
3 *thin slices ginger root*
1 *teaspoon salt*
2 *tablespoons lemon juice or 1 tablespoon lime juice*

Shell and devein shrimp, then wash and drain on absorbent paper. Melt butter in skillet and add shrimp and onion. Toss until tender. Add ginger root and stir. Sprinkle with salt. Remove skillet from heat and pour lemon juice over all. Serves 6.

Savoy Shrimp

¾ *pound cooked shrimp*
3 *tablespoons salad oil*
4 *tablespoons butter*
1 *small green pepper, chopped*
2 *tablespoons chopped onion*
1 *clove garlic, minced*
½ *teaspoon celery seeds*
⅛ *teaspoon each of salt, pepper, dry mustard, cayenne, paprika and thyme*
Grapefruit and orange sections

Heat salad oil and butter. Add chopped pepper, onion, shrimp and minced garlic. Toss until soft. Add celery seeds and seasonings. Heat again. Serve on platter garnished with grapefruit and orange sections. These may be heated but should be drained. Serves 6.

TIP: Canned fruit may be used.

Iron Skillet Shrimp

1½ *pounds raw shrimp*
6 *slices bacon*
1 *medium-size green pepper, in strips*
2 *cloves garlic, minced*
French bread

Shell, devein, wash and dry shrimp. Cook bacon in heavy iron skillet until crispy brown. Drain on absorbent paper. Strain drippings and return them to skillet. Add shrimp, green pepper, cut into strips, and garlic, finely minced. When shrimp and pepper are tender remove from skillet to a hot platter and sprinkle crumbled bacon over the top. Serve with hot buttered French bread. Serves 6.

Shrimp-Mushrooms on Toast

1½ *pounds raw shrimp*
4 *tablespoons oil or other fat*
1 *can (4 ounces) mushrooms*
½ *teaspoon salt*
1 *small green pepper, chopped*
2 *tablespoons grated lemon peel*
6 *slices buttered toast*

Peel shrimp and remove sand veins. Wash and drain on absorbent paper. Drain mushrooms, saving the liquid. Heat oil. Add shrimp, salt, mushrooms, green pepper and lemon peel. Cook until shrimp and pepper test soft, or about 10 minutes. Add reserved liquid. Serves 6. Spoon over buttered toast or Chinese noodles.

Chafing Dish Shrimp with Almonds

1 *pound cooked shrimp, peeled and deveined*

1 cup blanched, slivered almonds
½ cup butter or margarine, melted
½ teaspoon salt
Dash pepper
2 tablespoons chopped parsley
Toast points

Sauté almonds in butter until lightly brown. Remove almonds. Add shrimp and sauté until lightly brown. Add seasonings, parsley, and almonds. Serve on toast points. Serves 6.

Shrimp Tipsy

1 pound small raw shrimp
¼ cup olive oil
2 tablespoons lime juice
2 tablespoons butter
1 whole clove garlic
½ cup chopped almonds, blanched
2 tablespoons dry white vermouth
Yellow rice

Shell and devein shrimp. Wash and dry. Combine the olive oil, lime juice, pour over shrimp and let stand several hours, turning shrimp twice. Drain and reserve the marinade.

Melt butter and cook the whole garlic and shrimp until soft. When both are tender and shrimp pink, remove from heat. Discard garlic and spoon shrimp on plate.

Sauté almonds in small amount of fat in the pan until evenly browned. Add reserved marinade and vermouth. Heat and pour over shrimp. Serve on cooked rice, with a pinch of saffron added for the golden tint. Serves 4.

TIP: For a change substitute sherry for vermouth and add 1 teaspoon ground ginger. Serve over cooked white rice.

Shrimp Cantonese

1½ pounds raw shrimp, peeled and
    deveined
⅓ cup butter or other fat, melted
1 cup boiling water
2 chicken bouillon cubes
2 cans (4 ounces each) sliced
    mushrooms, drained
2 cans (5 ounces each) Chinese
    bamboo shoots, drained
2 tablespoons soy sauce
½ cup water
3 tablespoons flour
1 teaspoon ground ginger
Dash each of salt and pepper
Fluffy cooked rice

Wash shrimp and dry, then cook in the melted butter until shrimp are tender and pink. In the boiling water dissolve bouillon cubes. Add mushrooms, bamboo shoots, soy sauce. Mix water and flour thoroughly. Add together with other ingredients, except rice, to the shrimp and cook until thick, stirring constantly. Serve over rice. Serves 6.

Shrimp Olive and Tomato

1½ pounds raw shrimp
2 tablespoons corn oil
½ teaspoon garlic salt
¼ teaspoon pepper
Dash red pepper
⅓ cup white wine or dry white
    vermouth
1 tomato, chopped
¼ cup ripe olives, chopped

Heat oil in skillet. Add shrimp, shelled and deveined. Add seasonings and cook, stirring until shrimp are tender. Add wine. Cover and cook 2 minutes. Add tomato and olives. Toss and serve hot. Serves 6.

With this delicious shrimp dish, we suggest rice pilaf, green asparagus with lemon sauce, lettuce hearts and a light custard dessert.

Sautéed Shrimp on Pancakes

1 pound raw shrimp
4 tablespoons butter or margarine
½ cup chopped celery
1 can (4 ounces) mushrooms
½ teaspoon salt
2 tablespoons grated lemon peel
Silver-dollar-size pancakes

Shell and devein shrimp. Drain mushrooms, reserving liquid. Melt butter and add shrimp, celery and mushrooms. Sauté until shrimp are pink and the celery is tender, about 10 minutes. Add mushroom liquid. Serve on hot silver-dollar-size pancakes. Serves 4.

Hoecake Shrimp with Salad

HOECAKES:
1 cup white corn meal (not
  self-rising)
1 tablespoon salt
1½ cups hot water

Mix corn meal and salt; stir in hot water, mixing well. Batter should be thin. Heat a large greased griddle, pour the batter on, as for pancakes, but making one large cake. Turn heat to low When underside is brown, turn hoecake with a wet plate turned over it Brown other side. Keep warm while preparing shrimp.

SHRIMP:
1 pound raw shrimp
1 clove garlic, finely minced
1¼ cup butter or margarine
Dash Cayenne pepper
½ teaspoon salt

Sauté shrimp and garlic in butter. Add seasonings and serve hot over hoecakes to 4.

Good with this dish—LETTUCE AND BACON SALAD, made this way: Cook 2 to 3 slices bacon until crisp. Remove from skillet and in drippings mix 1 tablespoon tarragon or plain vinegar, 1 tablespoon lemon juice, ⅛ teaspoon pepper. Pour hot sauce over chopped lettuce and serve immediately. For dessert we suggest ambrosia.

In some sections of the country jumbo shrimp are called scampi, *an Italian word.*

Gourmet Flamed Scampi

1 pound raw jumbo shrimp
2 tablespoons olive oil mixed with
  1 tablespoon butter
1 tablespoon minced onion
1 tablespoon minced celery
1 tablespoon minced parsley
¼ cup brandy, warm
2 large ripe tomatoes, diced
½ cup water
2 tablespoons lemon or lime juice
1 teaspoon salt
⅛ teaspoon pepper
8 drops Tabasco sauce
½ cup heavy cream
1 tablespoon butter
1 teaspoon flour

Shell, devein, wash and dry shrimp. Heat olive oil and butter mixture.

Sauté minced onion, celery and parsley until soft. Add shrimp and cook until they turn pink and are tender. Remove pan from heat.

Pour the warmed brandy over shrimp mixture and light it with a match. When it flames and dies down, return mixture to heat. Add tomatoes with all other ingredients. Simmer for 10 minutes. Remove the shrimp to a hot dish. Reduce the sauce over high heat until it is quite thick. Force it through a sieve. Stir in the cream and 1 tablespoon butter creamed with 1 teaspoon flour. Reheat the sauce and pour it over the shrimp just before serving. Serves 6.

Shrimp Rarebit

¾ pound cooked shrimp
2 tablespoons butter or margarine, melted
2 tablespoons green pepper, chopped
3 tablespoons flour
¾ teaspoon salt
¼ teaspoon pepper
1 cup tomato juice
1 cup grated American cheese
¼ cup milk

Cut shrimp in pieces if they are large. In melted fat cook the green pepper. until soft. Blend in flour, salt and pepper. Add tomato juice, stirring constantly until thickened. Add the cheese and milk alternately, stirring constantly. Fold in the shrimp and heat again. Serve on toasted buns or toast points. Serves 4.

Shrimp Newburg

¾ pound cooked shrimp
½ cup butter or other fat, melted
2 tablespoons flour
1 teaspoon salt
⅛ teaspoon nutmeg
Dash cayenne
1½ cups coffee cream
2 egg yolks, beaten
2 tablespoons sherry
Toast points

Cut shrimp in half. Blend flour and seasonings in melted fat. Add cream gradually. Cook, stirring, until thick and smooth. Stir a little of the sauce into the beaten egg yolk, then gradually recombine, stirring constantly. Add shrimp and heat. Remove from heat and pour in the sherry slowly. Stir and serve while still hot on toast points. Serves 6.

TIP: The reason for adding a little of the sauce to the beaten egg and then gradually combining is to prevent the egg from coagulating quickly, resulting in a lumpy sauce.

Boiled Shrimp Hot and Cold

*

Shrimp Boiled in Shells

1½ pounds raw shrimp
1 quart water
1 lemon, sliced
¼ cup salt

Wash shrimp. Add salt and sliced lemon to water and bring to boil. Add shrimp and cover. When water boils again reduce heat and simmer 5 minutes. Drain and cool shrimp.

TO SHELL AND DEVEIN

Hold tail end of shrimp in right hand. Slip thumb under shell between feelers. Lift off 2 or 3 segments in one motion. Then, still holding firmly to tail, pull out shrimp from remaining section. Cut along the back of shrimp and wash out the black vein. Chill before serving.

NOTE: 1½ pounds of raw (sometimes called "green") shrimp will yield ¾ pound when shelled and cooked, or enough for 6 servings.

SHRIMP BOILED AFTER PEELING

If you prefer to peel shrimp before boiling simply shell and devein as described above and place the shrimp in enough boiling salted water (add lemon and spices if desired) to cover. When water boils again, turn down heat and simmer about 3 minutes, according to the size of the shrimp. Test for tenderness. Do not overcook, as this causes the shrimp to become tough and leathery. Drain water from shrimp and chill.

SPICES FOR 1½ TO 2 POUNDS SHRIMP

8 to 12 whole allspice
1 bay leaf
1 onion, sliced

Or use a commercial shrimp boil (spices). For convenience, place spices in an aluminum tea ball, with chain. Put in water with shrimp, salt and a sliced lemon.

Steamed Shrimp

Wash 1½ pounds raw headless shrimp thoroughly several times. Lift out of rinse water into heavy saucepan with tight fitting lid. Add no more water than clings to the shells. Place over heat, cover tightly, and steam for 3 minutes.

Remove from pan and serve in shells with cocktail or lemon-butter sauce. Serves 6. These are really delicious.

COLD BOILED SHRIMP

Marinade Sauce for Shrimp

1 cup olive oil
½ cup tarragon or plain vinegar
⅓ cup prepared mustard
1 teaspoon salt
2½ tablespoons paprika
¾ teaspoon cayenne pepper
1 cup chopped celery
2 tablespoons chopped green onion
2 tablespoons minced parsley
2 hard-cooked eggs, chopped

Combine the oil, vinegar and seasonings and mix well. Add the vegetables and eggs and stir them in well. Chill, if desired. Best if sauce is made enough in advance so that it can stand to blend flavors. Serves 6.

TIP: For a quick sauce, omit the celery, parsley and eggs, but add the minced onion to the oil and vinegar mixture.

MARINATED BOILED SHRIMP

Mix the dressing ingredients in *Marinade for Shrimp*. Combine the vegetables, egg and ¾ pound cooked shrimp. Pour over the marinade and marinate in refrigerator for several hours, stirring several times, lifting marinade from the bottom of the bowl. Serves 6.

Stuffed Shrimp with Marinade Sauce

Serve *Marinade Sauce for Shrimp* separately in a small bowl with stuffed shrimp.

French Shrimp

2 pounds cooked shrimp
3 egg yolks, mashed
3 tablespoons hot water
3 tablespoons vinegar
3 tablespoons pepper sauce
1½ tablespoons olive oil
1 teaspoon horseradish
1 teaspoon salt
½ teaspoon creole mustard
¼ teaspoon celery seed

Shell and devein boiled shrimp. Mash egg yolks and stir in the water. Add vinegar and pepper sauce. Stir well. Add other ingredients. Pour over shrimp and refrigerate for several hours. Serve as appetizer or salad on lettuce. Enough appetizers for 12, salad for 6.

Shrimp Saucy

¾ pound cooked shrimp

SAUCY

1 can (8 ounces) tomato sauce
1 cup mayonnaise
¼ cup sweet pickle relish
1 hard-cooked egg, chopped
½ teaspoon grated onion (or onion flakes)
½ teaspoon prepared mustard
1 tablespoon lemon juice

Blend tomato sauce with mayonnaise. Add other ingredients, mixing thoroughly. Chill. Serve with cooked shrimp. Makes 2½ cups *Saucy*.

Shrimp New Orleans Style

3 pounds large raw shrimp
1/4 cup Spanish olive oil
1 teaspoon salt
2½ tablespoons paprika
½ teaspoon cayenne
2 cloves garlic, minced
1/3 cup tarragon vinegar
1/3 cup horseradish mustard (Dijon)
2 tablespoons catsup
½ cup chopped green onions and
    tops or 1 large onion, chopped
2 hard-cooked eggs, minced

Boil the shrimp in shells using only salt and black pepper in the water. Drain, shell and devein. Pour shrimp into shallow bowl and cool at room temperature, then chill in refrigerator. Combine all the other ingredients, mixing well. Pour over shrimp and let stand in the refrigerator overnight or longer. Serve as appetizer or salad.

Note: Be sure to use real olive oil and Dijon or New Orleans horseradish mustard to turn out the authentic dish.

HOT BOILED SHRIMP

Shrimp in Beer

1½ pounds raw shrimp
3 cups stale beer
1 cup water
2 teaspoons salt
1 bay leaf
1 teaspoon celery seeds

Shell and devein shrimp. Bring beer-water mixture to a boil and add seasonings. Drop in shrimp. When beer boils again, turn heat to simmer and allow to cook 3 to 5 minutes, according to size. Try one and if shrimp is tender, pink, but still a little crisp, drain. Serve as other boiled shrimp. Serves 6.

Note: Alcohol always evaporates when cooked. Beer simply is used to give shrimp a slightly different flavor.

Hot Shrimp with Red Devil Sauce

2 pounds large raw shrimp, peeled
    and deveined
1 lime, sliced
3 tablespoons pickling spices
1 tablespoon salt
1 teaspoon pepper
1 tablespoon tarragon vinegar

To enough water to cover shrimp, add all other ingredients. Let water boil vigorously before putting in shrimp. When it comes to the second boil (after shrimp are added), cover pan and remove from heat. Let shrimp stand in water for 5 minutes. Drain and keep warm. Serve hot with:

RED DEVIL SAUCE

¼ cup salad oil
½ cup minced onion
2 cloves garlic, minced
3 tablespoons chili sauce
¾ teaspoon salt
1 tablespoon Worcestershire sauce
1 teaspoon prepared mustard
6 drops Tabasco or pepper sauce

Sauté onion and garlic in salad oil. Add other ingredients and simmer for 3 minutes. Stir well. Serve hot over spiced shrimp or other cooked seafoods. Serves 6 to 7.

Quick Shrimp Wiggle

¾ pound cooked shrimp
1 can condensed celery soup
¼ can water
1 small can tiny peas (1 cup cooked peas)
1 teaspoon Worcestershire sauce

Cut large shrimp in half. Heat soup mixed with water. Add peas, Worcestershire sauce, and shrimp. Stir thoroughly. Serve in patty shells, toast cups, or on toast. Serves 6.

TIP: For a variation omit the peas and Worcestershire sauce. To the soup add ¼ can of milk with the water. Stir in 2 tablespoons chopped pimento with seasonings to taste.

Shrimp and Mushrooms à la Crème

¾ pound cooked shrimp
1 pound mushrooms (or 1 4-ounce can)
¼ cup butter or salad oil

¼ cup chopped onion
2 tablespoons flour
2 tablespoons milk
1 cup commercial sour cream
Salt, pepper, paprika

Cut cooked shrimp in half crosswise and set aside. Clean and slice fresh mushrooms or drain if canned.

Melt butter and sauté onion until lightly browned. Sprinkle with flour. Add milk and ½ cup sour cream, stirring constantly; bring to simmer. Add sliced mushrooms, salt, pepper, paprika to taste. Stir and simmer 5 minutes. Add remaining sour cream and shrimp. Heat thoroughly and serve with tossed salad, broccoli and cherry pie. Delicious! Serves 6.

Quick Creamed Shrimp with Broccoli

2 cups cooked shrimp
2 packages frozen broccoli or 1½ pounds fresh
2 cans frozen cream of shrimp soup
1 cup sour cream
¼ teaspoon salt
⅛ teaspoon pepper
½ cup almonds, toasted

Shell and devein shrimp and cut into pieces; reserve several whole for garnish. Heat soup over low heat; add sour cream and heat again. Do not boil. Add seasonings. Toast or brown the blanched, slivered almonds in a little butter. Drain. Cook the broccoli, drain and place on plates. Pour the shrimp sauce over it and top with the almonds. Garnish with whole shrimp. Serves 6.

TIP: Asparagus, whole green beans or cauliflower may be substituted for broccoli.

Shrimp Coquilles

¾ pound small cooked shrimp
1 can cream of mushroom soup
1 teaspoon finely chopped onion
2 tablespoons lemon juice or sherry
1 cup fine bread crumbs
¼ cup grated Parmesan cheese

Cut shrimp in half, after shelling and deveining. Heat the mushroom soup. Add shrimp, onions and lemon juice or sherry. Let stand 5 minutes. Spoon mixture into cooking shells, coquilles or small custard cups. Top with a mixture of bread crumbs and cheese. Place cups or shells in broiler pan and have broiler rack in oven about 4 inches from heat. Let cook until golden brown. Serve garnished with parsley. Serves 6 as appetizer or side dish.

Shrimp Aloha

¾ pound cooked shrimp
1½ teaspoons cornstarch
¾ teaspoon salt
¼ teaspoon cayenne pepper
½ teaspoon curry powder
1 pint cream (or half and half evaporated milk and plain milk)

Combine cornstarch with seasonings. Bring cream to a boil, but do not allow to boil. Add to cornstarch mixture and return to heat. Cook over low heat until smooth and thick. Add shrimp. Serve over cooked rice. Serves 6.

TIP: Heat pineapple chunks, drained, and serve with *Shrimp Aloha.* Grated fresh coconut is also good with toasted almonds as condiments.

Quick Curry of Shrimp

1 pound shrimp, shelled and deveined
2 cans frozen condensed shrimp soup
1 cup sour cream
1 teaspoon curry powder
Cooked rice

Cook shrimp in boiling salted water for 3 minutes. Drain and cut into pieces, saving several whole for garnish. Heat soup according to package instructions. Add sour cream, curry powder, and shrimp pieces; heat again. Serve on fluffy cooked rice with small bowls of curry condiments, if desired.

CURRY CONDIMENTS

Chopped salted peanuts
Chopped hard-cooked eggs
Chutney
Flaked or grated coconut
Crumbled salted crackers
Chopped green onions and tops
Chopped tomatoes
Chow mein noodles

Rice is placed in plate first, then the curry spooned over it, and tiny portions of each condiment placed on top. Or serve condiments in little bowls. It is good this way when you have a party. It is also good without condiments, if you prefer it that way.

Basic Shrimp Curry

¾ pound cooked shrimp, peeled and deveined
3 tablespoons butter or other fat
3 tablespoons chopped onion
3 tablespoons flour
1 teaspoon salt
⅛ teaspoon white pepper
¼ teaspoon ground ginger

2 cups milk
Cooked rice

Cut shrimp in half. Melt butter and cook onion until tender; blend in flour and seasonings. Stir in milk gradually and cook until thick, stirring constantly. Add shrimp and heat. Serve with fluffy cooked rice. Serves 6.

Serve minute spinach, a crisp green salad, hard rolls and citrus dessert with shrimp curry. Also two or more curry condiments, given above.

Easy Shrimp-Apple Curry

¾ pound cooked shrimp
2 cans (10½ ounces each) condensed cream of chicken soup
½ cup grated onion
1 cup applesauce
1½ teaspoons curry powder
½ teaspoon salt
⅛ teaspoon white pepper
3 cups fluffy cooked rice
Curry condiments (listed above)

Cut cooked shrimp into bite-size pieces, reserving 6 whole for garnish. Combine soup with applesauce, curry powder, salt and pepper. Heat in large saucepan until well blended. Add shrimp. When hot again, serve on a bed of rice. Pass several curry condiments in small dishes to be spooned onto plate around the curry. Serves 6.

TIP:
Curry powder is not a special spice but a combination of various spices. If you have tried one brand and didn't like it, by all means try others until you find a curry powder suited to your taste. There is some difference in the blends.

Curried Shrimp with Mushroom Soup

1 pound cooked shrimp, peeled and deveined (or two 5-ounce cans, drained)
1 small onion, chopped
½ teaspoon curry powder
2 tablespoons butter or margarine
1 can (10½ ounces) condensed cream of mushroom soup
⅓ cup water
3 cups cooked rice (1 cup uncooked or 4 ⅝-ounce package precooked)

In skillet, cook onion with curry powder in butter, until onion is tender. Stir in soup, water and shrimp. Cook over low heat about 10 minutes. Stir occasionally. Serve over rice with a side dish of flaked coconut. Serves 6.

Busy-Day Shrimp Creole

¾ pound cooked shrimp
1 No. 2 can stewed tomatoes
1 teaspoon onion flakes
¼ teaspoon salt
⅛ teaspoon each Tabasco, mace, and thyme

Cut shrimp in half crosswise, or pieces if they are large. Heat stewed tomatoes; add other ingredients including shrimp. Cover and cook 5 minutes, or until all is heated. If sauce is too thin, add 2 tablespoons water blended with 1 tablespoon flour. Cook and stir until creole thickens. Serve over rice or toasted bread cubes. Serves 6.

Shrimp Creole Quickie

1½ pounds cooked, cleaned shrimp
1 small onion, chopped

½ cup green pepper, chopped
3 tablespoons salad oil
1 clove garlic, minced
1 teaspoon salt
Pepper
2 cups canned tomatoes

Sauté onion and pepper in oil until soft. Add garlic, salt, dash pepper, and tomatoes. Simmer 30 minutes. Add cooked shrimp and heat thoroughly. Serve over fluffy steamed rice. Serves 4 to 6.

Shrimp Creole

2 cups shrimp, cooked and cleaned
1 large green pepper, sliced
1 large onion, sliced
1 small garlic clove, minced
2 tablespoons salad oil, or other fat
1 can (10½ ounces) condensed
    tomato soup
2 teaspoons lemon juice
½ teaspoon salt
Dash black pepper
3 cups cooked rice

In skillet, cook green pepper, onion and garlic in fat until vegetables are tender. Stir in soup, lemon juice, salt, black pepper and shrimp. Cook over low heat about 10 minutes. Stir now and then. Serve over rice. Serves 6.

Creole Shrimp St. Augustine

2 pounds raw shrimp
2 tablespoons butter or margarine
2 medium onions, chopped
2 cloves garlic, minced

1 green pepper, chopped
2 teaspoons chopped parsley
1 large can tomatoes
1 tablespoon flour
½ teaspoon red pepper
2 bay leaves
1 teaspoon salt
½ teaspoon celery seeds
1 teaspoon powdered thyme
2 teaspoons Worcestershire sauce

Shell and devein shrimp. Rinse and set aside. Melt fat in large kettle. Add onion, garlic, green pepper and parsley. When lightly browned add tomatoes. Mix flour with a little water and add. Stir in seasonings and cook, covered tightly, for 45 minutes. Add shrimp and continue cooking 15 minutes. Add 2 teaspoons Worcestershire sauce and serve in large soup tureen. Serves 6 to 8.

Shrimp and Ham Creole

2 cups cooked, cleaned shrimp
¾ cup diced ham
2 tablespoons shortening, melted
½ cup chopped green onions and
    tops
3 cloves garlic, minced
2 cans stewed tomatoes
½ teaspoon salt
1 bay leaf
½ teaspoon whole crushed thyme
1 lemon slice
Dash Tabasco or red pepper sauce
1 cup uncooked rice

Cut shrimp in half, if large. Sauté ham in shortening. Add onion and garlic. Cook until tender. Add tomatoes, seasonings, lemon, Tabasco and rice. Cover and cook, stirring occasionally, until rice is almost done, then add shrimp. Serves 6 to 8.

Old South Gumbo Filé

Filé is used instead of okra, serving the same purpose in the gumbo, but filé is never added until the last minute before serving. Okra is cooked with the soup.

1½ pounds large shrimp
1 slice lean ham
¼ pound lean veal
1 tablespoon butter
1 large onion
1 cup canned tomatoes
1 teaspoon chopped parsley
1 tablespoon flour
1 bay leaf
1 teaspoon salt
Dash each of cayenne, thyme and
   black pepper
2 quarts hot water
2 tablespoons filé powder

In a separate saucepan scald the shrimp in water seasoned with bay leaves and salt. Let shrimp cool in water before shelling them. Cut the ham and veal into small pieces (1 cup each) and dredge with salt and pepper.

Put a tablespoon of butter into a frying pan and when hot sauté sliced onion until it is soft. Add the chopped

meat. Cook and stir until lightly browned. Add tomatoes and seasonings, except the filé. Cook 2 minutes. Transfer to a soup kettle and add 2 quarts hot water. Add a quarter of the shrimp cut into pieces to be absorbed into the soup for flavor. Bring soup to a slow boil and let it simmer 2 hours. Put in remainder of shrimp and cook 5 minutes longer. Sprinkle in the gumbo filé. *Do not let gumbo boil after filé is added.* Serve with fluffy rice. Serves 8 to 12.

NOTE: Gumbo filé powder is found on most specialty and spice counters at your grocer's.

Shrimp Gumbo New York

¾ pound cooked cleaned shrimp or
   2 cans (4½ ounces each)
2 cups sliced fresh okra or 1 package
   sliced frozen
⅓ cup fat, melted
½ cup chopped green onions and
   tops
½ teaspoon garlic salt
¼ teaspoon pepper
1 No. 2 can stewed tomatoes
¼ teaspoon Tabasco sauce
1½ cups cooked rice

Cut cooked shrimp into bite-size pieces. Sauté okra in fat until it appears dry. Add seasonings and stewed tomatoes. Stir in Tabasco and shrimp. Cover and simmer for 10 minutes. Serve spooned over cooked rice. Serves 6.

TIP: Substitute 2 cans of combined okra and tomatoes for the sliced fresh or frozen okra and the stewed tomatoes, if desired.

CRABS

Blue crabs are taken along the Atlantic and Gulf coasts. They live in waters ranging from salt to brackish and even fresh. While the blue crab is the most common variety; the larger Dungeness crab comes from the Pacific coast.

All varieties have the hard- and soft-shelled stages. Many people have the idea that the so-called "soft-shelled crab" is a distinct species, but it is not. The soft-shelled crab is simply a crab after the hard shell has been discarded and before the new one has hardened. Soft-shelled crabs are delicious broiled or fried and served sandwich style.

The blue and Dungeness hard-shelled crabs are available all year, but are most plentiful during the summer months. Crabs are sold alive or are plunged into boiling water as soon as they are caught, and the sweet white meat is picked from the cracked shells, legs, and claws. Commercially these different kinds (shell, leg, claw) are packed separately in cans. The meat is also sold fresh-cooked or frozen. The fresh-cooked meat is packed in cans and sometimes frozen. It also is available processed in cans like salmon and tuna, but the fresh crabmeat is usually packed in that form in cans as are oysters. Claw meat is white and body meat darker. It is mixed in the cans unless marked "white" or "deluxe." Also the claws are marketed in shells (also in cans) and are used for cocktails.

BOILING CRABS AT HOME

Have enough boiling salted water to cover the live crabs. Add to each 2 quarts of boiling water, ¼ cup vinegar, 1 tablespoon Tabasco sauce or paprika and 2 tablespoons salt. Cook crabs in the water, which should be rapidly boiling for 8 minutes. They will turn red with cooking. They may be steamed in a steamer for 30 minutes. After cooking, break off the claws and legs from the body and crack the shells. Break off the segment that folds under the body in rear. Discard sponge. Slip fingers under the top shell and pull body downward without breaking the top shell, which is saved for baking. Remove the digestive tract by running water over crab. Split center crease. Cut hard membranes along the outer edge. Use a nut pick to remove the tender muscles in each cavity. Pick out all shell particles and tissue. This meat can be used in any number of ways.

Whole Crabs

*

Boiled Hard-Shelled Crabs with Hot Butter and Lemon

6 or 8 hard-shelled crabs
2 quarts water
2 tablespoons salt
1 tablespoon red pepper
1 lemon or lime, sliced

Bring water to boil with salt, pepper, and lemon or lime slices in it. Drop in crabs. Boil hard for 5 minutes, then simmer for 15 additional minutes. Crabs will turn red when cooked.

Drain and cool at room temperature. Break off claws and crack with nut crackers. Break body apart with hands. Pick out meat and eat, dipping into hot butter and lemon juice.

Fried Soft-Shelled Crabs

Place live crabs on board with back up. Cut off the head ½ inch back of the eyes. Turn back the tapered pointed ends of the back about half way and scrape out the spongy part that is exposed. Peel off the apron which laps under the crab, together with the spongy substance under it. Wash crab in cold water. Place in a salt solution of 2 tablespoons salt to 1 cup water for several minutes.

Heat deep fat to 360 F. Drain crabs, dry, and dip them into a beaten egg, then roll in fine bread or cracker crumbs. Arrange in one layer in wire basket and lower into hot fat (not smoking). Fry until golden brown, turning once. Drain on absorbent paper and serve with *Tartare Sauce*. The entire crab is edible. Good served on toasted bread as a sandwich.

Sautéed Soft-Shelled Crabs

2 soft-shelled crabs per person
3 tablespoons butter
Salt, pepper
Lemon juice
Chopped parsley

Clean, wash and dry soft-shelled crabs. Heat butter in a large frying pan until it is hot. Add the crabs and sauté them quickly, browning on both sides. Season with salt and pepper. Add lemon juice and parsley to butter in pan where the crabs were cooked, adding more butter if needed. When warm, pour over the crabs.

Broiled Soft-Shelled Crabs

Dip the cleaned and prepared crabs in flour and brush with salad oil. Place on rack under broiler heat for 3 minutes on each side, about 4 inches from source of heat. Serve on toast with melted butter, seasoned with lemon or lime juice, heated and poured over the crabs. Serve *Tartare Sauce with Capers* separately.

TARTARE SAUCE WITH CAPERS

1½ cups mayonnaise
1 chopped dill pickle
4 minced green onions
1 tablespoon each of tarragon, parsley and capers
½ teaspoon lemon juice

Combine the ingredients. Thin the sauce with cream. Add lemon juice, salt and pepper to taste. Makes almost 2 cups.

Recipes Using Cooked Crabmeat

Crabmeat with Deviled Eggs

1 pound cooked crabmeat
½ cup sour cream
2 tablespoons mayonnaise
2 tablespoons tomato catsup
2 tablespoons pickle relish
½ teaspoon salt
⅛ teaspoon white pepper

Look over crabmeat for any shell or tissue. Place in large round shallow bowl. Mix together other ingredients which have been chilled thoroughly. Spoon this sauce over crabmeat. Place deviled eggs around dish and garnish with tomato quarters and ripe olives. Serves 6.

DEVILED EGGS

6 eggs
¾ cup mayonnaise
2 tablespoons prepared mustard
Salt and white pepper
½ teaspoon tarragon vinegar

The basic rule for boiling eggs is to put them in a pan of cold water and bring to a boil. Then immediately remove pan from heat. Cover and let stand for 20 minutes. Shell at once under cool running water. This prevents the dark discoloration which we all dislike. Slice the eggs in half lengthwise. Remove yolks and mash. Add mayonnaise, mustard, salt and white pepper to taste and tarragon vinegar and mix well. Spoon back into whites and decorate with strip of pimento.

Most recipes are not for the whole crab but for various ways of using boiled crabmeat.

Crab Louis

2 cups cooked crabmeat
Lettuce
Salt and pepper
Lemon juice

Shred lettuce in large bowl. Drain and add crabmeat, which has been sprinkled with salt, pepper and lemon juice. Cover with *Louis Dressing* (or toss crabmeat mixture with the dressing). Serves 6.

CRAB LOUIS DRESSING

¾ cup mayonnaise
3 tablespoons chili sauce
2 tablespoons cream
1 tablespoon sweet pickle relish
2 teaspoons lemon juice
¼ teaspoon salt.

Blend and chill. Makes 1½ cups.

Crabmeat Remick

1 can cooked claw crabmeat or 2 cups
1 cup mayonnaise
¼ cup tomato catsup
1 teaspoon prepared mustard
¼ teaspoon each salt, pepper, and
    paprika
6 drops pepper sauce
1 teaspoon lemon juice
2 tablespoons butter, melted
½ cup dry bread crumbs

Place crabmeat in a well-greased baking dish. Mix all other ingredients except butter and bread crumbs. Spoon mixture over the crabmeat. Mix melted butter with bread crumbs and spread over the crabmeat mixture. Broil 4 inches from heat for 5 minutes. Garnish with ripe olives and tomato slices. Serves 6.

Deviled Crab Sticks

2 packages frozen crab sticks (ready
    to heat)
1 tablespoon Worcestershire sauce
Dash of Tabasco or pepper sauce
1 tablespoon grated onion
1 teaspoon lemon juice
¼ cup soft butter or margarine
½ teaspoon prepared mustard
2 teaspoons dehydrated parsley flakes
    or 2 tablespoons fresh chopped
    parsley

Place crab sticks close together in broiler pan. Combine other ingredients and spread over sticks. Broil 8 minutes. Serve hot between split hot dog buns. Pass a bowl of cole slaw. Serves 6.

Or serve with a raw vegetable salad and quick-frozen spinach. Orange custard finishes the meal off deliciously.

Baked Crabmeat

Crab Imperial

½ pound cooked crabmeat
1 tablespoon butter
2 tablespoons chopped green pepper
1 tablespoon chopped pimento
1 tablespoon chopped onion
1 egg, beaten

2 tablespoons mayonnaise
1 teaspoon dry mustard

Heat butter. Add green pepper, pimento and onion and sauté until tender but not brown. Combine egg, mayonnaise, dry mustard and crabmeat. Add sautéed vegetables and mix. Spoon into individual baking dishes. Bake at 350 F for 15 minutes. Makes 4 servings.

Different Deviled Crab

1 cup cooked crabmeat
1 cup soft bread crumbs
1 cup mayonnaise
¾ cup milk
6 hard-cooked eggs, chopped
1 small onion, chopped
¼ cup stuffed olives, sliced
1 teaspoon salt
⅛ teaspoon pepper
½ cup soft bread crumbs, buttered

Mix all ingredients, except bread crumbs. Spoon into buttered crab shells or shallow baking dish. Cover with buttered crumbs. Bake in moderate oven, 350 F, for 20 minutes. Garnish with parsley. Serves 6.

Tangy Baked Crabmeat

1 pound fresh cooked crabmeat
Salt to taste
Juice of 1 lemon
⅓ cup mayonnaise
4 tablespoons Worcestershire sauce
1 teaspoon mustard
Few drops Tabasco sauce
⅓ cup milk
1 cup saltines, crumbled
Butter for topping

Pick over crabmeat carefully for shell pieces. Sprinkle with salt, add lemon juice and set aside. Add remaining seasoning to mayonnaise, then add milk and toss this mixture lightly with crabmeat. Place in buttered casserole, cover with crumbled saltines. Dot generously with butter. Bake 30 minutes at 350 F. Serves 6.

Baked Crab-Avocado Salad

2 cups cooked crabmeat
1 cup mayonnaise
1 tablespoon vinegar
1 teaspoon pepper sauce
2 teaspoons Worcestershire sauce
⅛ teaspoon ground red pepper
1 teaspoon salt
½ cup evaporated milk, chilled and
    whipped
3 tomatoes, peeled, seeded, chopped
½ cup onion, minced
½ green pepper minced
1 clove garlic, minced
2 large avocados
4 slices bacon

Remove any shell particles or connective tissue from crabmeat. Combine in a bowl the mayonnaise, vinegar, pepper sauce, Worcestershire sauce, red pepper and salt. Mix in the whipped milk, crabmeat, tomatoes, onion, green pepper and garlic. Spoon into greased baking dish. Peel and slice avocados and place slices over the top. Cover with bacon, cut into halves. Bake in moderate oven, 350 F, for 30 minutes. Serves 6.

TIP: With this dish serve whole green beans, cabbage-carrot salad, toasted French bread and apple pie for dessert.

Easy Crabmeat Casserole

1 pound cooked crabmeat
1 can (10½ ounces) condensed
    mushroom soup

½ cup cooked peas
Dash pepper
½ cup grated American cheese
Paprika

Remove any shell or cartilage from crabmeat. Combine soup, peas, pepper, and crabmeat. Place in well-greased casserole dish or 6 individual shells. Sprinkle cheese and paprika over top of crab mixture. Bake in moderate oven, 350 F, for 20 minutes or until brown. Serves 6.

Blue Sea Crabmeat Casserole

2 cups cooked flaked crabmeat
1½ cups milk
1½ cups soft bread crumbs
4 hard-cooked eggs
1½ teaspoons salt
½ teaspoon pepper
¼ teaspoon ground mustard
⅓ cup melted butter
¾ cup bread crumbs, mixed with 2
    tablespoons butter for topping

Mix milk with bread crumbs, stir in flaked crabmeat. Slice egg whites thin and add to fish-crumb mixture. Stir in mashed egg yolks and blend in seasonings and ⅓ cup melted butter.

Turn into greased casserole and top with crumb and butter topping. Bake at 350 F for 15 to 20 minutes, or until brown. Serves 6.

Seven Seas Deviled Crab

2 cups cooked claw crabmeat
2 eggs, beaten
½ cup cream
2 tablespoons melted butter
1 tablespoon minced onion
1 teaspoon prepared mustard
½ teaspoon salt

¼ teaspoon pepper
1 teaspoon Tabasco sauce
1 cup bread or cracker crumbs

Look over crabmeat and remove any shell particles or connective tissue. Combine beaten eggs, cream, butter and seasonings and mix thoroughly. Stir in crabmeat and half the crumbs. Fill crab shells with mixture, top with the remaining crumbs and dot with butter. Bake in moderate oven, 350 F, until crumbs are browned. Serve with *Easy Tartare Sauce.* Serves 6.

EASY TARTARE SAUCE

½ cup mayonnaise
1 teaspoon grated onion
2 tablespoons sweet pickle relish

Combine all ingredients in a small bowl and chill. Makes ⅔ cup.

Deviled Crab with Vegetable Base

1 pound cooked claw crabmeat
1½ cups chopped celery (stalk and
    leaves)
¼ cup chopped parsley
1 large onion, chopped
½ stick butter or margarine
6 drops Tabasco sauce
⅛ teaspoon pepper
¾ teaspoon salt
2 slices bread (white, whole wheat,
    corn bread or an equivalent
    quantity of crushed crackers)
1 egg, beaten

Remove any shell or connective tissue from crabmeat. Sauté celery, parsley, and onion in melted butter. Add seasonings. Mix crabmeat with bread, which has been finely flaked. Stir in beaten egg. Mix all together thoroughly. Spoon into cleaned, greased crab shells or use a casserole dish. Bake in moderate oven, 350 F, for about 30 minutes or until brown. Serves 6 to 8.

TIP: If desired, shape mixture into patties and bake on greased baking sheet until brown.

Crabmeat Spoon Bread

2 cups cooked crabmeat
3 cups milk
1 cup cream
1 teaspoon salt
¼ teaspoon pepper
1 cup corn meal
¼ cup melted butter
4 eggs, beaten

Look over crabmeat and remove any shell particles and connective tissue. Set aside. Combine milk, cream, salt and pepper. Heat until lukewarm, then stir in corn meal. Cook and stir until smooth. Stir in melted butter, crabmeat, and eggs. Stir over low heat for 3 minutes. Pour the batter into a buttered casserole, being sure it is not more than half full. Bake in preheated oven, 350 F, for 45 minutes. Serves 6.

Crab Spaghetti

2 cups cooked flaked crabmeat
⅓ cup chopped onion
½ clove garlic, minced
2 tablespoons butter or margarine
1 can cream of celery soup
1 can tomato soup
½ can water
½ teaspoon salt
½ small package spaghetti, cooked

Remove any shell particles or connective tissue from crabmeat. Sauté onion and garlic in melted butter until soft. Blend in soups, water and salt. Stir in the crabmeat. Heat. Combine with cooked spaghetti. Butter a 1½-quart casserole and add mixture. Cover and bake in moderate oven, 350 F, 35 minutes, stirring twice during cooking. Serves 6.

TIP: Chopped pimento and parsley flakes may be added for color and flavor.

With this dish we suggest you serve green peas, shredded lettuce with garlic French dressing, hard rolls and chocolate pudding.

Crab Mornay

1 pound cooked crabmeat
½ pound grated cheese
½ cup butter or margarine
3 tablespoons flour
2 teaspoons white pepper
1 teaspoon salt
2 cups milk

Make a thick cream sauce of the butter, flour, salt and white pepper, and milk. Into a greased baking dish put a layer of crabmeat, a layer of cheese and some of the cream sauce. Continue until all ingredients are used. Bake at 350 F for 25 to 30 minutes. This may be mixed ahead of time and kept in the refrigerator. Bake just 30 minutes before you plan to serve it. Serves 6.

Crab Loaf

2 cups flaked cooked crabmeat
1 cup milk
1½ cup soft bread crumbs

4 tablespoons melted butter
3 egg yolks, beaten slightly
2 tablespoons lemon juice
2 tablespoons minced onion
½ cup minced celery
½ teaspoon salt
⅛ teaspoon pepper
3 egg whites, beaten

Scald milk. Add bread crumbs and butter. Beat until smooth. Combine with crabmeat, egg yolks, lemon juice, onion, celery, salt and pepper. Fold in stiffly beaten egg whites. Grease loaf pan. Turn in fish mixture and bake at 350 F for 35 minutes. Serve hot with a tomato sauce. Serves 6.

Louise Wilder's Crab-Fondue Loaf

1½ cups soft bread crumbs
1½ cups scalded milk
Dash cayenne pepper
1 teaspoon prepared mustard
2 tablespoons butter
2 cups grated sharp cheese
1 teaspoon salt
3 egg yolks, beaten
½ cup crabmeat
2 tablespoons chopped green pepper
2 tablespoons chopped celery
2 tablespoons pimentos, chopped
3 egg whites

Combine first 7 ingredients. Add well-beaten egg yolks, crabmeat, chopped green pepper, celery and pimentos. Fold in stiffly beaten egg whites last. Sprinkle top with paprika. Bake at 350 F, 45 minutes. Serve immediately.

Easy Crab Soufflé with Almonds

2 cups cooked crabmeat
3 eggs, separated

¼ teaspoon paprika
1 can condensed cream of celery soup
1 teaspoon grated onion
½ cup dry bread crumbs
½ cup slivered blanched almonds

Remove shell particles and connective tissue from crabmeat. Beat egg yolks thoroughly. Add remaining ingredients except almonds. Beat the egg whites stiff and fold carefully into mixture. Pour into 1½-quart buttered casserole. Bake in pan of hot water in moderate oven, 350 F, for 50 minutes. Serve with almonds sprinkled over the top. Serves 6.

Crab Soufflé with Pecans

1 pound cooked crabmeat
1 cup cream sauce
½ cup water
3 egg yolks, beaten
½ teaspoon prepared mustard
2 teaspoons grated onion
1 teaspoon lemon juice
2 tablespoons chopped parsley
3 egg whites, whipped
Toasted chopped pecans

Remove shell particles or cartilage from crabmeat. Heat cream sauce. Add water, then stir a small amount of sauce into the beaten egg yolks. Return all to hot sauce. Cook 2 minutes, stirring constantly.

Add mustard, onion, lemon juice, parsley and crabmeat. Fold in stiffly beaten egg whites. Pour into greased 1½-quart casserole. Place in a pan of hot water and bake at 350 F for 1 hour, or until soufflé is firm in center. Serve at once. Sprinkle with toasted chopped pecans. Serves 6.

Crabmeat in Skillet and Saucepan

Crab Nuggets

1 cup cooked crabmeat, shredded fine
2 tablespoons butter
1 teaspoon flour
½ cup light cream
½ teaspoon dehydrated celery flakes
⅓ teaspoon paprika
½ teaspoon seasoned salt
1 egg white
Bread crumbs

Remove any shell particles or tissue from crabmeat. Shred or grind. Melt butter, blend in flour and slowly add cream. Add celery flakes, paprika and seasoned salt. Stir and cook until mixture thickens. Add crabmeat and bring just to a boil. Set aside to cool. Form into small balls. Brush with egg white and roll in dry bread crumbs. Place in a basket of deep-fat fryer and fry at 350 F, a few at a time until brown, about 2 to 3 minutes. Makes 12 nuggets.

Crab Patties

1 pound cooked claw crabmeat
4 tablespoons butter
1 medium onion, chopped
½ cup celery, chopped
1 cup soft bread crumbs
2 eggs, beaten slightly
4 tablespoons minced parsley
1 teaspoon salt
¼ teaspoon pepper
¼ teaspoon ground ginger
½ cup cream
Cracker crumbs

Look over crabmeat and remove any shell particles and connective tissue. Melt butter and cook onion and celery until soft. Add bread crumbs, crabmeat, eggs and parsley. Add seasonings and stir in cream. (If not enough to hold mixture together, add a little more cream). Shape into patties and fry in 1 inch of fat until brown. Turn and brown other side. Drain on absorbent paper. Serves 6.

Good with these patties are baked potatoes with sour cream, buttered asparagus, lettuce and tomato salad and cherry tarts.

Crab-Almond Sauté

2 cups cooked crabmeat
½ cup blanched, slivered almonds
½ cup butter or margarine
½ teaspoon salt
¼ teaspoon white pepper
1 tablespoon paprika
2 tablespoons lime or lemon juice

Fry almonds in butter until lightly browned. Remove. Add seasonings and crabmeat. Toss all together until heated. Add lime juice. Mix in almonds. Serve on toast points. Serves 6.

Crabmeat Dewey

1 pound cooked crabmeat
2 tablespoons butter
1½ cups cream sauce
½ teaspoon salt
⅛ teaspoon white pepper
¼ cup coffee cream
½ cup sliced cooked mushrooms
  or 1 4-ounce can, drained

Remove any shell particles and connective tissue from crabmeat. Heat the butter and sauté the crabmeat in it for about 5 minutes, tossing constantly. Combine the crabmeat with the hot cream sauce, season with salt and pepper and heat again. Stir in the coffee cream and mushrooms. Serves 6.

Spicy Crabmeat

1 pound cooked claw crabmeat
1 medium-size onion, chopped
1 green pepper, chopped
3 tablespoons butter, melted
½ teaspoon salt
½ teaspoon pepper
½ teaspoon crushed basil
¼ teaspoon paprika
1 tablespoon tarragon vinegar
¼ cup sherry

Remove any shell or tissue from crabmeat. Sauté onion and pepper in melted butter. Add crabmeat and toss until heated thoroughly. Add seasonings, except sherry. Stir and cook 2 minutes. Add sherry. Serves 6.

TIP: *Spicy Crabmeat* is delicious with sesame seed crackers.

Crab Paprika

2 cups cooked claw crabmeat
5 tablespoons melted butter or
  margarine
1 teaspoon paprika
½ teaspoon ground mustard
½ teaspoon pepper
⅛ teaspoon salt
2 tablespoons tarragon vinegar

Flake crabmeat lightly. Remove any shell particles. Melt butter. Add other ingredients, except crabmeat, and heat, stirring. Pour hot sauce over crabmeat. Serve with tomato and cucumber slices and top with slices of hard-cooked eggs. Serves 4.

Crabmeat Flambé I

2 cups cooked claw crabmeat
4 tablespoons melted butter
6 green onions, chopped
1 small green pepper, chopped
½ teaspoon salt
¼ teaspoon pepper
Pinch of tarragon
¼ cup sherry
¼ cup chopped parsely
⅓ cup cognac, warmed

Sauté the onions and pepper in the melted butter until tender. Add the crabmeat, seasonings, and sherry and toss until mixture is heated. Stir in the chopped parsley. Pour over the mixture the cognac, which has been heated. Ignite with a match and serve the crabmeat flaming. Spoon it over pecan pilaf—cooked rice with ¼ cup chopped pecans stirred in. Serves 6.

Chopped parsley
Paprika

Crabmeat Flambé II

1 pound cooked crabmeat
2 cans condensed cream of chicken
    soup
1 can light cream
½ teaspoon white pepper
¼ cup butter
¼ cup brandy
4 tablespoons cooking sherry
1 teaspoon ground mustard, dissolved
    in 1½ tablespoons wine vinegar
    and 1 tablespoon water

Look over crabmeat and remove any shell particles or tissue. Set aside. Mix soup and cream and heat thoroughly. Add white pepper.

In a large skillet heat the butter. Add crabmeat. Stir until heated. Heat brandy and sherry in a very small container. Ignite with a match and pour over the crabmeat. When flame dies, stir in the mustard mixture and the sauce. Simmer 3 minutes. Sprinkle top with chopped parsley and paprika. Serves 8.

SAUCEPAN CRABMEAT

In these recipes, the sauce is made first, then crabmeat added.

Crab-Orange De Luxe

1 pound de luxe crabmeat
1 can cream of mushroom soup
1 cup commercial sour cream
1 tablespoon grated onion
¼ teaspoon salt
¼ teaspoon grated nutmeg
5 tablespoons orange wine (optional)

Look over crabmeat for any shell particles. Set aside. In large saucepan heat soup, add sour cream, onion, salt and nutmeg. When thoroughly heated, add crabmeat, reduce heat and simmer 5 minutes.

Remove from heat and stir in 5 tablespoons orange wine (optional). Serve on a bed of chow mein noodles. Garnish with minced parsley and orange sections. Serves 6.

Crabmeat Rosy

2 cups cooked crabmeat
5 tablespoons butter
5 tablespoons flour
1 cup milk
1 cup light cream (evaporated milk
    can be used)
1 teaspoon salt
5 tablespoons tomato paste
½ teaspoon garlic juice
5 drops Tabasco sauce
⅛ teaspoon each of curry powder and
    ginger
1 tablespoon brandy (optional)

Look over crabmeat for any shell particles and connective tissue which should be removed. Set aside. In a saucepan melt butter, remove from heat, and add flour, mixing well. Return to heat and stir in milk gradually. Add cream. Cook and stir until sauce is thick. Add tomato paste and seasonings. Add crabmeat and heat again. Stir in brandy just before serving. Spoon mixture around a bed of cooked rice on a large platter. Garnish with parsley. Serves 6.

Crabmeat Rosy is good with asparagus, onion-ring salad and pocketbook rolls. For dessert serve lime sherbet.

Crabmeat Curry on Asparagus

1 cup cooked crabmeat
1 can cream of celery soup
1 tablespoon curry powder
½ tablespoon onion flakes
Salt and pepper to taste
2 hard-cooked eggs, chopped
1 10-ounce package frozen asparagus spears or 1 No. 2 can green asparagus

Heat soup. Add curry powder, onion flakes, salt and pepper. Stir until smooth. Add eggs and crabmeat. Heat again. Meanwhile, cook asparagus as directed on package. Drain well and arrange on platter. Pour curried crabmeat over asparagus. Serves 6.

Crab-Mushroom Sherry

2 cups cooked crabmeat
1 can (4 ounces) mushrooms, drained
2 tablespoons butter
1 cup sour cream
2 tablespoons grated onion
½ teaspoon grated nutmeg
½ teaspoon salt
¼ cup sherry or lemon juice

Remove any shell particles or connective tissue from crabmeat. Brown the mushrooms lightly in melted butter. Add sour cream, onion, nutmeg and salt. Stir in crabmeat. Heat thoroughly, remove from heat and stir in the sherry. Serve on Chinese noodles or cooked rice. Serves 6.

TIP: With *Crab-Mushroom Sherry*, serve green beans and apple-raisin salad; for dessert lime pie would be good.

Crab à la King

2 cups cooked crabmeat
1 cup celery, cut fine
2 hard-cooked eggs, chopped
1 tablespoon melted butter
1 pint cream
3 tablespoons sherry
Salt and white pepper to taste

Look over crabmeat and remove any shell particles or connective tissue. Simmer celery in a small amount of water until tender. Drain and add eggs, melted butter, cream. Heat thoroughly. If sauce seems too thin, combine 1 tablespoon cornstarch with 2 tablespoons water and stir this into sauce, cooking until thickened. Do not boil. Add crabmeat and sherry. Taste and add salt and pepper as needed. Serves 6.

Crab and Rice Supreme

2 cans (2 cups) cooked crabmeat
1 can condensed tomato soup, undiluted
1 tablespoon dehydrated onion flakes

1 cup cream
½ cup sherry
1 tablespoon lemon juice
1 teaspoon salt
⅛ teaspoon pepper
⅛ teaspoon mace
Dash of cayenne (or red) pepper
Dash of paprika
Cooked rice

Heat soup in a saucepan. Add onion, cream, sherry, and lemon juice. Add salt, pepper, mace, cayenne pepper and paprika. Carefully fold in crabmeat and heat over low heat, stirring occasionally. Serve over hot, cooked rice. Serves 6.

Crab-Chick Delight

2 cups cooked crabmeat
2 cups cooked chicken, cut into pieces
6 slices bacon
1 package frozen asparagus, broccoli or peas
2 cans condensed cream of chicken soup
¼ can water
¼ teaspoon garlic salt
⅛ teaspoon ground nutmeg
6 drops Tabasco sauce
1 cup commercial sour cream

Look over crabmeat and remove any shell particles or connective tissue. Place crabmeat in colander and pour over it 2 cups boiling water. Put crabmeat and cut-up chicken aside.

Cook the bacon crisply. Drain. Cook asparagus or other vegetable. Drain. Combine soup and water; add other ingredients, except sour cream. Heat, then stir in sour cream slowly. Add crabmeat and chicken meat. Mixing lightly, add bacon. Serve in large bowl, surrounded with cooked vegetable. Serves 6.

Easy Crabmeat Rarebit

2 cans prepared Welsh rarebit (9 ounces each)
1 3-ounce can broiled sliced mushrooms
1 cup claw (dark) cooked crabmeat
Salt and pepper to taste
2 tablespoons cooking wine, such as dry white vermouth
Chow mein noodles or toast

Heat Welsh rarebit over low heat. Add drained mushrooms and crabmeat (be sure to remove any shell particles before adding).

Stir in salt and pepper. Stir in cooking wine. Serve over chow mein noodles or toast. Garnish with a sprig of parsley. Serves 4.

Crab Confetti

2 cups dark cooked crabmeat
3 tablespoons butter or margarine
1 cup finely chopped pared apple
⅓ cup minced onion
2 tablespoons flour
2 teaspoons curry powder
2 cups milk
1 teaspoon salt
3 cups chow mein noodles

Heat butter in skillet. Add apple and onion and cook until tender. Stir in flour and curry powder. Stir in milk, slowly, and cook, stirring, until mixture thickens. Add salt and crabmeat. Heat thoroughly. Serve over crisp noodles. In fluted shells serve condiments such as chopped ripe tomatoes, flaked coconut, tangerine pickles or other combinations. Serves 6.

STONE CRABS

Stone crabs have huge claws and this species lives near the rocks on beaches and bays. In most states where they are found the law says only one of the giant claws from the male may be taken, and the open season is short. In some states it is unlawful to take the female stone crab.

Boil the claws about 20 minutes in salted water to cover. Serve with melted butter and a wedge of lime or lemon. Have nut crackers and picks handy for cracking and getting out the meat. Meat may be used in any recipe calling for cooked crabmeat.

Stone Crab in Shells

2 cups cooked stone crabmeat
1 onion, minced
1 clove garlic, minced
2 tablespoons butter
1 bay leaf
1 teaspoon thyme
1 tablespoon chopped parsley
Bread crumbs

Remove crabmeat from shells and cut or shred finely. Sauté onion and garlic in the melted butter until soft, but not brown. Add crabmeat, bay leaf, thyme and parsley. Cook and toss until heated thoroughly.

Remove from heat. Add just enough dry bread crumbs to hold mixture together. Stuff into crab shells or individual baking shells. Sprinkle top of crabmeat with buttered bread crumbs. Bake in hot oven, 450 F, just until brown—about 10 minutes. Serves 6.

Stone Crabs Creole

Boil stone-crab claws. Remove meat and serve with creole sauce.

CREOLE SAUCE

2 tablespoons butter
1 3-ounce can mushrooms, drained
  (save liquid)
2 green onions, chopped
1 small green pepper, chopped
2 tomatoes, peeled, seeded and
  chopped
1 pimento, chopped, or 2 tablespoons,
  canned
½ cup tomato sauce
½ cup cream
2 tablespoons flour

Melt butter in a skillet and sauté mushrooms, onions and green pepper until soft. Add other ingredients, including mushroom liquid, and cook until well blended, 10 to 15 minutes. Add cream with flour stirred in, for thickening. Makes about 1 cup of sauce.

Stone Crab Cakes

1 dozen stone crab claws
¼ pound butter or margarine
½ cup flour

1 cup milk
1 egg yolk
Salt, pepper, and cayenne pepper
Cracker crumbs
Cooking oil

Prepare stone-crab claws by boiling. Cool and remove the meat from the claws. Chop or shred finely.

In a saucepan melt butter. Stir in flour slowly. Have heat low. Add milk gradually, blending until mixture leaves sides of pan. Remove pan from heat and mix in the egg yolk. Add crabmeat and stir. Season to taste with salt, pepper and a dash of cayenne pepper or Tabasco.

Shape cakes by removing 1 tablespoon of the crab mixture at a time, using enough cracker crumbs to hold together. Let stand in the refrigerator an hour. Fry in hot (but not smoking) cooking oil. Drain and serve with lemon or lime wedges. Serves 6 to 8.

Outdoor Recipe for Stone Crab with Barbecue Sauce

Wash stone-crab claws and plunge into boiling, salted water for 10 to 15 minutes. Drain. Crack and when cool, remove meat from shell with the help of a pick. Place meat on a piece of heavy aluminum foil, spoon barbecue sauce over the top and put on outdoor grill until sauce bubbles.

BARBECUE SAUCE

1 cup chili sauce
2 tablespoons Worcestershire sauce
½ teaspoon salt
⅛ teaspoon pepper
2 teaspoon dry mustard
2 tablespoons lime juice
¼ cup water
2 tablespoons grated onion

Mix all ingredients well. Makes 1½ cups sauce.

LOBSTERS

The lobster is one of the largest of the crustaceans, which also include crabs and shrimp. Two varieties are found in the United States: the true lobster, taken from cool waters of the North Atlantic coast, and the spiny or rock lobster, found in Florida and southern California waters.

Both northern lobsters and spiny lobster tails are highly valued for their supply of proteins, vitamins and minerals. Both are frequently served boiled or broiled in the shell; however, the meat is used in main dishes, cocktails, salads, stews and sandwiches. The meat of either lobster is used also in recipes calling for crabmeat. The recipes are interchangeable, and lobster meat may be substituted for many shellfish ingredients in other dishes.

NORTHERN LOBSTER

The northern lobster is among the most highly valued of all shellfish. With modern handling, freezing and transportation methods, this "king of the shellfish" is available in many inland sections. Lobsters are taken along the Atlantic coast from Labrador to North Carolina, but the largest catches are along the Maine and Massachusetts coasts.

Lobsters can be caught throughout the year, but they are most plentiful in the summer when they come closer inshore. Some states have closed seasons for conservation purposes.

When taken from the water the lobster is a dark bluish-green color, but turns pink-red during cooking. The tail should curl under the body and not hang down when the live lobster is picked up. They are cooked while alive and kicking.

The northern lobster may weigh from ¾ pound to 2½ or 3 pounds. However, they have been known to weigh up to 20 pounds. Jumbos are 2½ pounds, usually; chickens ¾ to 1 pound; quarters, 1¼ pounds; large 1½ to 2¼ pounds. The most popular size is 1 pound.

Whole cooked lobsters, red in color, are sold in the markets, fresh and frozen. The tail of a cooked lobster should spring back quickly after it has been straightened out.

Cooked meat picked from the lobster is marketed fresh, frozen and canned. Frozen lobster meat can be purchased in 6-, 14- and 16-ounce cans. The 14-ounce can is the most popular size.

SPINY LOBSTER

The spiny lobster got its name because of the numerous spines on the body and legs. It lacks the large claws of the northern lobster; the meat comes entirely from the large wide tail. The spiny lobster is sometimes called a crawfish. It is most plentiful during the summer months.

Live spiny lobsters are available in some parts of Florida and California. They should be alive at time of cooking, as the northern lobster should. The shells turn pink when cooked; the meat is snowy white with tinges of red. Whole cooked lobsters may be purchased, although the cooked meat is more often canned for the market. Also some cooked frozen meat is marketed in 6-ounce cans; it must be kept under refrigeration.

Frozen spiny-lobster tails are popular and available throughout the United States. The frozen tails of several species are sold on the market. They weigh from 4 ounces to more than a pound each. They differ in the smoothness or roughness of the shell and the absence or presence of spots. Since the color of the frozen tails varies widely, it cannot be relied on. Spiny lobsters from Florida, the Bahamas and Cuban waters have a smooth shell and large creamy or white spots on the first segment of the tail, which generally has a brown-green color. The tails from western Australia are medium smooth with small white dots on most of the tail segments, which are red-brown in color. Spiny-lobster tails from southern California and the west coast of Mex-

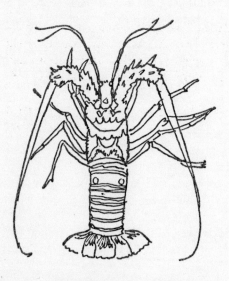

Spiny lobster or rock lobster

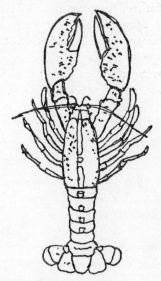

Northern lobster

Florida or Cuman spiny lobster tail

Western Australian spiny lobster tail

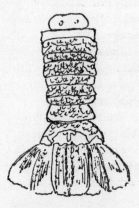

South African spiny lobster tail

ico have smooth shells without any spots or stripes, and the color varies from dark red to orange and brown.

Spiny-lobster tails from South Africa, New Zealand and eastern Australia have rough shells and no spots, and are brownish red in color. A more recent species on the American market is a lobster from the Mediterranean and southwestern part of Europe. It has a rough shell, reddish tan in color, with a number of white streaks and spots.

When using spiny-lobster tails for recipes calling for cooked lobster meat remember that 1½ pounds frozen spiny lobster tails yield approximately ¾ pound cooked lobster meat.

HOW TO EAT A NORTHERN LOBSTER

Many people do not enjoy the delicacy of lobster in the shell because of their hesitancy to tackle what they think is a complicated job of cracking the shell and removing the meat. Once they try it, this mistaken idea is corrected and their bashfulness is overcome. Lobster is so delicious everyone should eat it often, either at home or in restaurants. Here are a few tips if you are a novice:

Use a lobster or nutcracker to break the shell of the big claws. Chunks of delicious white meat are inside.

Use a small lobster or cocktail fork to remove the meat from the claw and tail.

With knife and fork, cut the lobster meat and dip each morsel as you eat it into melted butter.

Pull off each small claw and suck out the sweet nutty piece of meat. Lastly, use the small fork to get out small pieces of meat under the shell. Don't stop eating until every single morsel is found and enjoyed.

Boiled Northern Lobsters

*

These are delicious served hot or cold.

Plain Boiled Lobsters

2 live lobsters, 1 pound each
3 quarts boiling water
3 tablespoons salt
Melted butter

Plunge lobsters head first into boiling water with the salt added. Cover and return to boiling point. Simmer for 20 minutes. Drain. Place lobster on its back. With a sharp knife cut in half lengthwise. Remove the stomach, which is located just back of the head. Remove the intestinal vein running from stomach to tail. Cool lobster and serve broiled or remove the meat for other recipes. Do not discard the green liver and coral roe. They are delicacies.

Two live lobsters, 1 pound each, yield about ½ pound cooked meat.

Hot Spicy Lobsters

Add ½ cup packaged pickling spices to the salted water. Or mix together

1 cup vinegar
2 carrots, sliced
1 onion, sliced
2 stalks celery
1 lemon or lime, sliced

Add this mixture to the water with salt and pickling spices. Let vinegar-spice mixture boil for 30 minutes. Plunge in the lobsters. Cover and return to boiling. Simmer for 15 to 20 minutes. Drain and proceed as above.

Boiled Spiny Lobster Tails

6 spiny-lobster tails (5 to 8 ounces
each) or 1 per person
2 quarts boiling water
⅓ cup salt
Melted butter

Bring salted water to a boil. Place lobster tails in the water. Cover and return to boiling point. Simmer for 10 to 15 minutes, according to the size. Drain. Cut in half lengthwise. Serve with melted butter. Serves 6.

Cold Lobster

*

Lobster Cocktail

½ pound cooked lobster meat
Lettuce
Cocktail sauce

Cut lobster meat in pieces. Chill. Arrange lettuce in 6 cocktail glasses. Place lobster meat on top and cover with cocktail sauce.

COCKTAIL SAUCE FOR LOBSTER

⅓ cup mayonnaise
¼ teaspoon salt
¼ teaspoon paprika
2 teaspoons lemon juice

Combine all ingredients and chill. Serves 6.

Lobster Greco

2 cooked lobsters or 2 cups cooked
    lobster meat
⅓ cup Spanish olive oil
3 tablespoons tarragon vinegar
2 tablespoons lime juice
1 tablespoon chopped parsley
½ cup minced onion
1 teaspoon ground mustard
1 teaspoon salt
¼ teaspoon pepper

Cut the lobster meat into cubes. Place in a shallow bowl. Mix the other ingredients thoroughly, pour over the lobster and chill. Serves 6. Serve with buttered asparagus, little whole carrots, hot rolls and cherry tarts.

Broiled Lobster

*

Plain Broiled Lobster

The dealer will peg the claws if requested, to prevent the lobster from pinching the person handling it.

Place the live lobster with pegged claws on its back on a cutting board, and kill it by inserting a sharp knife between the body and tail segments: this cuts the spinal cord.

Cross the large claws. Using heavy scissors or knife, make a deep cut lengthwise through underside of the body, starting at the head, ending at end of the tail. Be careful not to cut the stomach or "lady" (a hard sack near the head at the back). Pull the two halves apart without breaking. Remove the "lady" and the intestinal vein, which runs through the middle of the underside of the body and tail. Remove and discard the stomach and intestinal vein. The spongy substance on either side of the body is harmless and need not be removed. The red coral and the greenish liver or tomaly are also edible and left in the lobster.

Broiled Lobster

2 live lobsters, about 1 pound each
1½ tablespoons butter or margarine,
  melted
Salt
White pepper
Dash paprika
¼ cup butter or margarine, melted
1 tablespoon lemon or lime juice

Prepare lobster as outlined above.
Place lobster, shell side down, on a
broiler pan. Open as flat as possible.
Brush the exposed meat with butter.
Sprinkle with salt, pepper and paprika. Broil 4 to 5 inches from source
of heat for 12 to 15 minutes or until
lightly browned. Combine butter and
lemon juice; serve with the lobsters.
Serves 2.

To remove the meat after broiling
use scissors or sharp knife, cutting
loose from the shell on the ends and
edges. The meat can be pulled out
then in one piece.

Quick Broiled Lobster
with Olive Stuffing

2 medium lobsters
Salt, pepper
1 cup crumbled Saltine crackers
¼ cup chopped ripe olives
½ cup melted butter
¼ teaspoon paprika

Have the lobsters split. Thaw if frozen. Crack the claws. Place in greased
broiler pan. Sprinkle lightly with salt
and pepper. In a small bowl mix the
crumbled crackers, ripe olives, melted
butter and paprika. Spoon this mixture over lobster meat and tail. Spoon
some melted butter over claws. Broil
about 4 inches from source of heat

for 12 to 15 minutes or until lightly
browned. Serves 2 to 4.

TIP: Serve extra melted butter with
lemon juice added if you wish. Good
with this dish are corn on the cob,
lettuce and tomato salad and lemon
pie.

Broiled Lobster Amandine

4 boiled lobster tails, split
3 cups soft bread crumbs
1 cup chopped, blanched almonds
½ cup butter
1 clove garlic, peeled and crushed
6 drops Tabasco sauce
1 teaspoon dried tarragon
½ teaspoon salt
⅛ teaspoon pepper

Place split boiled lobsters in greased
broiling pan, split side up, and brush
with melted butter. Broil about 10
minutes. Sauté crumbs and almonds
in butter until light brown, stirring
often. Add other ingredients and mix
well. Remove lobsters from broiler.
Spoon stuffing over tail and body cavity, if whole lobsters are used. Return
to broiler just long enough to brown.
Serves 4 to 6.

Lobster Meat Broil
with Curry

1 pound cooked lobster meat
¼ cup lemon juice
4 tablespoons olive oil
½ teaspoon garlic salt
1 teaspoon curry powder
½ teaspoon salt

Combine lemon juice, olive oil, garlic
salt, curry powder and salt. Pour over

lobster meat and let marinate for several hours. Place lobster with marinade in bottom of broiler pan. Broil about 3 inches from source of heat for 3 to 4 minutes. Turn and broil the other side. Baste several times with the marinade. Serves 6.

TIP: Serve chinese noodles, asparagus tips, yellow rice and fresh citrus sections with this dish.

Barbecued Lobster

2 cups cooked lobster meat
¼ cup salad oil
⅓ cup green onions, chopped
1 cup chili sauce
⅓ cup lime juice
2 tablespoons brown sugar
2 teaspoons prepared mustard
2 tablespoons Worcestershire sauce
½ teaspoon salt

Cut lobster into bite-size pieces. Set aside. In saucepan heat salad oil, add minced onions and sauté until tender but not brown. Add other ingredients, except lobster, and simmer covered, 10 minutes.

While the sauce is cooking, line broiler pan with foil and spoon lobster meat onto it. Pour sauce over lobster and place in oven broiler about 3 inches from heat. Broil 5 minutes. Serves 6.

French Fried Spiny Lobster Tails

6 spiny-lobster tails (5 to 8 ounces each)
2 eggs, beaten
6 tablespoons milk
1½ teaspoons salt
¼ teaspoon pepper
½ cup flour
½ cup dry bread crumbs or cracker meal

Thaw lobster tails. Cut in half lengthwise. Remove meat in one piece from each half. Mix together the eggs, milk, and seasonings. Combine flour and crumbs. Dip lobster meat in egg mixture, then roll in flour mixture. Have fat hot in deep fat fryer (350 F). Place breaded lobster meat in fry basket and fry for 4 to 5 minutes, or until golden brown. Serve with lime or lemon wedges and garnish with parsley. Serves 6.

TIP: Fry in 1 inch of fat heated in heavy frying pan on top of stove if desired.

Oven Lobster

Roasted Lobster Aflame

2 live lobsters, split lengthwise, cleaned and claws cracked
Salt and pepper

4 tablespoons melted butter
⅛ teaspoon each of dry mustard, thyme and basil
2 cups soft bread crumbs
2 tablespoons grated onion

Prepare lobsters as for *Plain Broiled Lobster* and crack claws. Place lobsters meat side up in greased broiler pan. Combine all other ingredients and spoon stuffing in cavity and tail of lobsters. Roast in hot oven at 400 F for 20 minutes, basting with additional butter if needed. Serve with pan juices poured over lobsters.

At table pour over lobsters 3 ounces of warmed cognac and light it with a match. Baste again with ¾ cup melted butter and 3 tablespoons lime or lemon juice. Serves 2 to 4.

TIP: Serve with this dish avocado and grapefruit salad with Roquefort dressing, fresh spring green peas and mocha ice-cream pie.

ROQUEFORT SALAD DRESSING

Soften ½ pound Roquefort (blue) cheese at room temperature. Mash and cream until smooth. Add cheese to 1½ cups French dressing and mix. Add ½ teaspoon sugar. Mix all together thoroughly. Makes about 2 cups dressing.

Lobster Hors d'Oeuvres

½ pound cooked lobster meat
3 tablespoons butter or margarine
2 tablespoons grated American cheese
1 large egg yolk, beaten
1 teaspoon lime juice
6 drops Tabasco sauce

Grind lobster meat. Cream the butter and cheese until smooth. Add egg yolk, lime juice, Tabasco and lobster meat. Form into balls by pressing into a teaspoon. Place balls on a well-greased cooky sheet. Bake in a hot oven, 400 F, for 5 minutes. Makes about 45 hors d'oeuvres.

Baked Stuffed Lobster Tails

6 frozen spiny-lobster tails (5 to 8 ounces each)
4 tablespoons butter or other fat
2 cups soft bread crumbs
2 tablespoons grated onion
1 tablespoon dry savory
¼ teaspoon garlic salt

If not precooked place lobster tails in boiling salted water. Cover and return to the boiling point. Simmer the tails for 10 minutes; a little longer if tails are large. Drain.

Cut tails in half lengthwise. Mix the other ingredients and heat in a skillet. Remove and spoon the stuffing over tail meat. Place in a shallow baking pan. Bake until browned, about 10 to 15 minutes in a hot oven, 400 F. Serves 6.

Lobster Loaf

2 cups cooked lobster meat, cut in ¼ inch pieces
Salt and pepper to taste
1 cup bread crumbs
1 tablespoon minced onion
½ green pepper, minced
2 eggs, beaten
½ cup milk

Mix lobster meat, seasonings, crumbs, onion, green pepper and beaten eggs. Add milk. Pour into greased loaf pan or dish. Bake until firm, about 30 minutes, in a pan of hot water in a slow oven, 325 F. Serves 6.

Baked Lobster-Asparagus

2 packages frozen asparagus spears or
  2 pounds fresh asparagus
2 cups cooked lobster meat, cut into
  pieces
2 cans condensed cream of mushroom
  soup
1 cup mayonnaise
1 teaspoon lime juice
½ teaspoon curry powder
½ cup cheddar cheese, shredded
1 tablespoon butter or margarine
1 cup soft bread crumbs

Cook asparagus in salted, boiling water. Drain. Transfer to an oblong baking dish or pan. Arrange lobster meat on top of asparagus. Blend soup, mayonnaise, lime juice, and curry powder. Spoon sauce over lobster and sprinkle with cheese. Mix melted butter with the bread crumbs and cover asparagus-lobster mixture with this. Bake in a moderate oven, 350 F, 20 to 25 minutes, or until mixture is thoroughly heated and the crumbs are brown. Serves 6 to 8.

Lobster Creole

½ pound cooked lobster meat, in
  pieces
3 strips bacon
2 onions, chopped
1 cup sliced okra, fresh or frozen
1 cup tomato sauce
1 cup cooked rice
½ teaspoon salt
⅛ teaspoon pepper
Buttered bread crumbs

Fry bacon until crisp. Remove bacon and sauté the onions and okra in the bacon fat. Add tomato sauce, rice, lobster meat, salt and pepper. Spoon into greased 1½-quart casserole. Cover with buttered bread crumbs. Bake in a moderate oven, 350 F, for 15 to 20 minutes, or until brown. Serves 6.

Saucepan Lobster

✳

Company Lobster Barbecue

4 cups cooked lobster meat
3 tablespoons butter
3 tablespoons salad oil
1 large onion, sliced
2 cups chopped celery
½ cup brown sugar
1½ tablespoons salt
1 tablespoon dry mustard
2 teaspoons chili powder
4 cups tomato juice
1 can tomato paste
1½ cups water
½ cup tarragon or plain vinegar

Heat butter and salad oil. Sauté the onion and celery until soft. Add the next 4 ingredients. Mix in tomato juice, paste, water and vinegar. Simmer the mixture 30 minutes. Pour it over the lobster meat. Simmer 10 minutes longer. Serves 12.

TIP: Cut the recipe for a smaller family: half of it for 6; one-quarter for 3.

Lobster Thermidor

2 cups cooked lobster meat
3 tablespoons butter
½ cup sliced mushrooms, fresh or
    canned
½ cup sherry
¼ teaspoon salt
¼ teaspoon paprika
2 tablespoons flour
2 egg yolks
2 cups light cream
½ cup grated Cheddar cheese

If you have lobster shells, clean and dry them; or use 6 cooking shells or custard cups.

Melt butter and cook the mushrooms until tender. (Drain canned mushrooms first.) Add lobster meat and stir until heated. Add sherry, salt and paprika. Cook 2 minutes. Sprinkle with flour, stirring thoroughly. Beat egg yolks with cream and add to the hot liquid, a little at a time. Cook and stir until smooth and thickened. Spoon mixture into shells. Sprinkle with grated Cheddar cheese. Brown under broiler. Serves 6.

TIP: For a casserole, omit the cheese and top the dish instead with 1 cup dry bread crumbs mixed with 3 tablespoons butter. Bake (instead of broil) in a hot oven 425 F, for 10 minutes or until brown.

Lobster with Shrimp Newburg Sauce

2 cups cooked lobster meat

SAUCE

1 pound small shrimp
¼ cup butter
¼ cup plain flour
1 teaspoon salt
¼ teaspoon pepper
2 cups milk
2 egg yolks
2 tablespoons sherry
Paprika

Cook shrimp. Shell and devein. If large, cut into pieces. Set aside.

Melt butter and blend in the flour, stirring to mix well. Add salt and pepper. Remove pan from heat and stir in the milk. Cook the sauce, stirring constantly, until it is thickened. Beat the egg yolks. Stir a little of the hot sauce into the eggs, then stir all of it into the sauce. Add the shrimp and lobster meat. Heat quickly. Add sherry and sprinkle with paprika.

Serve with fluffy rice. Serves 6.

TIP: This Newburg is easily frozen. Double the recipe and freeze in aluminum containers, wrapped in freezer paper. When ready to serve remove top wrapping and thaw in the oven.

Lobster Fu Yung

1 cup cooked lobster meat
1 cup bean sprouts, drained
¾ cup celery, chopped
½ cup onion, chopped
3 tablespoons olive oil
5 eggs
1 tablespoon cornstarch
1 tablespoon soy sauce
1 teaspoon salt
¼ teaspoon cayenne pepper

Mix lobster meat and sprouts in large bowl. Cook celery and onion in the olive oil until soft, about 4 minutes; then add lobster and sprouts. Beat eggs, add cornstarch and soy sauce, salt and cayenne pepper. Mix with celery mixture, off the heat. Put mixture by tablespoonfuls on greased hot griddle and brown. Turn to brown other side. Keep on hot platter until all are cooked. Pour the following sauce over top. Serves 4.

SAUCE FOR LOBSTER FU YUNG

Mix 2 teaspoons cornstarch with ½ cup water until smooth. Add 2 teaspoons sherry and 1 tablespoon soy sauce. Cook until thick, stirring constantly.

TIP: Substitute crabmeat or tiny cooked or canned shrimp for *Shrimp* or *Crab Fu Yung*.

Lobster Chow Mein

2 cups cooked lobster meat (approximately 1 large lobster tail)
2 tablespoons butter
½ cup chopped onion
1 can condensed mushroom soup
1 cup sour cream
¼ cup catsup
1 3-ounce can broiled sliced mushrooms

Cut lobster meat into pieces. Melt butter and sauté onion. Combine soup, sour cream and catsup. Add sautéed onions. Stir until heated. Add mushrooms and lobster meat. Heat thoroughly again. Serve over cooked rice or chow mein noodles. Serves 4.

Herbed Lobster

2 cups cooked lobster meat
2 tablespoons butter or other fat
1 cup finely chopped onion
½ cup condensed cream of tomato soup
½ teaspoon garlic salt
¼ cup chopped parsley
1 teaspoon dried thyme leaves, crumbled
1 bay leaf, crumbled

Have the lobster meat cut into chunks. Melt butter in a large skillet. Sauté onion about 5 minutes, or until soft. Remove from heat. Stir in the remaining ingredients, except lobster. Bring sauce to a boil, reduce heat, cover pan and simmer 15 minutes. Stir in the lobster meat and simmer 5 minutes longer. Serve with rice or mashed potatoes. Serves 6.

OYSTERS

Oysters are among the oldest of foods; in early days the Greeks and Romans served oysters at their festivals and banquets. Early settlers in America enjoyed oysters and they are still served and classed as delicacies in this country. Indians, before the pioneers from Europe came to these shores, were eating oysters in large quantities, as evidenced by their huge shell mounds.

While oysters are marketed in every coastal state in the United States, the best-known varieties are Blue Points and Rockaways from Long Island, Cotuits from Massachusetts, and Lynnhavens from Virginia. Pacific coast oysters from Puget Sound are highly prized. The oyster found in Florida's coastal waters is the same as the commercial species of the Eastern seaboard and Gulf of Mexico. Oysters from Apalachicola, Florida have been known and used by consumers for centuries. Most of these are canned for distribution to the consumer market all over the United States.

The idea that oysters can be eaten only in months with an "R"—that is from September through April—is no longer accepted. The spawning period was thought to be from May 1st to September 1st. In actuality, this season differs in different localities, and with different varieties. Oysters are edible and available from some source all year and may be eaten without hesitation.

Prices may be higher in the summer due to scarcity, and some states prohibit their shipment and sale during certain months, but frozen oysters are now available year round.

Oysters are high in nutrition, yet low in calories. They contain more protein than milk, and are rich in copper, iron and iodine. Also they supply essential calcium. Oysters are a good source of vitamins A, B and C. They can be eaten raw or cooked. They are good roasted, steamed, fried, in stews, casserole dishes and in the creole style.

PURCHASING OYSTERS

Oysters are marketed live in the shell, or shucked in fresh or frozen form, and in cans. They can also be found in frozen form prebreaded and ready to cook. Also frozen stews and soups.

SHELL OYSTERS

Oysters in the shell are sold by the dozen. They must be alive when purchased and when alive the shells are tightly closed. Gaping shells that do not close upon handling mean that the oysters are dead and no longer usable. If shell oysters are stored in the refrigerator at about 40 F, they will remain good for quite some time.

SHUCKED OYSTERS

These are oysters removed from the shell and sold by the pint or quart. They should be plump and have a natural cream-gray color, with clear liquor, free of shell particles. Fresh shucked oysters are packed in metal containers or waxed containers which should be refrigerated or iced. They remain fresh for a week or 10 days when properly handled.

The Eastern oysters are generally packed in the following commercial grades:*

GRADE	OYSTERS PER GALLON
Counts or extra large	Not more than 160
Extra selects or large	Not more than 161 to 210
Selects or medium	Not more than 211 to 300
Standards or small	Not more than 301 to 500
Standards or very small	Over 500

Shucked oysters are sold according to size from extra large to small, making it difficult to state the number in each container.

* From *How to Cook Oysters* by Home Economists, Branch of Commercial Fisheries, U.S. Department of the Interior.

QUANTITY TO PURCHASE

The quantity of oysters needed depends somewhat on how they are to be served. Served raw, allow 3 dozen shell oysters for 6 people or 1 quart of shucked oysters or two No. 1 cans. A pint, raw, serves 4 people. A pint stretched with other ingredients serves 6.

Cold Oysters

✳

SHUCKING OYSTERS

Wash and rinse oysters thoroughly in cold water. Open or shuck. Place oyster on a table, flat shell up, and hold it with the left hand. With the right hand force a heavy oyster knife between the shells at or near the thin end. To make it easier to insert the knife, the thin end or "bill" may first be broken off with a hammer. Now cut the large abductor muscle close to the flat upper shell to which it is attached and remove the shell. Cut the lower end of the same muscle, which is attached to the deep half of the shell. Leave the oyster loose in the shell, if it is to be served on the half shell, or drop it into a container.

After shucking, examine the oysters for bits of shell, paying particular attention to the muscle, to which pieces of shell sometimes adhere.

Raw Oysters on the Half Shell

36 shell oysters
Cocktail sauce

Shuck oysters, leaving them in the deep shells. Arrange beds of crushed ice in 6 shallow bowls. Place 6 half-shell oysters on the ice with a small container of cocktail sauce in the center. Garnish with lemon or lime wedges. Serves 6.

TIP: Prepared cocktail sauces are available or make your own from some of those suggested in this book.

Oyster-Grapefruit Cocktail

½ pint oysters, chilled
1 grapefruit (or 1 No. 2 can grape-
  fruit sections)
Lettuce

Place a small piece of green lettuce leaf in each of cocktail glasses. Chop a little of the head on top. Arrange 3 oysters and 4 sections of grapefruit around lettuce. Serves 4. Spoon on top this zippy sauce, chilled:

COCKTAIL SAUCE FOR OYSTERS I

¾ cup chili sauce
3 tablespoons lemon juice
1½ tablespoons Worcestershire sauce
¾ teaspoon salt
Combine all well. Serves 4.

Oysters Tasty

1 quart large oysters, chilled and
drained

Serve 4 to 6 oysters per person. Place in cocktail glass and spoon in this delicious sauce:

COCKTAIL SAUCE FOR OYSTERS II

½ cup tomato sauce
1 teaspoon soy sauce
¼ teaspoon salt
⅛ teaspoon pepper
1½ tablespoons mayonnaise
2 teaspoons lemon juice
Blend all ingredients and chill.

Old South Pickled Oysters

1 quart oysters
1 cup white vinegar
12 whole allspice
12 whole cloves
1 teaspoon salt
¼ teaspoon pepper
⅛ teaspoon cayenne

Pour oysters into a saucepan. Warm, then drain thoroughly. Mix vinegar and seasonings. Pour over the oysters. Heat until oysters curl around the edges. Remove from heat and set aside to cool. Chill oysters. Serve on lettuce with mayonnaise, as an appetizer. Serves 6.

TIP: Good with this dish are fried fish sticks, broiled shrimp, tiny hot rolls, crisp raw vegetable platter and a citrus dessert. Serve buffet style.

Oyster Salad in Puff Shells

1 quart oysters
1 cup chopped celery
2 tablespoons lemon juice
2 teaspoons grated onion
½ teasoon salt
Dash hot pepper sauce
Mayonnaise

Boil oysters in their own liquid until edges curl. Drain them and chop. When cool, mix with chopped celery, lemon juice, grated onion, salt, dash hot pepper sauce and enough mayonnaise to hold mixture together. Makes 2½ cups salad.

Cut tops from puff shells. Fill each shell with 3 teaspoons salad.

PUFF SHELLS

½ cup flour
⅛ teaspoon salt
¼ cup butter
½ cup boiling water
2 eggs

Sift flour and measure. Add salt and sift second time. Boil water and add butter. When butter is melted add flour all at once and stir hard until mixture forms a ball away from sides of pan. Remove from heat. Add the unbeaten eggs, one at a time, beating after each addition. Beat until dough is stiff. Drop by teaspoonfuls on a greased cooky sheet. Bake shells in hot oven, 450 F, 10 minutes. Reduce heat to 350 F and continue baking 10 minutes longer. Makes 60 small shells.

Broiled Oysters

*

Broiled Oysters on the Half Shell

24 shell oysters
¼ cup lemon juice
½ teaspoon salt
⅛ teaspoon pepper
½ cup bread crumbs
2 tablespoons butter
Paprika

Shuck and drain oysters. Pour lemon juice over oysters and let stand 15 minutes. Drain off before using. Place oysters on deep half of shells. Season with salt and pepper. Sprinkle buttered crumbs on top. Dust with paprika. Broil about 3 inches from heat for 5 minutes. Serves 4.

Oysters Wrapped in Bacon

1 pint oysters
12 slices bacon, cut in half
½ teaspoon salt
⅛ teaspoon pepper
⅛ teaspoon paprika

Drain oysters. Place an oyster on each half slice of bacon. Sprinkle with seasonings. Roll bacon around oyster and fasten with a toothpick. Place oysters on preheated broiler pan about 3 inches from heat and broil 3 minutes; turn and broil other side 2 minutes, or until bacon is crisp. Remove toothpicks and serve plain or on toast. Serves 6.

Oysters Remick

1 pint oysters
1 cup mayonnaise or salad dressing
¼ cup chili sauce
1 teaspoon prepared mustard
¼ teaspoon salt
¼ teaspoon paprika
3 drops Tabasco sauce
Dash pepper
1 teaspoon lemon juice
2 tablespoons butter or other fat, melted
½ cup dry bread crumbs

Drain oysters and arrange on a shallow well-greased baking dish. Mix salad dressing, chili sauce, mustard, salt, paprika, Tabasco, pepper and lemon juice. Spoon over oysters. Mix melted butter with bread crumbs. Spread over top and broil about 3 inches from source of heat for 5 minutes, or until edges of oysters begin to curl. Serves 4.

TIP: Oysters may be cooked in their own liquid for 3 minutes (or until edges curl) before placing in baking dish. Drain most of liquid off and cut broiling time to 2 minutes.

Oyster Casserole Quickie

1 pint oysters
½ cup butter or margarine
¼ cup cream or evaporated milk
2 cups cracker crumbs

¼ cup sherry
1 teaspoon salt
⅛ teaspoon white pepper
6 drops Tabasco sauce
½ cup additional cracker crumbs,
    mixed with
¼ cup butter or margarine for top-
    ping

Drain oysters thoroughly. Melt butter in skillet, add oysters and cook until they curl around edges. Add cream, 2 cups crumbs, sherry, salt, pepper, and Tabasco sauce. Cover with the topping of additional crumbs and butter. Put broiler rack at lowest point from direct heat and broil oysters in skillet 3 minutes, or until lightly browned. Watch carefully to prevent burning. Serves 6.

Fried Oysters

*

Basic Fried Oysters

1 quart large oysters
2 eggs, beaten
2 tablespoons lemon juice
1 teaspoon salt
¼ teasoon pepper
½ cup flour
1 cup bread crumbs

Drain oysters. Beat eggs, add lemon juice, salt and pepper. Dip oysters first in flour, then in beaten egg mixture, and roll in crumbs.

Fry in hot fat heated to 375 F, a few at a time, about 2 minutes or until brown, or in a heavy skillet in 2 inches of fat. Be sure to drain on absorbent paper. Keep warm and serve with lemon quarters. Serves 6.

TIP: Dipping first in flour prevents the breading and oyster separating.

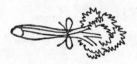

Simple Batter-Fried Oysters

1 pint large oysters
1 egg, beaten
3 tablespoons flour
1 teaspoon salt
Dash pepper
½ cup salad oil

Drain oysters. Combine egg, flour, salt and pepper. Add oysters and coat by stirring. Heat oil in large skillet and fry oysters, turning to brown on all sides. Serves 4. Serve with *Tartare-Dill Sauce:*

TARTARE-DILL SAUCE

½ cup mayonnaise
1 teaspoon grated onion
2 teaspoons diced dill pickle
1 teaspoon lemon juice

Combine all ingredients and chill.

Cracker Meal Fried Oysters

1 pint oysters
1 egg
2 tablespoons lemon juice
2 cups cracker meal
½ teaspoon salt
⅛ teaspoon pepper

Drain oysters. Beat egg and add lemon juice. Mix salt and pepper with 1 cup cracker meal. Spread another cup of cracker meal in another plate. Roll each oyster in seasoned cracker meal first. Then dip in egg mixture and lastly in plain cracker meal. Place breaded oysters singly on a tray and allow to stand in refrigerator for ½ to 1 hour or longer.

Line (one layer only) deep fat fry basket with oysters and lower into hot salad or peanut oil, 400 F, and fry until golden brown. Drain and serve to 4.

Quick Oysters on Toast

1 pint large oysters
4 tablespoons butter or margarine, melted
2 tablespoons lemon or lime juice
½ teaspoon salt
Dash pepper
¼ teaspoon Worcestershire sauce

Simmer oysters in their liquor for about 5 minutes or until edges begin to curl. Drain. Add melted butter and seasonings. Bring to boil, then add Worcestershire sauce. Serve on toast halves to 4. Good with this dish are baked potatoes, bacon-seasoned green beans, lettuce and tomato salad, and mixed fruits for dessert.

Fried Oysters in a Boat

1 loaf Italian, French or homestyle unsliced bread
3 dozen oysters
2 tablespoons lemon juice
2 eggs, beaten
½ teaspoon salt
½ teaspoon pepper
Cracker meal
Half salad oil and half butter

Cut a top layer off the bread. Hollow out inside. Heat 3 pieces of bread in a slow oven to crisp but not brown. Roll these fine crumbs to coat oysters. Mix lemon juice with the beaten eggs. Add salt and pepper. Roll drained oysters in crumbs and set aside until deep fat is hot, but not smoking.

Dip breaded oysters into egg mixture, then again in crumbs. Fry a few at a time until golden brown. Drain and pile into bread shell. Serve on a platter with sliced tomatoes and lemon wedges in nests of parsley. Stick stuffed olives with toothpicks and put around edges of "boat." Carrot curls and celery tops add to the decoration, if desired. Serves 6.

Crab-Fried Oysters

2 dozen medium-sized oysters, drained
1 pint (2 cups) flaked crabmeat
1 cup fine bread crumbs
¼ teaspoon salt
Dash Tabasco sauce
⅛ teaspoon nutmeg
1 egg, beaten
1 tablespoon milk
½ cup fat or salad oil

Set oysters aside while preparing crabmeat mixture by mixing the crabmeat with bread crumbs, salt, Tabasco sauce and nutmeg. In another bowl combine egg and milk. Dip oysters in this mixture, then in crab mixture.

Heat fat or salad oil in a large skillet and fry oysters about 2–3 minutes, turning to brown other side. Serve with lemon or lime wedges. Serves 4.

Baked Oysters

*

Oyster Pan Roast

1 pint oysters
2 tablespoons butter
½ teaspoon salt
⅛ teaspoon pepper
Toast

Drain oysters and place in shallow baking dish. Melt butter, add salt and pepper. Pour over oysters. Bake in oven at 400 F for 12 minutes, or until edges curl. Serve on plain or buttered toast. Serves 4.

Zippy Oysters

1 pint large oysters
½ cup minced green pepper
6 slices bacon, cooked and crumbled
1 tablespoon lemon juice
¼ teaspoon mixed black pepper and paprika
Dash cayenne or Tabasco sauce

Drain oysters. Pour into a shallow baking dish or pie plate. Sprinkle with minced green pepper, crumbled bacon, lemon juice and seasonings. Bake in hot oven, 450 F, 10 minutes, or until the oysters curl around the edges. Serves 4.

Oysters Rockefeller

This dish is said to have been invented by one Jules Alciatore, who called it by this name because, he said, "I know of no other rich enough to describe it." There are many versions of it.

36 shell oysters
2 cups spinach, cooked
4 tablespoons minced onion
1 tablespoon minced parsley
½ teaspoon celery salt
½ teaspoon salt
⅛ teaspoon pepper
6 drops Tabasco sauce
2 tablespoons lime juice
½ cup bread crumbs
6 tablespoons butter

Shuck and drain oysters. Place on deep half of shells. Add other ingredients to the spinach. Cook in a small saucepan for about 5 minutes. Add bread crumbs and mix well. Spread mixture over oysters, dot with butter and bake in hot oven, 400 F, for 10 minutes. Garnish with lemon or lime wedges. Serves 6.

Devilish Oysters

36 shell oysters or 1½ pints select
  oysters
2 tablespoons butter
3 tablespoons onion, minced
4 tablespoons flour
1½ cups milk (half evaporated
  milk-half water may be substituted)
1 teaspoon salt
¼ teaspoon nutmeg
⅛ teaspoon cayenne
1 teaspoon prepared mustard
1 tablespoon soy sauce
1 teaspoon parsley, chopped
  (optional)
1 egg, beaten
½ cup bread crumbs
2 tablespoons butter, melted

Shuck and chop oysters. In the butter
cook the onion until it is tender. Blend
in flour, add milk and cook until thick,
stirring constantly. Add seasonings,
beaten egg and chopped oysters. Heat.
Fill deep halves of oyster shells with
this creamed mixture. Cover with buttered crumbs. Bake in a hot oven,
400 F, for 10 minutes, or until brown.
Serves 6.

TIP: 1½ pints select oysters may be
used when shell oysters are not available.

Meme's Oyster Pie

1 quart oysters
2 slices bacon, fried crisply and diced
1 small onion, minced
1 tablespoon minced parsley
1 tablespoon chopped green pepper
½ teaspoon salt
¼ teaspoon black pepper
½ teaspoon paprika

Dash cayenne pepper
Juice of 1 lemon
Butter
Biscuit dough

Sauté onion in bacon fat until soft.
In a shallow greased baking dish arrange half the oysters. Over them
sprinkle half the sautéed onion and
diced bacon together with a mixture
of half of the rest of the ingredients
except butter and biscuit dough. Repeat layer with remaining oysters and
seasonings. Dot with butter and cover
with rich biscuit dough. Pierce top
with a knife. Bake in a hot oven,
450 F, 20 minutes or until brown.
Serves 6.

Oyster Pie Maryland

1 pint oysters
½ small green pepper, chopped
½ cup chopped celery
4 tablespoons butter, melted
5 tablespoons flour
2 cups milk
1 teaspoon salt
⅛ teaspoon pepper
2 tablespoons pimento, chopped
Pastry

Cook oysters in their own liquor until
the edges curl. Drain. Sauté green
pepper and celery in the butter until
soft. Blend in flour, add milk and cook
until thick, stirring constantly. Add
oysters and seasonings, and heat again.
Pour into a casserole and top with
pastry. Bake in a hot oven, 425 F, 15
minutes, or until the crust is brown.
Serves 6.

Oyster-Noodle Surprise

1 pint oysters
½ cup butter
1 cup milk

2 tablespoons flour
2 tablespoons water
1 tablespoon Worcestershire sauce
1 teaspoon salt
⅛ teaspoon pepper
1 8-ounce package noodles
2 cups grated Cheddar cheese

Drain oysters. Heat oysters in butter until edges curl. Mix flour with water. Add milk to oysters and flour-water paste. Stir until slightly thickened. Add Worcestershire sauce, salt and pepper. Remove from heat.

Cook noodles until tender in boiling salted water. Drain. Place half of noodles in shallow buttered baking dish. Cover with half of oyster mixture. Sprinkle with half of the cheese. Repeat with noodles, oysters and remaining cheese. Bake 20 minutes in a moderate oven 350 F. Serves 6.

Escalloped Oysters

1 pint oysters
½ cup butter
½ cup dry bread crumbs
1 cup cracker crumbs
¼ teaspoon salt
⅛ teaspoon pepper
2 tablespoons to ¼ cup milk
¼ cup oyster liquor

Melt butter in a skillet, add combined bread and cracker crumbs; heat and stir until delicately browned. Spread a layer of ⅓ of the buttered crumbs on the bottom of a shallow baking dish; cover with half the oysters and sprinkle with pepper and salt. Combine milk and oyster liquor and add part of the liquid. Add a second layer of crumbs and oysters, season and add remainder of the liquid. Cover top layer of oysters with the last of the crumbs. Bake at 350 F for 30 minutes. Serves 6.

Quick Scalloped Oysters

1 pint oysters
2 cups whole oyster crackers
½ teaspoon salt
⅛ teaspoon pepper
½ cup butter (not margarine, in this case)
¼ teaspoon Worcestershire sauce (optional)
1 cup milk

Drain oysters. Place a layer of one-third of the crackers on bottom of buttered baking dish; then put in one-third of the oysters and sprinkle with some of the salt and pepper. Dot generously with butter. (If possible use butter, as this is the secret of a delicious dish.) Mix Worcestershire sauce with milk and pour in one-third of this mixture. Repeat layers, ending with crackers on top. Dot with butter to prevent crackers from burning. Bake in moderate oven, 350 F, for 30 minutes or until brown. Serves 6.

Holiday Oyster Scallop

1 quart oysters
1 3-ounce can broiled mushrooms
1 cup crumbled oyster crackers
1 teaspoon salt
¼ teaspoon pepper
¼ teaspoon ground thyme (optional)
½ cup butter (not margarine, in this case)
2 cups milk
½ cup soft bread crumbs
¼ cup additional butter

Combine oysters and mushrooms, with liquid from both, in a saucepan. Cook just until oysters plump and curl around edges. Add salt, pepper and thyme. Place a layer of crumbled crackers on the bottom of a buttered casserole. Add a layer (one-third) of oyster mixture. Dot generously with butter. Repeat layer, ending with oysters on top. Pour milk over all.

Mix soft bread crumbs (untoasted) with melted butter. Sprinkle over top of casserole. Reserve several large oysters for top. Bake in moderate oven, 350 F, for 20 minutes. Serves 6 to 8.

Corn Bread—Oyster Stuffing

1 pint small oysters
1 cup butter
1 cup minced onion
¾ cup chopped celery
⅓ cup chopped parsley
1 tablespoon dry savory or poultry
  seasoning
1½ teaspoons salt
¾ teaspoon pepper
5 cups stale bread cubes
5 cups crumbled corn bread, made
  with eggs but without sugar

Drain and dice oysters. Melt butter in skillet. Add all ingredients, except bread cubes and corn bread. Cook for 5 minutes. Add crumbs. Use as stuffing for turkey. If too dry, stir in ¼ cup or more turkey broth. Makes 10 cups.

Oyster Stuffing for Duck

1 pint small oysters
1 medium onion, minced
1½ cups celery, diced
⅓ cup butter
1⅓ cups cooked rice
1 cup water chestnuts, chopped
2 teaspoons mixed herbs
Salt
Pepper

Drain and chop oysters. Cook onion and celery in butter until soft. Add remaining ingredients, mixing lightly. Stuff duck. When serving duck, garnish with kumquat preserves and spiced crab apples. Makes 4 cups.

Skillet and Saucepan Oysters

✳

Barbecued Oysterburgers

1 pint oysters
1 cup chili sauce
¼ cup brown sugar
2 tablespoons lime or lemon juice
2 tablespoons Worcestershire sauce
1 teaspoon prepared mustard
6 drops hot pepper sauce

Pour oysters into saucepan and cook in own liquid until edges curl. Remove and set aside.

Combine other ingredients in a skillet and simmer for 10 minutes. Add oysters.

Split and toast 6 hamburger buns. Spoon barbecued oysters on buns. Serve with cole slaw, mixed pickles and orange tarts. Serves 6.

Oysters in the Pink

1 quart oysters
¼ cup butter
1 medium onion, minced
2 stalks celery, chopped very fine
1 carrot, chopped very fine
1½ cups oyster liquor (fill out with
*   chicken stock or bouillon cube*
*   and water)*
1 tablespoon chopped parsley
1 teaspoon salt
¼ teaspoon dried thyme
¼ teaspoon marjoram
Dash cayenne pepper
1 cup light cream
1 tablespoon tomato paste
¼ cup flour

Drain oysters and reserve liquor.
    Cook onion, celery and carrot in butter until soft. Add oyster liquor and chicken stock. Cook until almost all of liquor has evaporated. Add seasonings and simmer 3 minutes. Add oysters and simmer until they curl around edges. Stir in cream and tomato paste.
    Blend ¼ cup of flour with enough water to make a paste. Add to oyster mixture. Stir and cook until thickened. Add salt to taste and dash of Tabasco, if needed. Serves 6.

TIP: Serve with baked potatoes, green salad and a mixed citrus-fruit dessert.

Oyster-Lima Mingle

1 pint oysters
1 package frozen lima beans
1 pint sour cream
4 tablespoons tomato paste
5 strips crisply cooked bacon,
*   crumbled*

Cook oysters in own liquid until they curl around the edges. Drain. Cook lima beans according to package instructions and drain. Combine and add remaining ingredients. If needed, stir in 3 tablespoons milk. Heat all together, without boiling. Serves 6.

TIP: Serve with baked potatoes, mixed greens and tomato salad, hard rolls and gingerbread with orange sauce.

Oysters and Cabbage Palm

1 pint oysters
1 heart of cabbage palm (see below)
8 slices bacon (cut into 4 pieces each)
5 tablespoons bacon drippings
1 cup cream or ¾ cup evaporated
*   milk*
Salt and pepper to taste

Break 1 cabbage palm into pieces (better than cutting) and cook in enough salted water to cover until tender, or about 20 minutes. Drain. Cook cut-up bacon until crisp. Add bacon, drippings, cream, salt and pepper to cabbage palm. Stir and simmer for about 5 minutes. Serves 6.

TIP: Green cabbage may be substituted, but if you are in a subtropical area do use palm cabbage or swamp cabbage, as it is also called.
    Swamp cabbage is the heart of the so-called cabbage palm of Florida and other subtropical and tropical climates. The palms used are about 4 feet in

height. They are cut down and the heart taken out. It is tender after the outside layers of bark are peeled off. The recipe is to take one cracker (human kind, of course) and let him get the heart of palm for you. It is crisp and has a nutlike flavor similar to chestnuts. It is delicious, too, in salads, raw, slivered like cabbage for slaw.

NOTE: Canned hearts of palm may be used in above recipe. A 1-pound can, drained, is sufficient.

Oyster-Asparagus Orlando

1 pint small oysters
3 tablespoons butter
1 pound fresh mushrooms, sliced
1 tablespoon minced onion
3 pounds fresh asparagus
½ tablespoon flour
1 cup heavy cream
½ teaspoon salt
½ teaspoon pepper
⅛ teaspoon nutmeg

Heat oysters in their own liquid until they curl around the edges, about 3 minutes. Set aside.

Sauté in 2 tablespoons melted butter the sliced mushrooms and onion. In the meantime break off tips of asparagus, trim and wash. Cover with boiling salted water and cook 10 minutes or until tender.

Heat in a skillet 1 tablespoon butter and blend in flour. When lightly browned add cream. Stir constantly over low heat until sauce is thickened. Add salt, pepper and nutmeg. Stir in the mushrooms, onions, and drained oysters. Keep warm.

Drain asparagus and arrange it in a warm serving dish. Top with the oyster-mushroom sauce. Serves 6.

Creamed Oysters in Green Peppers

6 green peppers
1 quart oysters
1 cup thick white sauce
Grated rind of 1 lemon
½ teaspoon salt
⅛ teaspoon cayenne

Remove seeds of peppers and cut in half lengthwise. Parboil and drain.

Heat oysters in liquor until the edges curl, about 3 minutes. Drain, reserving liquor. Mix with the white sauce, lemon rind, salt and cayenne. Place in top of double boiler over hot water and heat for 5 minutes. Serves 6.

Stuff pepper halves with creamed oysters. Sprinkle tops with buttered crumbs. Bake in moderate oven, 350 F, for 10 minutes or until brown. Serves 6.

THICK WHITE SAUCE

Make a *roux* by melting 3 tablespoons butter in saucepan and blending in 3 tablespoons flour with ¼ teaspoon salt. Stir until smooth. Add 1 cup milk or cream, stirring, and cook until sauce comes to a boil. Cook and stir until thick. Add 2 extra tablespoons butter.

Oyster Sauce for Chicken or Turkey

Serve slices of leftover chicken or turkey with this quick tasty oyster sauce.

½ pint small oysters
2 tablespoons melted butter

1 small onion, chopped
½ clove garlic, chopped
1 can condensed cream of chicken
    soup
2 teaspoons prepared mustard
2 tablespoons tomato catsup
1 teaspoon ground ginger
½ teaspoon salt
¼ teaspoon paprika
6 drops Tabasco sauce

Drain and chop oysters. Set aside. Melt butter in a skillet. Add onion and garlic. Sauté until soft but not brown. Add soup and other ingredients. Add oysters last. Heat thoroughly. Makes about 2 cups.

This is an old southern recipe.

Oyster-Egg Bread Stuffing for Chicken or Turkey

RICH EGG BREAD:

3 eggs
2 cups buttermilk
3 tablespoons melted shortening
2 teaspoons salt
2½ cups sifted water ground white
    corn meal
3 teaspoons baking powder
1 teaspoon soda

Beat eggs until light. Add milk, shortening and salt. Add corn meal, a small amount at a time, beating smooth after each addition. Grease and heat baking pan. Stir in the baking powder and dissolve the soda in a spoonful of cold water. Add to corn-meal mixture and stir well. Bake in hot oven, 450 F, 20 minutes, or until brown.

STUFFING:

1 pint small oysters, drained
½ cup butter
1 onion, chopped
1 cup chopped celery
1 cup chicken or turkey stock

Let bread cool, then crumble and pulverize crust with a fork.

Melt butter in a skillet and sauté the onion and chopped celery until tender. Add the drained oysters. Cook just until oysters curl around edges, tossing. Pour from skillet into crumbled egg bread and add 1 cup of chicken or turkey stock. Mix well.

Use to stuff turkey or chicken as directed.

The traditional oyster stew will be found in the soup section. This one is more truly a "stew."

Oyster Stew Surprise

1 quart oysters
1 green pepper, chopped
1 carrot, thinly sliced
3 medium potatoes, thinly sliced
1 small chopped onion
2 stalks celery, sliced
3 cups water
4 tablespoons butter
¼ teaspoon salt
¼ teaspoon pepper
¼ teaspoon chili powder
⅛ teaspoon ground cloves
⅛ teaspoon mace
6 drops hot pepper sauce

Cook vegetables in the water to which the butter and the seasonings have been added. When vegetables are tender add undrained oysters and simmer until they curl around the edges. Makes 8 servings.

Quick Oyster Gumbo

1 pint oysters
2 cups or 1 package frozen cut okra
2 tablespoons melted fat
2 tablespoons flour
2 tablespoons water
2 cups canned stewed tomatoes
1 tablespoon onion flakes
2 tablespoons parsley, chopped
¼ teaspoon Tabasco sauce
¾ teaspoon salt

Drain oysters.

Thaw frozen okra. Melt fat in skillet. Add okra and cook until fairly dry but not brown. Add tomatoes and heat. Mix flour with water to make a paste. Add this to tomato mixture. Cook until thickened. Add oysters and seasonings. Simmer about 5 minutes, or until edges of oysters begin to curl. Serve over cooked rice. Serves 6.

CLAMS

There are numerous species of clams. The market varieties of the east coast are different from those of the west.

On the Atlantic coast are found in the markets the hard clam, the soft clam, and the surf clam. The hard-shell is called quahog in New England, where "clam" generally means the soft-shell variety. In the middle Atlantic states and southward, "clam" is usually the name for the hard clam.

Littlenecks and cherrystones are dealers' names for the smaller-sized hard clams, generally served raw on the half shell. The larger sizes of hard clams are called chowders and are used in chowders and stews. The larger sizes of soft clams are known as in-shells and the smaller sizes as steamers.

On the Pacific coast, the most common market species are the butter, littleneck, razor and pismo clams. These are different from the hard clam.

There are many recipes for serving clams. They have a fine sea flavor and are high in the "protective" nutrients, including proteins, minerals and vitamins.

Clams and oysters are very much alike. The preparation and recipes are interchangeable. All recipes given for oysters are good using clams.

BUYING CLAMS

Clams may be bought in three forms: In the shell, shucked and canned.

SHELL CLAMS

These are usually sold by the dozen or by the pound. They should be alive when bought. With hard clams, the shells must be tightly closed. Gaping shells that do not close when handled mean the clams are no longer usable. With other varieties, there will be some constriction of the siphon or neck when the clam is touched. If fresh shell clams are kept in the refrigerator at about 40 F, they will remain alive for several days.

SHUCKED CLAMS

Shucked clams are the clam meats that have been removed from the shells; they are generally sold by the pint or quart. Shucked clams should be plump, with clear liquor, free from shell particles. Fresh shucked clams are packed in metal or waxed containers, which should be refrigerated. When properly handled they stay fresh for a week or 10 days.

In some places, shucked clams are available packaged and quick-frozen. In this form they can be stored for as long as a year. They should not be thawed until ready to use and, once thawed, they should not be refrozen.

CANNED CLAMS

You will find whole and minced clams canned. They come in 3½-ounce to 4-pound cans. The juice and nectar are also available canned or bottled.

HOW MUCH TO BUY—A good rule is to buy 3 dozen shell clams, 1 quart of shucked clams, or two 7-ounce cans for 6 persons.

WASHING CLAMS—After digging clams be sure to wash off all surfaces with sea water. Cover clams with clean sea water or 2 percent brine (⅓ cup salt to 1 gallon of water) and let stand for 15 or 20 minutes to allow the clams to cleanse themselves of sand. Salt water is necessary for the clams to open and discharge the sand, which will settle to the bottom of the pan. Change the water and let the clams stand several times. This cleansing is important if the clams are to be steamed or eaten from the shell.

SHUCKING HARD CLAMS—Wash the shell clams thoroughly, discarding any broken-shell or dead clams. To open a hard clam, hold it in the palm of one hand with the shell's hinge against the palm. Insert a slender, strong sharp knife between the halves of the shell and cut around the clam, twisting the knife slightly to pry open the shell. Cut both muscles free from the two halves of the shell. If clam is to be served on the half shell, remove only one half of the shell. If clam is to be used in one of the other recipes, remove and rinse the meat.

Soft clams do not have tight-fitting shells, so are easier to open.

An alternate method is to place the shell clams, after washing, in a small quantity of boiling water. Cover and steam them 5 to 10 minutes, or until they are partially open. Drain, remove and take the meat from the shells.

New England Steamed Clams

6 pounds shell clams
½ cup boiling water
Butter or margarine
Lemons or limes

Wash clams thoroughly, as directed. Place in a steamer, add water and cover. Steam for 5 to 10 minutes, or until clams open. Serve hot in the shell with melted butter. Pass lemon or lime wedges. Serves 6.

Clams on the Half Shell

36 shell clams (littleneck or
    cherrystones)
Cocktail sauce
Lemon or lime

Shuck clams. Arrange a bed of crushed ice in 6 shallow bowls or plates. Place 6 half-shell clams on the ice with a small container of cocktail sauce in the center. Garnish with lemon or lime wedges. Serves 6.

COCKTAIL SAUCE

½ cup catsup
¼ cup lemon juice
1 tablespoon horseradish
3 drops Tabasco sauce
½ teaspoon celery salt
¼ teaspoon salt

Blend all ingredients and chill. Serves 6.

Lemon-Fried Clams

1 quart clams
1 egg, beaten
1 tablespoon lemon juice
1 teaspoon salt
⅛ teaspoon pepper
⅛ teaspoon paprika
1 cup dry bread crumbs or cracker
    meal
3 slices lemon

Drain clams. Combine egg, lemon juice and seasonings. Dip clams in egg mixture and roll in crumbs. Place 3 slices of lemon in deep hot fat. Fry clams in a basket at 375 F for 3 minutes or until brown. Drain and serve plain or with *Tartare Sauce*. Serves 6.

Batter-Fried Clams

1 quart clams
1 cup sifted flour
1 teaspoon salt
1 egg, slightly beaten
1 cup cold milk
4 tablespoons melted fat
Lemon or lime wedges

Drain clams. Combine all other ingredients except fat and lemon or limes. Heat the fat in a frying pan (about ⅛ inch fat). Dip clams in batter and fry until golden brown on all sides. Drain on absorbent paper. Serves 6. Garnish with lemon or lime wedges and serve plain or with a sauce.

Plain Fried Clams

1 quart clams
1 egg, beaten
1 tablespoon milk
1 teaspoon salt
⅛ teaspoon pepper
1 cup dry bread crumbs or cracker crumbs

Drain clams. Combine other ingredients except crumbs. Dip clams in egg mixture and roll in crumbs. Heat ⅛ inch fat in skillet and fry clams at moderate heat until brown, turning once. Cook 5 to 8 minutes. Drain on absorbent paper. Serve plain or with a sauce. Serves 6.

NOTE: Deep-fat fry the same way except fry in basket in deep fat 375 F for 2 to 3 minutes or until brown.

Clam Fritters

1 pint clams
2 cups sifted flour
1½ teaspoons baking powder
1 teaspoon salt
Dash pepper
⅛ teaspoon mace
2 eggs, beaten
1 cup milk
2 teaspoons grated onion
1 tablespoon melted butter or margarine

Drain clams and chop. Sift dry ingredients together. Combine eggs, milk, onion, butter and clams with the dry ingredients. Drop mixture by spoonfuls into deep hot fat, 375 F, and fry until brown. Drain on absorbent paper. Serves 6.

TIP: Good with clam fritters are stewed tomatoes, green peas, apple-raisin salad and layer cake.

This is an outdoor recipe, for a crowd.

English Roasted Clams

4 dozen clams in the shell
1 cup melted butter or margarine
Salt, pepper, paprika
5 tablespoons chopped parsley and chopped green onion

Shuck clams and return each to a half shell. Place each clam on a piece of foil cut large enough to completely cover clam. Divide melted butter among clams with salt, pepper and paprika. Sprinkle with parsley and green onion. Wrap each clam in its foil, sealing completely. Put packages directly on hot coals or gas briquettes of outdoor grill for 4 minutes. Serves 8.

Roast Clams

6 pounds shell clams
Butter or margarine

Wash clams thoroughly. Place in a baking pan. Roast in a very hot oven, 450 F, for 15 minutes or until clams open. Serve hot in the shell with melted butter. Serves 6.

Baked Clam-Mushroom in Shells

1 dozen large shell clams ("chowders")
3/4 cup chopped onion
1 4-ounce can mushrooms, drained and chopped
4 tablespoons butter or other fat, melted
3 tablespoons flour
1 1/2 teaspoons celery salt
Dash pepper
2 tablespoons butter or other fat, melted
1/2 cup dry bread crumbs

Drain clams, or shuck as directed. Chop them. Wash shells thoroughly or use other shells.

Cook chopped onion and mushrooms in butter until soft. Blend in flour and seasonings. Add clams and cook until thick, stirring constantly. Fill greased clam shells. Combine butter and crumbs and sprinkle over top of each shell. Bake in a hot oven, 400 F, for 10 minutes or until brown. Serves 6.

TIP: For a party dinner serve also green beans with almonds, tossed salad and banana-cream pie.

Clam Paella

1 pint clams
1 small Spanish onion
1 small green pepper
2 cloves garlic
1/2 cup Spanish olive oil
3/4 cup stewed whole tomatoes (canned may be used)
Pinch of saffron
1/2 teaspoon yellow coloring
1 teaspoon salt
2 cups seafood broth or clam juice (canned or bottled is fine)
1 cup Valencia or yellow rice

Drain clams, saving liquor. Chop finely the onion, pepper and garlic. Simmer in heated olive oil until limp. Add clams. Cook for 3 minutes. Add tomatoes, saffron, coloring, salt and broth, using reserved liquor to make 2 cups. When this comes to a boil, add rice. Remove and place in moderate oven, 350 F, for 15 minutes. Serve garnished with cooked peas, strips of pimento and parsley sprigs. Serves 6.

TIP: If no clam chowder or juice is available, but you do have some fish or other seafood on hand make broth this way: Cover fish fillets or other seafood with water to which is added a sliced lemon; stalk of celery, chopped; several sprigs of parsley and 1 bay leaf. Salt and pepper to taste. Simmer until fish turns white and flakes easily and remove from liquid. Continue to cook liquid until celery is soft. Strain. Fish or other seafoods may be stored in refrigerator or frozen for future use.

Stuffed Clams with Bacon

2 cups minced clams or 2 7-ounce cans
⅓ cup minced green pepper
½ cup minced celery
1½ cups dry bread crumbs
1 cup heavy cream or evaporated milk
2 eggs, beaten
2 tablespoons butter or other fat, melted
2 teaspoons prepared mustard
1½ teaspoons salt
1 teaspoon pepper

Mix all ingredients together. Spoon into clam or scallop shells. Bake in moderate oven, 350 F, for 20 minutes. Remove, sprinkle top with grated Parmesan cheese and place half a strip of bacon across top of each shell. Return to oven until bacon is crisp. Serves 6.

Spaghetti Baked with Clam Sauce

1 8-ounce package spaghetti
1 pint clams
2 tablespoons butter, or other fat
2 tablespoons flour
½ teaspoon salt
Dash pepper
1 can condensed celery soup
¼ cup milk
2 tablespoons butter or other fat
½ cup dry bread crumbs

Cook the spaghetti. Do not let it get too soft. Drain.

Drain clams and chop finely. Melt butter and sauté chopped clams for 5 minutes, stirring constantly. Blend in flour, salt and pepper. Add soup and milk gradually and cook, stirring, until thick. Add spaghetti to sauce. Turn mixture into greased 1½-quart casserole. Mix butter with crumbs. Spoon over top of casserole. Bake in a hot oven, 400 F, for 10 minutes or until golden brown. Serves 6.

Clam-Vegetable Medley

2 cups minced clams or 2 7-ounce cans
¼ cup melted butter or margarine
1 large onion, chopped
¼ cup flour
⅛ teaspoon pepper
2 cups clam liquor and milk
½ cup diced cooked carrots
½ cup chopped cooked celery
3 hard-cooked eggs, chopped
1½ cups seasoned mashed potatoes

Drain clams, saving liquor. Melt butter and cook onion until tender. Blend in the flour and pepper. Add clam liquor and cook until thick, stirring constantly. Add carrots, celery, egg and minced clams. Grease a 1½-quart casserole. Spoon clam mixture into it and cover with the potatoes. Bake in a hot oven, 425 F, for 20 to 25 minutes, or until brown. Serves 6.

Scalloped Clams

1 pint clams
1 cup cracker crumbs
1 cup dry bread crumbs
½ teaspoon salt
⅛ teaspoon pepper
½ cup butter or margarine, melted
1 cup combined clam liquor and milk

Drain clams and save liquor. Chop. Combine crumbs, salt, pepper, and butter. Sprinkle one-third of this mixture in a greased casserole. Cover with one-third of the clams. Add some of the liquid. Repeat, ending layers with crumbs. Bake in a moderate oven, 350 F, for 25 to 30 minutes, or until brown. Serves 6.

Clam and Potato Scallop

1 pint clams
3 tablespoons butter or margarine
3 tablespoons flour
1 teaspoon salt
⅛ teaspoon pepper
⅛ teaspoon mace or thyme
¾ cup clam liquor
¾ cup milk
2 cups sliced cooked potatoes
¼ cup chopped onion
1 cup dry bread crumbs, buttered

Drain clams, reserving liquor. Chop. Melt butter and blend in flour, salt, pepper, and mace. Add liquor and milk gradually and cook until thick and smooth, stirring constantly. Add chopped clams. Place half of the sliced potatoes in a greased casserole, add one-half the chopped onion and cover with one-half the sauce. Repeat layers. Top with buttered bread crumbs. Bake in moderate oven, 350 F, for 45 minutes, or until brown. Serves 6.

Clam Mornay

1 pint clams
¼ cup butter or margarine
¼ cup flour
½ teaspoon salt
¼ teaspoon nutmeg
2 cups clam liquor and milk, mixed
Dash Tabasco sauce
1 egg yolk, beaten
Bread crumbs for topping
1 cup Parmesan cheese

Drain clams and save liquor. Melt butter, blend in flour and seasonings. Gradually add liquor and milk, then stir in Tabasco sauce. Cook until thick and smooth, stirring constantly. Stir a little of the hot sauce into egg, add to remaining sauce, stirring constantly.

Add clams. Spoon mixture into 6 scallop shells or other shells. Top with soft fine bread crumbs and grated cheese. Place under broiler heat until nicely browned. Serves 6.

Clams with Sunshine Sauce

1 pint clams
1 tablespoon minced onion
4 tablespoons butter or other fat, melted
4 tablespoons flour
1 cup milk and liquor from clams, combined
Salt and pepper
6 hard-cooked eggs
Cooked rice

Drain clams, saving liquor. Cook onion in butter and when soft, gradually blend in flour. Stir in milk and liquor from clams. Season with salt and pepper to taste. Cut eggs in half lengthwise. Add eggs and clams to sauce. Cook and stir 3 minutes, or until clams curl around the edges and the eggs are heated thoroughly. Serve on a heated platter, surrounded by hot buttered rice. Serves 6.

Scrambled Eggs with Clams

1 pint clams or 2 7-ounce cans
5 eggs, beaten
¼ cup milk
Salt and pepper
2 tablespoons butter

Drain clams and mince. Break eggs, add milk, salt and pepper and clams. Stir lightly. Melt butter in frying pan and add clam-egg mixture. When eggs begin to set, stir with a fork. Toss and serve hot to 6.

TIP: Add 1 cup diced ham, which has been fried in a little butter until brown, to the clams. Then add to egg mixture. Serve on toast sprinkled with grated cheese and parsley, for a change.

Cool Clam-Madrilene

2 cups madrilene (canned)
1 cup clam juice
1 tablespoon lime juice

1 teaspoon grated lime rind
⅛ teaspoon dried tarragon
1 tablespoon fresh dill, chopped
    (optional)
¼ cup yoghurt

Mix all ingredients together and chill. When ready to serve add ¼ cup cold yoghurt to soup and beat with a whisk until blended. Serves 4.

COQUINA OR DONAX CLAM

This is really the Donax clam, called sometimes the coquina. Webster's Dictionary defines coquina as shellfish, cockle, a soft, whitish limestone, of broken shells and corals cemented together, used in the southern U.S. for building, etc. These very tiny clams are variable wedge-shell and butterfly-shell and are sometimes incorrectly called periwinkles. The shells are the substance of coquina rock, used in much of the first construction of St. Augustine, Florida. The gay rainbow colors are found arranged so that they produce plaid and striped color patterns. The clams are usually abundant along the Atlantic coast in April and through the summer months. After the receding waves have washed the sand from them, the little clams can be seen by the hundreds quickly burrowing back into the sand. They scarcely reach ½ inch in length.

There is little or no commercial market for these clams, but people living on the ocean or visitors to the seashore enjoy gathering them in colanders, washing away the sand through a screen.

COQUINA BROTH AND SOUP

Wash coquinas thoroughly in their shells in cold water. Place them in a kettle of hot water just to cover. Do *not* add salt as this is not needed. When the water boils vigorously, strain the coquina shells out, leaving the juice. Season this to taste with salt and pepper. Serve cold, with a dash of lime juice and Tabasco sauce, for a cocktail, or warm as a broth. For soup, serve hot with milk or cream added to taste, and melted butter.

SCALLOPS

Scallops are delicious, all-meat shellfish, highly prized. Because they are always marketed as dressed meat, without shells, many people do not know that they are shellfish at all. Similar to oysters and clams, scallops have two shells, hence they are "bivalves." The part of the scallop that is eaten is the large muscle, or eye, of the scallop. This muscle controls the opening and closing of the shell, the snapping of which spurts out a stream of water and provides locomotion for the scallop. This excellently flavored muscle is cut from the shells and marketed all over the United States. In Europe, we are told, the entire scallop is eaten, not just the muscle.

There are two varieties of scallops: the bay scallop, which is small and creamy-pink in color, and the sea scallop, which is larger, sometimes growing as large as 8 inches in diameter. The muscle may be as large as 2 inches in diameter. The sea scallop is taken from the waters off the Northern and Middle Atlantic states, centering around Maine and Massachusetts.

The smaller bay scallop differs very little from the ocean scallop. The shell of the bay scallop is grooved and has scalloped edges. The abductor muscle, or eye, of the bay scallop is about half an inch across. This mollusk is taken from inshore bays and estuaries from New England to the Gulf of Mexico.

Scallops are at their best from November to April, but they are marketed all year around. All are creamy pink in color. They are available fresh or frozen, but *only* in the form of dressed meat, as the scallops are opened, packed and iced at sea. Fresh scallops and thawed frozen scallops have a pleasant deep-sea fragrance. Packages are almost entirely free of liquid.

Both scallops have high levels of protein, little or no fat, and many of the vitamins and minerals necessary for good health.

Scallops are available in some form in almost every section of the country. Breaded and ready to cook, precooked and in many other forms, they are now conveniently packaged.

Either bay or sea scallops may be used in any recipe calling for scallops. They are good as cocktails, appetizers, in salads, soups and main dishes; fried, broiled, baked and barbecued.

Scallops are purchased by the pint or pound—fresh and frozen. A pint or pound serves 6.

Scallops may be substituted for shrimp in most recipes, and in many recipes used in the place of flaked, cooked fish.

Boiled Scallops

1 pound scallops, fresh or frozen
1 quart boiling water
2 tablespoons salt

Thaw frozen scallops. Remove any shell particles and rinse well. Place in boiling salted water. Cover and return to the boiling point. Simmer for 3 to 4 minutes, depending on size. Drain. Serves 6.

NOTE: This is the basic recipe for cooked scallops called for in many recipes.

SCALLOP COCKTAIL

Serve boiled cold scallops, 3 or 4 per serving, as you would shrimp or other seafood, as a cocktail.

COCKTAIL SAUCE FOR SCALLOPS

2 tablespoons salad dressing
2 tablespoons tomato catsup
2 tablespoons chopped celery
1 tablespoon chopped onion
¼ teaspoon salt
Dash curry powder
⅛ teaspoon pepper

Combine all ingredients and chill. Serves 6.

Scallops on Skewers

1 pound fresh sea scallops
¼ cup melted butter mixed with ¼ cup salad oil (makes a nice brown color)

Rinse scallops in cool water. Dry thoroughly with paper towel. Thread scallops on skewers and brush with melted butter and salad oil. Broil 3 inches from source of heat for 5 minutes. Turn and brush with fat. Broil 3 to 5 minutes longer. Serve with this sauce:

QUICK SEAFOOD SAUCE

¾ cup tomato catsup
½ cup minced celery
2 tablespoons lemon juice
½ teaspoon Tabasco or pepper sauce
½ teaspoon salt
¼ teaspoon pepper

Mix all ingredients and chill. Serves 6.

Scallop-Bacon Rolls

8 strips bacon, cut in half
16 fresh scallops (about 1½ pounds)

Wash and dry scallops. Sprinkle lightly with salt and pepper. Wrap a half slice of bacon around each scallop and fasten with toothpick. Broil 4 inches from heat 10 minutes, or until bacon is crisp and scallop tender.

Serve with sauce made by blending ½ cup tomato catsup with 2 tablespoons lemon juice. Salt and pepper to taste. Serves 4.

Tangy Pan-Broiled Scallops

1 pound or 1 pint scallops, fresh or
   frozen
2 tablespoons butter
½ teaspoon salt
⅛ teaspoon pepper
¼ teaspoon paprika
2 tablespoons minced onion
2 tablespoons lemon or lime juice

Thaw frozen scallops. Remove any shell particles and wash. Cut large scallops in half. Heat next 4 ingredients until bubbling hot. Add onion. Drop in enough scallops to cover the bottom of frying pan. Cook and turn until brown, or about 5 to 6 minutes. Remove from pan. When all scallops are cooked, pour lemon juice in butter where scallops were cooked. Pour over scallops for serving. Serves 4.

TIP: For a change substitute sherry or a white wine such as dry vermouth for the lemon or lime juice.

Scallops with Grapefruit

1 pound scallops, fresh or frozen
2 grapefruit, cut in half
1 teaspoon salt
¼ teaspoon pepper
¼ cup brown sugar
¼ cup butter or margarine
½ teaspoon soy sauce

Thaw scallops, if frozen. Wash and dry scallops. If scallops are large, cut in half, crosswise. Halve and core grapefruit. Place in baking pan. Fill centers of grapefruit with scallops. Sprinkle with salt, pepper and brown sugar. Melt butter and add soy sauce. Spoon over top of scallops. Broil 10 minutes, or until brown.

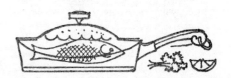

Garlic Scallops

1½ pounds scallops
2 or 3 cloves garlic, split
2 tablespoons butter
2 tablespoons minced scallions
  (or green onions)
2 tablespoons chopped parsley
½ teaspoon dried tarragon
½ teaspoon salt
¼ teaspoon pepper

Wash and dry scallops. Brown garlic in butter, then remove garlic and discard. Add onions and seasonings. Place scallops in shallow baking dish and pour the seasoned butter over them. Let them stand in refrigerator until just before serving time, then broil 3 to 4 minutes, turn and broil same length of time on other side. Baste and serve bubbling and brown. Serves 6.

Scallop Kabobs

1 pound scallops, fresh or frozen
4 slices bacon, cut into squares
1½ cups pineapple chunks, drained
¼ cup butter or other fat, melted
1 teaspoon salt
¼ teaspoon pepper
½ teaspoon paprika

Thaw frozen scallops. Remove any shell particles and wash. Use 6 skewers, 7 inches each. Alternate scallops, bacon and pineapple chunks on each skewer. Place on a greased broiler pan. Combine butter and seasonings. Brush kabobs with butter mixture. Broil about 3 inches from heat for 5 minutes. Turn carefully. Brush other side with butter and broil 4 to 5 minutes. Serves 6.

TIP: For a change omit pineapple and use 1 4-ounce can button mushrooms, drained, and 1 green pepper, cut into 1-inch squares.

Batter-Fried Scallops

1 pint scallops, fresh or frozen
1 cup flour
1 cup milk
1 egg, beaten
½ teaspoon salt

Remove any shell particles from scallops. Rinse and dry. Mix other ingredients thoroughly. Dip scallops in batter and fry in deep hot fat, 375 F, until brown on all sides. Serves 4.

NOTE: This basic batter recipe can be used for frying all fish and shellfish.

Batter-Fried Scallops with Mustard Sauce

Prepare *Batter-Fried Scallops.* Serve hot with this sauce:

MUSTARD SAUCE

½ cup sour cream
3 tablespoons prepared mustard
2 tablespoons prepared horseradish
⅛ teaspoon cayenne
⅛ teaspoon Tabasco sauce
1½ teaspoons salt

Combine all the ingredients and chill in refrigerator until ready to serve. Makes about ¾ cup sauce.

Deep-Fat Fried Scallops

1 pound scallops
2 tablespoons lemon juice
¼ teaspoon celery salt

2 tablespoons grated onion
1 egg, beaten
¼ cup milk or water
Cracker or fine dried-bread crumbs

Wipe scallops with damp cloth. Mix together lemon juice, celery salt and onion. Pour this over scallops, cover and let stand 1 or more hours.

Drain scallops. Mix beaten egg and milk or water. Dip scallops in mixture, then in crumbs. Fry in preheated deep shortening, 370 F, until golden brown. Serves 6.

Fried Scallops with Cucumber Sauce

1 package frozen scallops or 1 pint
  fresh scallops
1 egg, beaten
1 tablespoon cold water
1 teaspoon salt
⅛ teaspoon pepper
½ cup flour
½ cup bread crumbs or cracker meal

Thaw frozen scallops. Wash and dry. Combine egg, water, and seasonings. Combine flour and crumbs.

Dip scallops in egg mixture and roll in flour-crumb mixture. Fry scallops in frying pan with ⅛ inch of fat or in a basket in deep hot fat, 350 F, for 2 to 3 minutes or until brown. Drain on absorbent paper. Serves 4. Serve Cucumber Sauce separately.

CUCUMBER SAUCE

1 medium-size cucumber
½ cup mayonnaise
1 tablespoon lemon juice
½ teaspoon paprika
¾ teaspoon salt
4 drops Tabasco sauce

Cut cucumber into very small dice. Blend other ingredients together and add cucumber. Makes about 1½ cups sauce.

Scallops with Green Pepper and Mushrooms

1½ pounds scallops
6 slices French bread
5 tablespoons butter
1 small green pepper, chopped
1 4-ounce can button mushrooms
1 tablespoon paprika
1 teaspoon celery salt
¼ cup cooking sherry (optional) or
  lemon juice

Wash and dry scallops. If very large, cut in half, crosswise. Toast French bread in oven, while preparing scallops.

Melt 4 tablespoons butter in skillet, add scallops and sauté until tender and lightly browned. Remove scallops and set aside. Add an additional tablespoon butter to pan. Spoon in green peppers and mushrooms, add paprika and salt, and sauté until brown.

Add sherry. Stir and cook about 2 minutes. Place scallops on toast, then spoon mushrooms and sauce over them. Serves 6.

TIP: For a change substitute port wine for the sherry.

Scallop and Shrimp Creole

1 pound shrimp
1 pound scallops
1 No. 2 can stewed tomatoes
1 tablespoon dehydrated onion flakes
½ teaspoon garlic juice
1 large carrot, grated
1 tablespoon butter
2 tablespoons lemon juice

1 teaspoon salt
½ teaspoon black pepper
Pinch of red pepper
⅛ teaspoon crushed saffron
2 tablespoons chopped parsley
2 tablespoons flour
2 tablespoons water

Shell and devein shrimp. Rinse with scallops in cool water. Drain and cut scallops in half, crosswise, if they are large. Set aside.

In a large saucepan mix stewed tomatoes with onion flakes, garlic juice, carrot and butter. Add the lemon juice and seasonings, except parsley. Cover and simmer 10 minutes. Add shrimp, scallops and parsley. Simmer 10 minutes longer. Mix flour and water and stir it into mixture. Cook 5 minutes. Serve hot in soup bowls, over a mound of fluffy cooked rice. Serves 6.

Vermouth Scallops

1½ pounds scallops
1 can frozen cream of shrimp soup
¼ cup butter
1 3-ounce can mushrooms, drained
1 teaspoon salt
¼ teaspoon fresh ground pepper
2 tablespoons dry vermouth
¼ cup bread crumbs, buttered

Thin soup with hot water according to instructions on can. Wash and dry scallops. Slice crosswise if large. Melt 2 tablespoons butter in skillet and sauté scallops for 3 to 4 minutes. Remove and set aside.

Add rest of butter to pan and sauté mushrooms 3 minutes. Return scallops and add salt and pepper. Stir soup until smooth and add to the scallop mixture. Add vermouth. Divide mixture among 8 custard cups. Sprinkle top with buttered crumbs. Bake in

hot oven, 425 F, 10 minutes, or until heated and browned on top. Serves 8.

Scalloped Scallops

1 pound scallops
2 cups cracker crumbs (oyster crackers)
1 cup soft bread crumbs
¾ cup melted butter
½ teaspoon salt
⅛ teaspoon pepper
1 cup light cream or milk

Wash scallops in cold, running water. Drain. Cut in half, crosswise. Combine cracker crumbs, butter or margarine, salt and pepper. Alternate layers in greased baking dish, ending with buttered bread crumbs. Pour cream over all. Bake in moderate oven, 350 F, for 25 to 30 minutes. Serves 6.

TIP: Serve with green peas with tiny green onions, lettuce and tomato salad, hot rolls and lemon refrigerator pie.

Deviled Scallops

1 quart scallops
½ cup butter or margarine
1½ teaspoons prepared mustard
¾ teaspoon salt
1 teaspoon Worcestershire sauce
Dash Tabasco sauce
1 cup hot milk
Buttered bread crumbs

Chop scallops, heat and pour into baking dish. Beat softened butter, creaming in mustard, salt, Tabasco and Worcestershire sauce. Add to scallops and pour in milk. Cover with buttered bread crumbs and bake in moderate oven, 350 F, for 20 minutes. Serves 6.

Soups, Salads

and Sandwiches

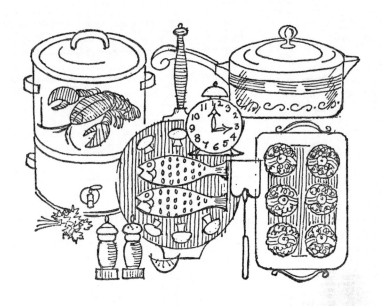

SOUPS AND CHOWDERS

SEAFOODS *in fish and chowders are always delicious. Almost all varieties may be used in the recipes given here. This is an extremely nutritious way of preparing fish and shellfish, as all the highly prized nutrients are reserved in soups and chowders. Some are full meals in themselves. Served with salads and desserts, they are party foods and are enjoyed by most families. Recipes may be cut for smaller portions. Of course, recipes serve more if portion is for a first course, less if it is a main course.*

TIP: *A cup of chopped cooked seafoods—all varieties—is good added to all canned soups. This is a change-of-pace hint, and we think you will like it.*

This old-fashioned recipe, which is popular for picnics in the south and especially in South Carolina, got its name because in early days the kettle, which was over an open fire outdoors, would be covered with pine boughs to keep in the flavor.

Pine Bark Stew

2 pounds fish fillets, fresh or frozen
6 slices bacon, chopped
1 cup onion, chopped
2 cans (1 pound 13 ounces each)
  tomatoes
2 cups diced potatoes
1 cup catsup
2 tablespoons Worcestershire sauce
2 teaspoons salt
½ teaspoon pepper

Thaw fillets if frozen. Skin fillets and cut into cubes. Fry bacon until lightly browned in a large kettle over a hot fire, or top burner of your range. Remove bacon; add onion to bacon drippings and cook until soft. Return bacon to kettle and add other ingredients except fish. Cover and simmer for 20 minutes, stirring occasionally. Add fish and continue cooking for about 10 minutes longer. Serves 6 to 8.

Blue Sea New England Fish Chowder

1 pound fish fillets, fresh or frozen
2 tablespoons bacon, chopped, or salt
  pork
½ cup chopped onions
2 cups hot water
1 cup diced raw potatoes
2 cups light cream or rich milk
¾ teaspoons salt
⅛ teaspoon pepper

Cut fillets in about 1-inch cubes. Fry bacon until crisp in heavy kettle. Add onions and brown slightly. Add water and potatoes. Cook 12 minutes or until potatoes are partially tender. Add fish and cook until it flakes easily. Add cream and seasonings and heat. Serve in hot bowls with unsalted crackers. Sprinkle soup with chopped parsley, if desired. Serves 6.

Fish Chowder with Potatoes and Carrots

1 pound fish fillets, fresh or frozen
2 cups milk
1 cup light cream
1 cup crushed saltines
¼ cup cubed salt pork
1 clove garlic, minced
½ cup chopped onion
¼ cup sliced celery
1 cup water
1 cup diced raw potatoes
½ cup sliced carrots
1 bay leaf
¼ teaspoon thyme
⅛ teaspoon nutmeg
¼ cup (½ stick) butter or margarine
Dash cayenne
¼ cup chopped parsley

Cut fillets into bite-size pieces. Mix milk, cream and saltines and set aside to soak. Cook salt pork in a large heavy saucepan until lightly browned. Add garlic, onion and celery and cook until vegetables are soft. Add water, potatoes, carrots, bay leaf, thyme and nutmeg. Cover and cook 10 minutes. Add fish, saltine-milk mixture and butter. Bring to a boil. Reduce heat, cover and simmer 5 to 8 minutes, or until fish flakes easily when tested with a fork.

Season with cayenne and serve with a sprinkling of chopped parsley. Serves 8.

Fish-Tomato Chowder

1 pound fish fillets, fresh or frozen
3 medium potatoes, chopped
1 large onion, chopped
2 1-pound cans stewed tomatoes
1½ tablespoons Worcestershire sauce
1 teaspoon salt
½ teaspoon pepper
2 tablespoons lemon juice
2 tablespoons butter

Cut fish into small pieces. Combine chopped potatoes and onion in a small amount of salted water and cook until almost tender. Add stewed tomatoes and fish. Stir in Worcestershire sauce, salt and pepper. Cook 15 minutes or until fish will flake when tested with a fork. Pour into serving dish, stir in lemon juice and top with butter. Serves 6.

Delicious Fish and Corn Chowder

1 cup flaked cooked fish
7 slices bacon
1 large onion, chopped
2 1-pound cans cream-style white corn
1 can cream of celery soup
1 tablespoon salt
¼ teaspoon pepper
1 quart milk
2 cups light cream
Parsley for garnish

Poach, drain and flake any variety of white-meated fish or use 2 small cans of canned fish flakes.

Cook bacon in a large skillet or Dutch oven or an iron pot for outdoors, until brown. Remove, crumble and set aside. Drain off all except 3 tablespoons drippings. Add onion and sauté until soft. Add all other ingredients, except bacon and parsley. Simmer for 15 minutes. Add bacon. Serve hot.

Garnish with chopped parsley, if desired. Makes 2½ quarts. Serves 8 to 12.

Quick Fish Flake Soup

2 cups flaked cooked fish or crabmeat
1 can cream of mushroom soup
1 can cream of celery soup
2 soup-cans water
⅛ teaspoon ground mustard
⅛ teasoon ground ginger
½ teaspoon paprika
1 tablespoon chopped parsley

Heat soups and water in a saucepan. Add fish, seasonings and parsley. When soup is hot again, serve in bowls with crisp crackers or croutons. Serves 6 to 8.

Creole Bouillabaisse

(*Bouilla-Baisse*)

The Picayune Creole Cook Book explains how this famous thick soup got its name. Two fishermen in Marseilles were disputing as to the best way to cook sturgeon and perch combined. Both took a try. One made a fine dish and the other a failure. The successful cook agreed to show his friend how to put the dish together. When the friend was putting the finishing touches to the recipe, the teacher, seeing that the moment had come when the fish must be taken from the heat or be spoiled, cried out

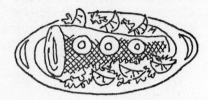

"Quand ça commence à bouiller, BAISSE!" (When it commences to boil, STOP!)

This recipe is taken from Mary Moore Bremer's interesting little cookbook entitled *New Orleans Recipes*.

"Get three slices each of redfish and red snapper, a half can of tomatoes, a cup of water, tablespoon of olive oil, an onion, one clove of garlic, a half lemon, a bay leaf, a sprig of parsley and of thyme, a few allspice, salt, black pepper and cayenne to taste.

"Mince the parsley, thyme, and bay leaf very fine, mixing in the allspice. Rub each slice of fish with this spice mixture. Be sure to do this, you want it to get into every part of the fish.

"Put a tablespoon of oil into a pan large enough to hold each piece of fish without touching; add a chopped onion to this and cover saucepan, letting it smother for ten minutes. Turn the fish once only.

"Take out and lay the fish on a dish. Pour into the pan the tomato and a cup of water, also a half of lemon, sliced. Season well with salt, pepper and cayenne and let this boil until it reduces considerably; then add a cup of white wine and return the fish carefully, each slice to itself, into the sauce.

"The moment it comes to a boil take it off. Lay each slice on a piece of toast which has been fried in butter. Pour sauce over all and add a pinch of saffron spread on top of fish. Serve at once, very hot."

Chefs later made more sauce and flaked the fish to make a soup, but either way it is very tasty.

Blue Sea Bouillabaisse

2 pounds fresh or frozen fillets, thawed
1 7½-ounce can crabmeat
1 7½-ounce can minced clams
1 pound shrimp, fresh or frozen, shelled and deveined
2 medium onions, sliced
⅓ cup salad or olive oil
2 1-pound can tomatoes
1½ bay leaves
½ cup chopped pimento
¼ cup chopped parsley
1 teaspoon garlic powder
½ teaspoon thyme
½ teaspoon saffron
1 cup lemon, lime juice or white wine

Cut the fish and crabmeat into strips. Sauté onions in oil until soft. Add all the fish and shellfish, tomatoes and bay leaves. Bring to a boil and cook for 15 minutes. Add pimento, parsley, garlic powder, thyme and saffron. Let simmer 10 minutes longer. Just before serving add lemon, lime juice or wine. Cover and let stand for 5 to 10 minutes longer. Serves 8.

Bouillabaisse American Style

1 pound halibut steaks or fillets, or other fish
½ cup chopped onion
½ cup chopped celery
1 clove garlic, finely chopped

¼ cup butter or other fat, melted
1 7-ounce can minced clams
1 5-ounce can shrimp, drained
1 can (1 pound 4 ounces) tomatoes
1 cup water
1¼ teaspoons salt
¼ teaspoon thyme
1 bay leaf, crushed
Dash pepper
Grated Parmesan cheese
6 slices French bread

Remove skin and bones from steaks and cut into ½-inch cubes. Cook onion, celery and garlic in butter until tender. Add remaining ingredients except cheese and bread. Bring to boiling point and simmer for 20 minutes. Sprinkle cheese over bread; toast. Arrange toast in large soup bowls and cover with bouillabaisse. Serves 6.

Tuna Chowder

1 7-ounce can tuna
1 cup raw diced potatoes
1 cup tomato juice
1 medium onion, sliced
½ cup chopped celery
1 cup boiling water
3 tablespoons butter or other fat
3 tablespoons flour
1 teaspoon salt
¼ teaspoon pepper
3 cups light cream or rich milk

Drain tuna and break it into large pieces. Combine potatoes, tomato juice, onion, celery, and boiling water. Cook for 15 to 17 minutes, or until potatoes and celery are tender. Add tuna.

In a skillet, melt butter and blend in flour and seasonings. Add milk gradually and cook mixture until thick and smooth, stirring constantly. Add

it to the tuna mixture and heat. Serve in hot bowls garnished with chopped parsley or celery tops. Serves 6.

Quick Tuna Chowder

1 7-ounce can tuna
¼ cup chopped bacon or salt pork
¼ cup chopped onion
1 cup boiling water
1 cup diced raw potatoes
¼ teaspoon salt
⅛ teaspoon pepper
1 quart milk

Drain tuna and break it into pieces. Fry bacon until lightly browned. Add onion and cook until tender. Add boiling water, potatoes, and seasonings. Cook for 15 minutes, or until potatoes are tender. Add milk and tuna and heat. Garnish with chopped parsley if desired. Serves 6.

TIP: For a real quickie fry breakfast bacon and crumble. Discard drippings. Combine 2 tablespoons onion flakes with water from 1 No. 2 can cooked potatoes. Dice 1 cup of the potatoes and add them with salt, pepper, 2 cans evaporated milk and 1 can of water, or 3 cups milk. Allow soup to come just to a boil. Add bacon. Remove from heat and serve.

Tuna and Cheese Chowder

1 7-ounce can tuna
¼ cup chopped onion
1 cup chopped celery
¼ cup butter or other fat, melted
3 tablespoons flour
3 cups milk
2 chicken bouillon cubes
2 cups boiling water
1½ cups grated cheese

Drain tuna and break it into large pieces. Cook onion and celery in butter until soft. Blend in flour. Add milk. Dissolve bouillon cubes in boiling water and add to onion-celery mixture. Cook and stir until thickened. Add cheese and tuna. Heat until cheese melts, stirring constantly.

Tuna, Carrot, Potato Chowder

1 7-ounce can tuna
½ cup chopped onion
2 tablespoons butter or other fat, melted
1½ cups boiling water
1 teaspoon salt
1 cup sliced carrots
1 cup diced potatoes
3 cups milk
2 tablespoons chopped parsley
¼ teaspoon paprika

Drain tuna. Break into pieces. Cook onion in butter until tender. Add boiling water, salt, carrots and potatoes. Simmer for 25 to 30 minutes or until vegetables are tender. Add milk, parsley and tuna. Heat. Garnish with paprika sprinkled over the top. Serves 6.

Tuna-Broccoli Cream Soup

1 7-ounce can tuna
1 10-ounce package frozen, chopped broccoli
3 tablespoons butter or other fat
2 tablespoons flour
1 teaspoon onion salt
Dash pepper
Dash nutmeg
1 quart milk
⅓ cup broccoli liquid or water

Drain tuna and break into pieces. Cook broccoli as directed on pack-

age; drain. Save liquid. Melt butter; blend in flour and seasonings. Add milk gradually and cook until mixture is thick and smooth, stirring constantly. Add broccoli, liquid and tuna; heat. Serves 6.

Salmon Chowder New Orleans

1 1-pound can salmon
1 chicken bouillon cube
1 cup boiling water
¾ cup chopped onion
½ cup chopped green pepper
1 clove garlic, finely chopped
¼ cup butter or other fat, melted
⅓ cup salmon liquid
1 1-pound can tomatoes
1 9-ounce can whole-kernel corn
1 cup sliced okra, fresh or frozen (optional)
½ teaspoon salt
¼ teaspoon thyme
⅛ teaspoon pepper
1 whole bay leaf

Drain salmon, reserving liquid. Break salmon into large pieces. Dissolve bouillon cube in boiling water. Cook onion, green pepper and garlic in butter until tender. Combine all ingredients and cook for 15 minutes, or until vegetables are tender. Remove bay leaf. Serve in hot soup dishes with crisp crackers. Serves 6 to 8.

Quick Salmon Chowder

1 1-pound can salmon
2 cans chicken gumbo soup
1 No. 2 can stewed tomatoes
½ cup water
1 8-ounce can whole kernel corn (optional)
⅓ cup salmon liquid
2 tablespoons butter

Drain salmon, reserving the liquid. Heat the 2 cans of chicken gumbo with the tomatoes and water. If desired, add the corn. Heat thoroughly, then stir in the salmon and liquid. Drop in the butter. Simmer for 2 minutes. Serves 6.

Shrimp Chowder

¾ pound cooked shrimp
¼ cup diced salt pork
1 large onion, chopped
1 cup chopped celery
4 medium potatoes, diced
1 teaspoon salt
¼ teaspoon pepper
2 cups boiling water
1 quart milk
2 tablespoons flour
2 tablespoons butter
Parsley and paprika

Cut shrimp into pieces. Set aside. Fry the pork in a deep kettle until crisp. Remove. Cook chopped onion and celery in the fat until soft. Add potatoes, salt, pepper and boiling water. Cook 15 minutes, then add the milk. Blend together the flour and butter and add to the mixture along with the shrimp. Cook and stir until slightly thickened. Serve in soup bowls. Sprinkle the chowder with minced parsley and paprika. Serves 6.

TIP: For *Shrimp-Tomato Chowder* substitute 2½ cups cooked strained tomatoes for the milk. Crumble oysterettes in the bottom of soup bowls and pour the chowder over them.

Easy Shrimp Chowder

1 cup cooked shrimp
¼ cup chopped onion
2 tablespoons butter or margarine

2 cans (10½ ounces each) condensed cream of celery soup
1 soup can milk
1 soup can water
2 tablespoons chopped parsley
Dash black pepper
Paprika, if desired

In a saucepan, cook onion in butter until tender. Blend in soup, milk and water and add shrimp, parsley and pepper. Heat thoroughly. Garnish each serving with paprika. Serves 6 to 8.

Shrimp Bisque

¾ pound cooked shrimp
3 tablespoons chopped onion
3 tablespoons chopped celery
4 tablespoons butter or other fat, melted
3 tablespoons flour
1½ teaspoons salt
⅛ teaspoon pepper
¼ teaspoon paprika
1 quart milk

Grind shrimp. Cook chopped onion and celery in butter. Blend in flour and seasonings. Add milk gradually and cook mixture until thick, stirring constantly. Add ground shrimp and heat. Garnish with chopped parsley, if desired. Serves 6.

Quick Shrimp Gumbo Soup

1 cup cooked shrimp
2 cans chicken gumbo soup
2 soup cans water
⅛ teaspoon salt
Dash pepper
Dash mace

Cut cooked shrimp into small pieces. Heat chicken gumbo soup. Add shrimp and seasonings. Serve in hot soup bowls with crisp crackers. Serves 6.

TIP: Other cooked seafoods may be used instead of shrimp. This is a real surprise and your family and guests will think you a real gourmet cook. Try it!

Jambalaya is sometimes served as a thick soup, and other times as a main dish with rice.

Shrimp Jambalaya

¾ pound cooked shrimp
¼ cup chopped bacon
3 tablespoons chopped onion
3 tablespoons chopped green pepper
1 clove garlic, finely minced
1 tablespoon flour
1 teaspoon salt
Dash cayenne
Dash paprika
½ teaspoon Worcestershire sauce
3 cups canned tomatoes with juice
2 cups cooked rice

Cut shrimp in half. Fry bacon until crisp. Add onion, green pepper and garlic; cook until tender. Blend in flour and seasonings; add tomatoes and cook until thick, stirring constantly. Stir in rice and shrimp; heat. Serves 6.

For a main dish meal reduce canned tomatoes to 2 cups.

Cold Shrimp-Avocado Soup

¾ pound cooked shrimp
2 tablespoons butter
3 tablespoons flour
1 cup milk

3 cups chicken broth (canned may be used)
1 tablespoon onion juice
½ cup cream
2 medium ripe avocados, mashed
Salt and pepper to taste
1 lemon

Cut shrimp crosswise into pieces. Melt butter, blend in flour. Add milk gradually; cook and stir until thickened. Add chicken broth, onion juice, cream and avocados. Season with salt and pepper. Chill. Serve cold garnished with wedges of lemon. Serves 6.

Quick Crab Soup

1 cup cooked white crabmeat, flaked
1 can condensed cream of celery soup
*1 can condensed cream of mushroom
  soup*
1 soup-can water
1 soup-can milk
Parsley
Paprika

Look over crabmeat and remove any shell particles. Combine soups and stir in the water and milk a little at a time. Heat to boiling point. Add crabmeat and heat again. Pour into soup bowls and place a pat of butter in each. Serve with minced parsley and paprika over the top if desired. Serves 6 to 8.

Sherried Crab Soup

½ pound cooked crabmeat
2 hard-cooked eggs
1 tablespoon butter or margarine
1 tablespoon flour
Grated peel of 1 lemon
Dash pepper

1 quart milk
½ cup cream
1 teaspoon Worcestershire sauce
1 teaspoon salt
¼ teaspoon pepper
¾ cup sherry

Look over crabmeat and remove any shell particles. Drain and set aside. Peel the hard-cooked eggs and mash to a paste using a fork. Add butter, flour, grated lemon peel and dash of pepper. Heat milk just to boiling point. Pour it gradually over the mashed egg mixture, blending it well. Return to heat and add crabmeat. Simmer for 5 minutes, add cream and bring just to boiling again, then add Worcestershire sauce, salt, pepper and sherry. Do not boil but heat thoroughly. Serve with crisp crackers or croutons. Enough for 6 to 8.

Corn-Crab Chowder

1 cup cooked crabmeat
¼ cup chopped bacon
½ cup diced onion
1 1-pound can cream-style corn
1 teaspoon salt
¼ teaspoon pepper
2 cups boiling water
2 cups milk
Paprika

Look over crabmeat and remove any shell particles. Cook bacon and remove it. Add onion to bacon drippings. When tender add other ingredients including crabmeat. Simmer chowder, but don't boil, for 12 minutes. Crumble bacon over top of soup and serve sprinkled with paprika. Serves 6.

Chili Crab Soup

2 cups cooked crabmeat
3 tablespoons butter or margarine
¼ cup chopped onion
½ cup chopped green pepper
2 1-pound cans tomatoes
1 cup canned okra
½ teaspoon salt
¼ teaspoon pepper
1 tablespoon chili powder

Look over crabmeat and remove any shell particles. Melt butter and cook onion and green pepper until soft. Add tomatoes with juice, okra, salt, pepper and chili powder. Simmer for 20 minutes or until tomatoes are cooked to pieces. Add crabmeat and heat again. Serve in hot soup bowls with golden croutons. Serves 6 to 8.

Golden Croutons

3 slices stale bread
¼ cup butter or margarine
Onion or garlic salt, optional

Trim crusts from bread and cut into ½-inch cubes. Melt butter in skillet. Add bread cubes and toss and stir until they are golden brown—about 5 minutes. Sprinkle with onion or garlic salt if desired. Makes 1½ cups.

Lobster Soup

¾ pound cooked lobster meat
1 teaspoon salt
¼ teaspoon paprika
⅛ teaspoon white pepper
Dash nutmeg
¼ cup butter or margarine, melted
1 pint milk
1 pint coffee cream
Minced parsley

Cut lobster meat into ½-inch pieces. Add seasonings and lobster meat to butter; heat. Add milk and cream and bring almost to boiling point. Garnish with parsley sprinkled over the top. Serves 6.

Lobster Gumbo

2 cups cooked lobster meat, cut into
    pieces
2 tablespoons bacon drippings
1 package frozen sliced okra
2 stalks celery, diced
1 small onion, minced
2 No. 2 cans stewed tomatoes (about
    4 cups)
2 tablespoons flour
2 teaspoons salt
½ teaspoon pepper
1 teaspoon garlic juice (optional)

Heat bacon drippings and add thawed okra, celery and onion. Sauté until soft but not brown. Add tomatoes and cook 5 minutes. Blend flour with a small amount of water and add to tomato mixture. Add seasonings and lobster. Simmer 5 minutes more.

Pour over mounds of fluffy cooked rice in hot soup bowls. Serves 6.

Lobster Stew

2 cups cooked lobster meat, in pieces
2 tablespoons butter
2 tablespoons flour
2 cups cream or 1 cup milk and 1
    cup cream
½ teaspoon salt
¼ teaspoon pepper
1 egg yolk (optional)

Melt butter and blend in flour. Add cream gradually, stirring constantly

and cooking until thick. Add salt, pepper and lobster. Heat thoroughly.

Beat egg yolk and stir some of the hot sauce into it. Stir it all back into stew. This makes the stew richer. Do not allow stew to boil after cream is added. Serves 4.

TIP: A dash of curry is a change-of-taste hint.

Basic Oyster Stew

1 pint small oysters
1 quart milk
4 tablespoons butter
1½ teaspoons salt
⅛ teaspoon pepper
Paprika
Oyster crackers

Heat milk and add oysters. Cook 3 to 4 minutes, or until edges of oysters curl. Do not allow to boil. Add butter and seasonings and heat. Serve garnished with oyster crackers over top. Serves 6.

Oyster Bisque I

1 pint oysters
1 slice onion
2 stalks celery
Sprig parsley
Bay leaf, small piece
1 quart milk
⅓ cup butter
⅓ cup flour
2 teaspoons salt
¼ teaspoon pepper

Drain oysters and chop. Add liquor, and heat slowly to boiling point. Add onion, celery, parsley and bay leaf to milk; scald; strain. Melt butter in top of double boiler and blend in flour, add milk and cook until thick, stirring constantly. Add oysters and seasonings and heat. Serve immediately with chopped parsley or paprika. Serves 6.

Oyster Bisque II

1 12-ounce frozen oysters, thawed,
  or 1 pint fresh oysters
1 cup oyster liquor
3 cups milk
1 cup light cream
¼ cup chopped celery
½ teaspoon onion salt
1 sprig parsley
1 bay leaf
⅓ cup melted butter or margarine
⅓ cup flour
¼ teaspoon pepper
½ teaspoon Tabasco sauce
Chopped chives

Drain oysters, reserving 1 cup liquor. Dice oysters and combine with liquor in a saucepan. Bring slowly to the boiling point. Remove from heat. Scald milk and cream, add celery, onion salt, parsley and bay leaf. Strain and reserve liquid. In a large saucepan, blend the butter with flour, pepper and Tabasco. Slowly stir in the scalded milk. Continue to cook and stir over low heat until thickened. Add oysters and liquor. Pour into soup bowls and garnish with chopped chives. Serve with oyster crackers. Serves 6 to 8.

Quick Oyster Bisque

1 pint oysters
1 pint cream
3 tablespoons flour
1 cup milk
Salt and pepper to taste

Mince oysters and drain, reserving liquor.

Heat cream in top of a double boiler. Blend flour into milk and add seasonings. Add this to cream and cook, stirring constantly until thickened. Add to sauce. Cook and stir for 10 minutes. Serve hot with crisp crackers. Serves 6.

Oyster Tomato Bisque

1 pint oysters
1 quart milk
1 slice onion
4 tablespoons butter
1 tablespoon flour
2½ teaspoons salt
¼ teaspoon pepper
1 can condensed tomato soup

Drain oysters and chop. Add liquor and heat slowly to boiling point. Scald milk with slice of onion. Melt butter in top of double boiler, blend in the flour, add milk, and cook until thick, stirring constantly. Add oysters, seasonings and tomato soup; heat to boiling point. Serve immediately with crackers or croutons. Serves 6.

Oyster Chowder

1 pint oysters
3 tablespoons onion, chopped
3 tablespoons butter
1 cup water
⅔ cup celery, diced
2 cups potatoes, diced
1 tablespoon salt
½ teaspoon pepper
1 quart milk
Parsley

Fry onion in butter until slightly brown. Add water, celery, potatoes, salt and pepper. Cover and cook until vegetables are tender. Add milk and let come to boiling point. Simmer oysters in their own liquor about 5 minutes or until edges curl. Drain. Combine with milk and vegetables. Serve immediately with chopped parsley sprinkled over the top. Serves 6.

Oyster-Clam Chowder

1 dozen each raw oysters and clams,
   chopped
3 tablespoons butter

1 tablespoon mixed chopped onion and
   1 garlic clove
3 cups light cream
1 teaspoon salt
Dash cayenne pepper
¼ cup chopped parsley

Drain oysters and clams, chop and set aside. In the butter saute onion and garlic until soft. Add oysters and clams, then the cream and seasonings. Bring to a boil but do not boil. Add chopped parsley, simmer and serve hot in individual bowls with oyster crackers. Serves 6.

Clam Chowders

✳

Boston Clam Chowder

3 dozen shucked soft-shell clams, with
   drained liquid
2 cups cold water
2 medium onions, sliced
¼ pound diced salt pork
2 tablespoons flour
½ teaspoon salt
¼ teaspoon pepper
2 cups diced potatoes
3 cups milk
1½ teaspoons salt
1 tablespoon butter or margarine

Cut off necks of clams and cut necks with scissors into fine pieces. Leave soft parts of clams whole. Place clams in saucepan with their own liquid. Add water and onions and bring to boil. Drain, reserving liquid.

In a large kettle sauté salt pork until brown. Add flour, salt and pepper and blend. Add reserved clam liquid and potatoes. Cover and cook 10 minutes, or until potatoes are soft. Add milk, remaining salt and butter. Heat. Serve hot in soup bowls. Serves 8.

Clam Chowder, Manhattan Style

1 pint clams
¼ cup chopped bacon or salt pork
½ cup chopped onion
½ cup chopped green pepper
1 cup chopped celery
1 cup combined clam liquor and water
1 cup diced potatoes
¼ teaspoon thyme
1 teaspoon salt
Dash pepper sauce or cayenne
2 cups tomato juice

Drain clams and save liquor. Chop clams. Fry bacon until lightly browned.

Add onion, pepper and celery and cook until tender. Add liquor, potatoes, seasonings and clams. Cook about 15 minutes, or until potatoes are tender. Add tomato juice and heat again. Serves 6.

Blue Sea New England Clam Chowder

1 pint clams
¼ cup chopped bacon or salt pork
¼ cup chopped onion
1 cup combined clam liquor and water
1 cup diced potatoes
½ teaspoon salt
Dash pepper
2 cups milk
Parsley

Drain clams and save liquor. Chop clams. Fry bacon until lightly browned. Add onion and cook until tender. Add liquor, potatoes, seasonings, and clams. Cook about 15 minutes or until potatoes are tender. Add milk and heat. Garnish with chopped parsley sprinkled over top. Serves 6.

Vichysoisse is a soup made of leeks or onions, potatoes, chicken stock, seasonings and the addition of seafoods if desired. It is served both hot and cold but usually cold. It originated at the French resort Vichy.

Blue Sea Scallop Vichyssoise

½ pound cooked scallops (see scallop section)
2 tablespoons butter
2 tablespoons flour
1 cup milk
3 cups chicken stock (bouillon or

canned broth may be used)
1 cup cooked cubed potatoes
½ cup cream
Chopped green onions or chives

Cut scallops in half. Combine butter and flour and add gradually to heated milk. Stir and cook until slightly thickened. Add chicken stock and potatoes with scallops. Heat again and stir in the cream last. Garnish with green onions or chives sprinkled over the top. Serves 6. This soup may be chilled and served cold.

Quick Scallop Vichyssoise

½ pound cooked scallops (see scallop section)
2 cans (10½ ounces each) frozen condensed cream of potato soup
1 pint milk
1 pint light cream
Salt and pepper to taste
Cut chives or chopped parsley

Cut large cooked scallops in half. Combine soup, milk, and cream and heat until soup is thawed. Add scallops and heat again. Serve from a heated soup tureen with chives or parsley sprinkled over the top. Serves 6.

Rich Scallop Soup

1 pound scallops
2 cups milk
1 cup heavy cream
2 tablespoons butter
2 teaspoons sugar
1½ teaspoons salt
¼ teaspoon pepper
1 teaspoon Worcestershire sauce
Paprika

Mix all ingredients, except scallops and paprika, in the top of a double boiler over boiling water. Heat thoroughly.

Chop scallops fine and add to cream mixture. Cook 7 minutes. Serve hot with paprika sprinkled over top. Pass crisp crackers. Serves 6.

TIP: Good with this is a crisp chopped tomato, celery, spring onion and lettuce salad and strawberry shortcake.

Scallop-Tomato Soup

1 pint of bay or ocean scallops, fresh
   or frozen
2 tablespoons butter or margarine
¼ cup minced onion
2 cans (10½ ounces each) tomato
   soup
2 cans water
2 bay leaves
1 teaspoon whole cloves
½ teaspoon salt
⅛ teaspoon pepper
⅓ cup dry cooking sherry

Rinse scallops in cool water. If large, cut crosswise into smaller pieces. Melt butter and sauté onion until soft. Add scallops, soup, water, bay leaves, cloves, salt and pepper.

Cover and simmer about 20 minutes. Remove bay leaves and cloves. Heat to boiling point. Add sherry just before serving. Serves 6.

Scallop Bisque

1 pound scallops, fresh or frozen
1 4-ounce can mushroom stems and
   pieces, drained
¼ cup butter or margarine, melted

½ teaspoon powdered mustard
1¼ teaspoons salt
⅛ teaspoon pepper
¼ cup flour
1 quart milk
Paprika

Thaw frozen scallops. Remove any shell particles and wash. Grind scallops and mushrooms. Combine butter, mustard, salt and pepper. Cook scallop mixture in seasoned butter for 3 to 4 minutes, stirring occasionally. Blend in flour. Add milk gradually and cook until thick, stirring constantly. Serve with paprika sprinkled over the top. Serves 6.

Mixed Seafood Chowder

1 pint oysters
1 cup scallops
1 cup clams
3 cups chicken broth or bouillon
1 cup cream or milk
3 tablespoons tapioca
3 egg yolks, slightly beaten
¼ teaspoon celery salt
¼ teaspoon mace
¼ teaspoon salt
⅛ teaspoon pepper

Drain oysters, reserving liquid. Cut scallops into 1-inch pieces. Drain clams, reserving liquid. In a saucepan place the oysters, scallops and clams. Pour in reserved liquid. Heat 5 to 6 minutes. Drain and reserve liquid.

Mix the liquid with the chicken broth and add cream. Bring to a boil. Blend a little of the cream with the tapioca and add. Stir some of the hot soup into the lightly beaten egg yolks, then return all to the soup mixture. Cook and stir over low heat 3 minutes. Add the oysters, scallops and clams. Stir in seasonings. Heat thoroughly. Serves 6.

SALADS

SALAD HINTS

Be sure to have greens and vegetables crisp. Wash as soon as possible after removing from grocery bag. Remove the outside leaves of lettuce and other salad greens. Drain and dry with an absorbent paper towel. Wrap in waxed paper and place in crisper of your refrigerator.

Peel carrots and other salad vegetables with potato peeler. Wrap in wax paper and place in crisper. The same goes for celery. If you wash and prepare as soon as you get home from the grocer's, you'll find salad making a real pleasure.

Seafoods for salads may be cooked in advance; some are marinated in French dressing and other sauces, if the recipe calls for it. When ready to mix the salad, cut the vegetables, fruits, meats, fish or shellfish into small pieces. Cabbage should be shredded finely and kept in ice water until ready to mix. Be sure to dry it quickly but thoroughly before using.

When planning your meals consider with care the salad and dessert. One or the other may be light. A heavy salad needs a light dessert like fresh fruit. Light salad needs a heavier dessert such as cake, pie and the like.

Chill salad plates icy cold for a real treat when serving summer salads. Chill plates in the crisper or lower shelf of the refrigerator. Cut tomatoes from stem down, in sections, instead of slicing around. This reduces bleeding.

Children like salads if everything is chopped finely. Remember that little hint. If you don't have a good sturdy chopping board, invest in one now.

Nearly all the recipes for seafood salads are good with other kinds of fish and shellfish than that indicated. The ingredients are interchangeable, so try the recipes with all seafoods.

Fish Flake and Cucumber Salad

2 cups cooked flaked fish
2 tablespoons chopped pimento
½ teaspoon salt
2 tablespoons lemon juice
1 cup diced cucumber
¼ cup chopped onion
Dash pepper
¼ cup mayonnaise

Combine all ingredients and serve very cold in crisp lettuce leaves. Serves 4 to 6.

Hot Potato-Fish Salad

1 cup cooked fish flakes or cooked
    chopped shrimp
2 cups hot mashed potatoes
¼ cup cream
2 tablespoons melted butter
¼ cup finely chopped onion
Salt and pepper to taste
2 egg yolks, beaten
3 teaspoons vinegar
1 teaspoon sugar

Add all ingredients to the hot mashed potatoes, blending well. Keep warm over hot water. Fold in cooked fish or shrimp. Garnish with pickled beets and celery tops. Serves 6.

This delicious hot salad may be served as a luncheon dish, or with other casserole dishes served buffet style.

Baked Fish Flake Salad

2 cups cooked fish flakes or crabmeat
⅔ cup mayonnaise
1 cup drained green peas
1 teaspoon salt
½ teaspoon black pepper
½ cup sliced stuffed olives
½ cup tomato sauce
½ cup grated American cheese

Flake cooked fish from bones and skin or use 1 7-ounce can of fish flakes. If crabmeat is used, look over and remove any shell particles. Flake lightly. Mix all other ingredients except cheese. Spoon mixture into a buttered shallow casserole and sprinkle cheese over the top. Bake in moderate oven, 350 F, 25 minutes. Serves 6.

Jellied Fish Salad

2 cups halibut flakes, or other fish
1 package lemon gelatine
1½ cups boiling water
¼ cup vinegar
½ teaspoon salt
1 cup grated carrot
¼ cup chopped green pepper
Lettuce
Mayonnaise or salad dressing

Dissolve gelatine in boiling water. Add vinegar and salt; chill until almost congealed. Fold in carrot, green pepper, and fish. Place in 6 individual molds; chill until firm. Unmold on lettuce; garnish with mayonnaise. Serves 6.

Fish Salad Ring

2 cups flaked fish
1 can (1 pound 4 ounces) crushed
    pineapple
2 packages lime gelatine
1½ cups boiling water
2 cups pineapple juice and water
¼ cup lemon juice
1 teaspoon salt
½ cup slivered toasted almonds
½ cup mayonnaise or salad dressing
1 teaspoon lemon juice
¼ teaspoon salt
Salad greens and radishes

Drain pineapple and save liquid. Dissolve gelatine in boiling water. Add pineapple juice and water, lemon juice and salt. Place in a 1-quart ring mold; chill until firm. Combine almonds, mayonnaise, lemon juice, salt, pineapple and fish. Chill. Unmold ring on salad greens and fill center with fish mixture. Garnish with radishes. Serves 6.

Fish Flake or Tuna Aspic

1 cup fish flakes or drained tuna
1 package lemon gelatine
1⅔ cups tomato juice
¼ cup tarragon vinegar
¾ teaspoon grated onion
1 teaspoon salt
¼ teaspoon paprika
¼ teaspoon cayenne pepper

Empty package of gelatine into a large bowl. Heat tomato juice to boiling point. Pour it over gelatine and stir until dissolved. Add other ingredients except fish. Cool.

Grease a mold and line it with half of the fish flakes. Pour half of tomato aspic mixture over flakes and allow it to set. Then add the rest of fish in a layer and the aspic. Chill until set.

When congealed turn mold over large plate or platter, unmold and serve with homemade mayonnaise or ½ cup sour cream mixed with 2 tablespoons mayonnaise. Serve on watercress or lettuce. Garnish with hard-cooked eggs, sliced, and stuffed olives. Serves 6.

Easy Tuna Aspic

1 7-ounce can tuna
1 tablespoon lemon juice
¼ teaspoon salt
1 3-ounce package lemon gelatine
1½ cups hot water
1 8-ounce can spaghetti sauce with
    mushrooms
Salt and pepper

Drain and flake tuna. Sprinkle with lemon juice and salt. Set aside.

Dissolve gelatine in hot water. Add other ingredients, testing for right amount of salt and pepper. Pour into molds or a glass dish and chill. When partly firm, add the tuna mixture. Stir and return to refrigerator until firm. Unmold on crisp lettuce, or garnish with other salad greens. Serves 6.

Tuna Christmas Salad

2 7-ounce cans tuna
1 cup diced unpeeled apples
½ cup chopped celery
¼ cup chopped walnuts or pecans
Dash salt
½ cup mayonnaise or salad dressing

Drain and flake tuna. Combine all ingredients and mix lightly. Chill and serve on crisp lettuce. Serves 6.

TIP: If made in advance, sprinkle the chopped apple with 1 tablespoon lemon juice to keep it from turning dark. This salad is good any day in the year, but during Christmas shopping it comes in mighty handy for a quick luncheon dish.

Country Kitchen Tuna Salad

1 7-ounce can tuna
½ cup chopped celery
1 medium-size cucumber, peeled and
    chopped
½ cup chopped stuffed olives
2 hard-cooked eggs, chopped
1 tablespoon tarragon vinegar
1 teaspoon prepared horseradish
Salad dressing to moisten

Mix all the ingredients, tossing with the salad dressing last. Serve on crisp lettuce leaves garnished with sliced ripe tomatoes. Serves 6.

Easy Salmon Salad

1 1-pound can salmon
½ cup chopped celery
½ small green pepper, chopped
1 medium-sized cucumber, pared and
    chopped
½ cup mayonnaise
2 tablespoons lemon juice
1 teaspoon grated onion
Lettuce and tomato slices

Drain salmon and flake into large pieces, removing small bones and skin. Combine with celery, green pepper and cucumber. Blend mayonnaise with lemon juice and onion. Toss with salmon mixture. Chill in refrigerator and when ready to serve, place in a salad bowl lined with lettuce and garnish with tomato slices. Serves 6.

Salmon Slaw Vinaigrette

1 can salmon, 7¾ ounce
½ medium-size cabbage
2 hard-cooked eggs, finely minced
¼ cup minced onion
2 tablespoons chopped parsley
    (optional)

Chill cabbage and shred it. Drain salmon and flake it. Combine cabbage, eggs, onion, parsley and salmon. At serving time, pour *Vinaigrette Sauce* over the salmon mixture and toss thoroughly. Serves 6.

VINAIGRETTE SAUCE

6 tablespoons olive oil
2 tablespoons vinegar
1 teaspoon salt
½ teaspoon dry mustard
2 tablespoons capers and juice
¼ teaspoon pepper

Combine all the ingredients, mix well, and let stand at room temperature as long as possible before using.

Tomatoes Stuffed
with Smoked Salmon Salad

1 7-ounce can smoked salmon or red
  salmon
2 hard-cooked eggs, chopped
¾ cup chopped celery
¼ cup peeled chopped cucumber
1 tablespoon minced onion
2 tablespoons chopped parsley
  (optional)
1 tablespoon lemon juice or 1½ teaspoons lime juice
⅓ cup salad dressing
6 medium-size tomatoes
¼ teaspoon salt

If smoked salmon is used, flake with a fork. Canned red salmon should be drained. Combine all ingredients except tomatoes and salt. Remove the centers from tomatoes by cutting them downward into sixths to the stem, but not all the way through. Salt tomatoes and fill with the salmon salad. Serve on crisp lettuce leaves. Serves 6.

SARDINE SALAD TIPS

- Add 1 can of sardines, coarsely broken, to a tossed salad, using French dressing instead of mayonnaise to bind.
- With spring salad vegetables, such as sliced tomatoes, green onions, radishes, etc., arrange two large sardines on each portion.
- A salad bowl of 2 cans sardines, chilled, 4 hard-cooked eggs, sliced, 8 pieces of sharp cheese and crisp salad greens will whet the appetite and it's so good with Russian dressing.

Sardine Tossed Salad

1 can (3¼ ounces) sardines
½ cup grated carrot
¼ cup chopped dill pickles
1 tablespoon minced onion
2 cups shredded lettuce
¼ cup French dressing
1 clove garlic

Break the sardines into pieces. Rub bowl with cut clove of garlic. Combine all the other ingredients and toss lightly until mixed. Serves 4.

TIP: Add sardines to your favorite potato salad with 2 cups diced, canned beets, for a Bohemian salad.

Maine Sardine
Red and Green Slaw

2 cans (3¼ ounces each) Maine
  sardines
2 slices bacon, diced
2 tablespoons minced onion
1 tablespoon flour
1 teaspoon dry mustard
2 tablespoons vinegar
½ cup water
2½ cups shredded red cabbage
2½ cups shredded green cabbage
½ cup diced green pepper
Salt and pepper
Lime or lemon

Fry diced bacon until crisp. Remove bacon and reserve. Add onion to bacon fat and cook slowly for one minute. Remove from heat. Stir in flour and mustard and add vinegar and water, mixing thoroughly. Cook mixture until slightly thickened. Cool dressing.

Combine cabbage, pepper, bacon and 1 can of sardines. Pour the dressing over slaw. Season to taste with salt and pepper. Garnish with remaining sardines and lime or lemon slices. Serves 4.

Sardine Potato Salad

2 cans sardines, 3¼ ounces each
½ cup sour cream
1 teaspoon prepared mustard
1½ teaspoons salt
⅛ teaspoon pepper
4 cups cold, diced, cooked potatoes
3 hard-cooked eggs
1 cup chopped celery
2 tablespoons minced onion

Mash one can of the sardines and add next 4 ingredients, mixing thoroughly. Set dressing aside.

Mix the potatoes with 2 of the eggs, chopped. (Slice the other egg for garnish.) Mix celery and onion with the potatoes and eggs. Toss with the sardine-sour-cream dressing. Chill and serve garnished with the other can of sardines and the sliced egg. Serves 6.

TIP: For a Bohemian-style salad, add 1 cup chopped canned beets.

Smoked Fish Salad I

1½ pounds smoked mullet or other fish

1 medium-size apple, peeled and cubed
2 tablespoons minced onion
4 small cooked beets, cubed
2 medium potatoes, cooked and cubed
2 tablespoons minced sweet pickles
2 tablespoons vinegar
¼ teaspoon freshly ground pepper
½ cup sour cream
2 tablespoons salad dressing

Bone, skin and cube smoked fish. Lightly mix with other ingredients. Toss last with sour cream and salad dressing (or use all salad dressing). Season to taste. Serves 8.

TIP: Serve with fresh green beans, citrus salad and strawberry-gelatine dessert.

Smoked Fish Salad II

1 pound smoked mullet or other fish, cut into strips
2 cups diced cooked potatoes
1 tablespoon minced onion
1 tablespoon minced scallions
2 tablespoons capers, drained
¼ cup olive oil
2 tablespoons tarragon vinegar
1 teaspoon prepared mustard
⅛ teaspoon salt
Freshly ground black pepper

Mix with care the fish, potatoes, onion, scallions and capers. Make a dressing with the olive oil and other ingredients, stirring well. Pour over the fish mixture and toss lightly. Chill. Serves 6.

TIP: Serve with green beans cooked with small white onions, sliced tomatoes and chocolate mousse.

Basic Shrimp Salad

2 cups cooked shrimp
1 cup diced celery
Salt and pepper to taste
Mayonnaise
Sweet green pepper

Shell and devein the shrimp. Pull them to pieces with a fork. Save several whole for garnish. Mix ingredients with enough mayonnaise to bind together. Place on shredded lettuce. Garnish with strips of the pepper and whole shrimp. Serves 4.

Blue Sea Shrimp Salad

1½ pounds raw shrimp
1 lemon, sliced
1 teaspoon salt
½ cup French dressing
1 cup diced celery
½ cup mayonnaise
½ teaspoon ground mustard
Salt and pepper to taste

Shell and devein shrimp. Add lemon and salt to enough boiling water to cover shrimp. Put in shrimp and when water comes to a boil again, remove from heat, cover and let shrimp remain in water for about 5 minutes. Drain and while shrimp are warm pour over them the French dressing. Set aside to cool. Then toss together with the remaining ingredients.

Place in refrigerator to chill. Serve on lettuce. Serves 6.

TIP: Serve with this salad string beans, pickled beets and hard rolls; for dessert, toasted pound cake topped with fresh peaches and whipped cream.

Garlic Shrimp Salad

1 pound cooked shrimp, shelled and
  deveined
¾ cup thin French dressing
6 cloves garlic, quartered
¼ cup ripe olives, pitted and halved
4 hard-cooked eggs
Salad greens or
Young spinach leaves (optional)

Mix the French dressing with the garlic and ripe olives. Set aside for 3 hours or more. Refrigerate shrimp. Cook the eggs. Shell and chop when cool. Tear pieces of salad greens into bowl. If fresh spinach is available use tiny leaves for this purpose. Over spinach scatter the shrimp and eggs. Pour the French dressing over all and toss. Serves 6.

Shrimp Salad with Hard-Cooked Eggs

1 pound cooked shrimp
2 tablespoons lemon juice
½ cup diced celery
2 hard-cooked eggs
½ cup mayonnaise
¼ teaspoon Tabasco sauce
Salt
Pepper
¼ teaspoon monosodium glutenate
Tomato slices

Chill and moisten shrimp with lemon juice. Combine with other ingredients. Season to taste. Serve on lettuce with tomato slices. Serves 6.

Golden Shrimp Salad

1 cup cooked shrimp
½ cup mayonnaise
2 tablespoons lime or lemon juice
½ teaspoon prepared mustard
2 hard-cooked eggs, chopped
1½ cups coarsely grated carrots
1 tablespoon minced onion
1 teaspoon salt
⅛ teaspoon pepper
*1 tablespoon celery seeds (soak 10
   to 15 minutes before using in
   1 tablespoon vinegar)*
Crisp lettuce

Blend mayonnaise with lime juice and mustard. Add shrimp, eggs, carrots and onion. Toss well with seasonings. Arrange lettuce on plates and spoon salad in the middle. Serves 6.

Shrimp Pecan Salad

1½ pounds medium shrimp
¼ cup thin French dressing
1 cup diced celery
2 hard-cooked eggs, chopped or sliced
¼ cup chopped pecans
Mayonnaise
Lettuce
Tomatoes
Sweet gherkin pickles

Shell and devein shrimp. Boil 3 minutes in salted water. Drain and pour over shrimp the French dressing. Set aside for 30 minutes.

   Mix with celery, eggs and pecans. Moisten all with mayonnaise. Serve on lettuce with quartered tomatoes and whole sweet gherkin pickles. Serves 6.

Citrus-Shrimp Salad with Tarragon-Ginger Dressing

1 cup cooked shrimp
1 large grapefruit
2 oranges
1 ripe avocado
Salad greens

Shell and devein shrimp. Peel citrus fruits and cut into sections. Peel avocado, remove seed and cut into slices. Sprinkle with lemon juice to prevent avocado turning dark.

   Mix all ingredients together. Toss with mixed chopped salad greens. Serve with *Tarragon-Ginger Dressing*. Serves 6.

TARRAGON-GINGER DRESSING

½ cup salad oil
4 tablespoons lemon juice
4 tablespoons tarragon vinegar
½ teaspoon powdered ginger
½ teaspoon salt

Combine in a jar, close lid tight and shake to combine flavors. About 1 cup dressing.

Shrimp-Apple Salad

3 cups cooked chopped shrimp
2 cups diced celery
1 apple, chopped
1 teaspoon salt
¾ cup Curry French Dressing
Salad greens

Combine all ingredients except *Curry French Dressing* and greens. Chill in refrigerator. Add dressing and serve on greens. Serves 6.

TIP: Serve *Shrimp-Apple Salad* with broiled pears sprinkled with ginger, slices of pineapple and peaches, on sauce dish.

CURRY FRENCH DRESSING

⅔ cup salad or olive oil
3 tablespoons vinegar
⅛ teaspoon salt
⅛ teaspoon white pepper
1 teaspoon curry powder

Beat all ingredients until well blended. Makes about ¾ cup.

Citrus-Shrimp Salad with Sour-Cream Dressing

1 pound cooked shrimp, shelled and deveined
2 oranges
1 grapefruit
1 No. 2 can pineapple chunks
1 ripe avocado
Lettuce

If shrimp are large, cut in bite-size pieces. Peel and divide in sections oranges and grapefruit. Drain pineapple chunks. Peel and slice avocado thin, then cut slices into smaller pieces. Set fruits and shrimp aside until you prepare *Sour Cream Dressing.*

Place fruits and shrimp on a bed of chopped lettuce and pour over the chilled dressing. Serves 6.

SOUR-CREAM DRESSING

1 cup sour cream
2 tablespoons orange juice (drained from orange sections)
1 tablespoon lime or lemon juice
⅛ teaspoon salt

Combine ingredients. Chill. Serves 6.

Grapefruit-Shrimp on Half Shell

Wash and cut grapefruit in half. Cut around each section, loosening from membrane, lift out. Cut around entire outer edge of fruit and underneath core and remove membrane. Return half the fruit with equal amount of cooked small shrimp. Serve with *Sauce Orlando.*

SAUCE ORLANDO

¼ cup butter or margarine
¼ cup chili sauce
3 tablespoons vinegar
1 teaspoon Worcestershire sauce
⅛ teaspoon salt
¼ teaspoon Tabasco

Combine all ingredients except Tabasco in saucepan. Bring to a boil over medium heat, stirring constantly. Remove from heat and stir in Tabasco. Serve hot or cold over grapefruit. Makes ¾ cup.

Florida Shrimp-Citrus Salad

*1 cup grapefruit sections (canned
    may be used)
1 cup orange sections
1 cup cooked shrimp
Lettuce
¼ cup French dressing
Ripe olives
Avocado slices*

Mix drained grapefruit and orange
sections with shrimp. Cut lettuce into
thin shreds. Toss with grapefruit and
orange sections, pouring on the French
dressing. Garnish with ripe olives and
avocado slices.

Shrimp Salad Vinaigrette

*1 pound small cooked shrimp (cut
    large shrimp in half)
2 tablespoons vinegar
4 tablespoons olive oil
1 teaspoon Dijon mustard
    (horseradish mustard)
¼ teaspoon salt and ⅛ teaspoon
    pepper*

Mix all dressing ingredients and pour
over shelled, deveined, cooked shrimp.
Chill in refrigerator. Serve with sliced
hard-cooked eggs and a spoonful of
mayonnaise. Delicious in halved avocados. Enough for 4.

*This is a delightful taste-tempter. Be
sure to shave the cabbage fine after
chilling.*

Partytime Shrimp-Coleslaw Salad

*3 to 4 cups shaved white cabbage
1 to 1½ cups cooked shrimp, small
    or cut into pieces*

*½ cup mayonnaise
¼ cup lemon juice
1 teaspoon salt
⅛ teaspoon white pepper*

Mix the cabbage with shrimp in a
large bowl. Combine mayonnaise,
lemon juice, salt and white pepper in
a small bowl. Toss with the cabbage-
shrimp mixture. Delicious with a seafood dinner. Serves 4 to 6.

French Shrimp Salad

*¾ pound cooked shrimp, shelled
    and deveined
¼ cup thin French dressing
1 cup chopped celery
½ teaspoon salt
⅛ teaspoon pepper
3 tablespoons mayonnaise
Salad greens*

Cook shrimp, then drain. While still
warm pour the French dressing over
them. When cool add other ingredients except mayonnaise and let stand
10 minutes. Drain if excess dressing is
in bowl. Toss shrimp mixture with the
mayonnaise. Chill and serve on salad
greens. Serves 6.

Curried Shrimp-Rice Salad

*1 cup cooked shrimp, chopped
3 cups cooked cold rice
1 cup chopped celery
¼ cup chopped green pepper
1 teaspoon instant onion
1 teaspoon curry powder
½ teaspoon dry mustard
¾ teaspoon salt
⅛ teaspoon pepper
¾ cup mayonnaise
2 tablespoons lemon juice
1 9-ounce can crushed pineapple,
    drained*

Mix together shrimp, rice, celery and green pepper. Mix the instant onion, curry powder, mustard, salt and pepper with mayonnaise. Stir in lemon juice. Toss the shrimp mixture with the mayonnaise mixture. Add pineapple last, folding in until well mixed. Serve on lettuce leaves with salted nuts sprinkled over top, if desired. Serves 6.

Cucumber-Shrimp Boats

2 large cucumbers
1 pound cooked shrimp
1 tablespoon fresh lime juice
½ cup chopped celery
2 teaspoons capers
1 tablespoon grated lemon rind
1 teaspoon salt
½ teaspoon white pepper
1 cup sour cream

Split cucumbers in half, lengthwise. Scoop out centers, leaving about ⅛ inch of peel. Chop and mix scooped out portion with other ingredients, tossing with sour cream. Spoon mixture back into cucumber shells. Serve on crisp lettuce. Serves 6.

TIP: With this delicious dinner salad, serve baked potatoes, green peas, clover leaf rolls and chocolate cake.

Shrimp-Cucumber Mold

1½ pounds cooked shrimp
2 cucumbers
2 tablespoons grated onion
1 tablespoon wine vinegar
2 envelopes gelatine
4 tablespoons water
¼ teaspoon salt
¼ teaspoon pepper

Set cleaned, cooked shrimp aside. Grate cucumbers, rind and all. Add grated onion and vinegar. Dissolve gelatine in the water. Melt it over hot water. Add to cucumber mixture and stir in salt and pepper. Pour into a greased ring mold. When set unmold on lettuce or other greens and fill center with boiled, spiced shrimp. Serve this dressing. Serves 6.

½ cup sour cream
½ teaspoon salt
⅛ teaspoon pepper
1½ teaspoon sugar
1 teaspoon tarragon vinegar
⅛ teaspoon prepared mustard

Mix all ingredients well. Chill before serving. Makes ½ cup.

Lemon-Shrimp Mold

1 cup cooked shrimp
2 chicken bouillon cubes
1 package lemon gelatine
1 cup boiling water
2 tablespoons tarragon vinegar
½ teaspoon salt
⅛ teaspoon ground ginger
1 cup thick cream
½ cup chopped cucumber, with rind
¼ cup chopped green pepper
2 tablespoons chopped green onions

Shell and devein the cooked shrimp. Cut into pieces, reserving several whole shrimp for garnish. Soften gelatine in a little water. Dissolve bouillon cubes and gelatine in boiling water. Add vinegar, salt and ginger. Chill until almost congealed. Add cream and beat until smooth. Add other ingredients, stirring in shrimp last. Pour into greased mold and chill until firm. Garnish with parsley sprigs and the whole shrimp. Serves 6 to 8.

Jellied Shrimp

1 pound cooked, peeled shrimp
1 No. 2 can tomatoes
1 tablespoon minced onion
3 whole cloves
1 teaspoon salt
½ teaspoon black pepper
1 tablespoon sugar
2 envelopes unflavored gelatine
½ cup cold water
½ cup boiling water
½ stuffed olives

Boil tomatoes with onion, cloves, salt, pepper and sugar for 15 minutes, then strain. Soak gelatine in cold water, add boiling water and stir until dissolved. Add strained tomato mixture. Arrange half the cooked shrimp in the bottom of a mold alternately with half the olives. Cover with a little of the liquid and set in refrigerator to congeal. Remove from refrigerator and add remaining shrimp, olives and gelatine mixture. Chill. To serve, remove from mold onto a bed of lettuce and garnish with thin cucumbers and mayonnaise.

This salad is delightful for a luncheon or buffet party. Serve it with sweet pickles. Tomato juice sparked with lemon and grated onion is also good with it.

Shrimp 'n' Ripe Olive Aspic

¾ pound cooked, peeled, deveined
   shrimp, fresh or frozen
¾ cup pitted ripe olives
2 tablespoons unflavored gelatine
½ cup cold tomato juice
1½ cups boiling tomato juice

2 tablespoons chopped sweet pickle
1 tablespoon lemon or lime juice
2 teaspoons horseradish
1 teaspoon grated onion
½ teaspoon salt
⅛ teaspoon pepper

Thaw shrimp if frozen (cooked). Cut large shrimp in half. Slice olives crosswise. Soften gelatine in cold tomato juice for 5 minutes. Add boiling tomato juice and stir until dissolved. Add the next 6 ingredients, shrimp, and ripe olives. Pour into an oiled mold and chill until firm. Unmold and garnish with additional shrimp and ripe olives. Serve with mayonnaise if desired. Serves 6.

Ruby Shrimp Ring

1 pound cooked shrimp, shelled and
   deveined
2 cups cranberries
1½ cups cold water
1 cup sugar
1 tablespoon unflavored gelatine
¼ teaspoon salt
½ cup chopped pecans
¾ cup diced celery
Pineapple slices

Wash cranberries and add 1 cup cold water. Cook until tender. Add sugar and simmer for 5 minutes. Soften gelatine in ½ cup cold water. Dissolve in hot cranberries. Add salt.

Chill until mixture begins to thicken. Add nuts and celery and mix thoroughly. Pour into oiled ring mold, chill until firm. Unmold on large round salad plate. Place lettuce leaves around salad. Arrange shrimp in center. Garnish with pineapple slices. Spoon dressing on half mayonnaise and half sour cream in center. Top with a ripe olive. Serves 8.

CRABMEAT SALADS

You can use cooked crabmeat in salads calling for shrimp, lobster and flaked fish, as well as those specifically naming crabmeat. Used plain or with sauces and condiments crabmeat is hard to beat. Try it for cocktails and appetizers. For information on buying and preparing crabmeat, see that section.

✳

Crab and Mixed Greens with Curry Dressing

Wash and cut in bite-size pieces mixed salad greens (may use packaged). Crisp in refrigerator until ready to serve. Then mix lightly with 1 can (2 cups) cooked crabmeat. Toss with *Curry French Dressing.* Serves 6 to 8. Use about 2 cups of cut salad greens. Recipe for the dressing is given with *Shrimp-Apple Salad.*

Crabmeat-Green Salad

2 cups fresh crabmeat
Salt and pepper
Lime juice
¼ cup sour cream
1 cup mayonnaise
2 tablespoons chopped parsley
2 tablespoons tarragon vinegar
1 clove garlic
Salad greens
Tomatoes or radishes

Pick over crabmeat and remove any shell particles and connective tissue. Sprinkle meat with salt, pepper, and lime juice. Set aside. Blend together sour cream, mayonnaise. Add chopped parsley, tarragon vinegar, and the peeled and crushed clove of garlic.

Chop lettuce, romaine and other favorite greens in salad bowl. Spoon crabmeat over it and top with the dressing. Garnish with quartered tomatoes or radish roses. Serves 6.

Crabmeat Salad with Capers

2 cups cooked crabmeat
1 cup celery
2 tablespoons lemon juice
2 tablespoons capers
1 teaspoon salt
½ teaspoon pepper
½ cup mayonnaise

Look over crabmeat and remove any shell particles. Combine with other ingredients. Chill and serve on lettuce, garnished with quartered tomatoes. Serves 6.

Crab and Avocado Salad with Special Salad Dressing

2 cups crabmeat
6 cooked artichoke hearts
6 tablespoons French dressing
3 large avocados
½ teaspoon salt
Special salad dressing (below)
1 pimento
2 tomatoes

Marinate artichoke hearts for an hour in the French dressing. Peel avocados and cut in half with a sharp knife, making a sawtooth edge. Remove pits. Mix crabmeat with salt and special dressing. Place one artichoke heart in each half of avocado. Surround with crabmeat. Arrange each avocado in a bed of crisp lettuce. Top with strips of pimento. Surround with small wedges of tomato. Serves 6.

DRESSING: Mix together the following:

1 cup mayonnaise
1 tablespoon finely chopped green
  pepper
2 teaspoons grated onion
3 tablespoons lemon juice
1 teaspoon Worcestershire sauce

Crab-Cantaloupe Salad

2 cups cooked crabmeat
1 teaspoon lemon juice
1 cup cooked rice
1 cup peeled, diced cantaloupe
1 cup light cream
1 teaspoon salt
⅛ teaspoon white pepper

Look over crabmeat and remove any shell particles. Sprinkle with lemon juice. Combine with other ingredients and mix lightly. Serve chilled on crisp lettuce. Serves 6.

Crab-Stuffed Oranges

2 cups cooked crabmeat
3 oranges
1 teaspoon salt
⅛ teaspoon white pepper
2 tablespoons lemon juice
½ cup homemade mayonnaise
Hard-cooked egg yolk

Prepare oranges as follows: Cut in half crosswise. With a sharp knife, or a scissors, cut around edges and clip at bottom to remove all pulp. Decorate shells by cutting a fluted design around tops. Turn upside down on absorbent paper to drain.

Mix crabmeat with salt, white pepper, lemon juice and ½ cup of orange sections removed from shells, and toss all with ½ cup homemade mayonnaise. Spoon into orange shells and sprinkle over the top grated hard-cooked egg yolk. Serves 6.

This pickled fish dish is served often in South America. Sometimes very small scallops, crab or red snapper are used. It is good with cocktails or as a salad and even as a first course, when whole-kernel corn and avocado may be added to the sauce.

Seviche
(Pickled Fish)

1½ pounds lemon sole, or other
  white fish
1 cup fresh lime juice
½ cup Spanish olive oil
¼ cup finely minced onion
¼ cup finely chopped parsley
2 tablespoons finely chopped, peeled,
  canned green chilis
1 minced clove garlic
1½ teaspoons salt
1 teaspoon freshly ground black
  pepper
6 drops Tabasco sauce
Fresh coriander (optional)

Cut fish into strips, then cover with the lime juice and let stand in the refrigerator 4 to 5 hours. Drain. Blend all the remaining ingredients and toss with the fish strips. Chill. Serve with chopped *cialantro* (fresh coriander) as a garnish. Serves 6.

Crab-Nut Salad

2 cups crabmeat, white or claw
1 cup sliced celery
1 cup nuts
¼ cup chili sauce
⅔ cup mayonnaise
2 tablespoons lemon juice
1 avocado
2 tablespoons lemon juice

Combine crab, celery and nuts. In a small bowl mix other ingredients, except avocado and extra lemon juice. Just before serving, peel, pit and slice avocado, pouring lemon juice over it. Serve salad on crisp lettuce with avocado slices around the edges.

Crab claws are a real delicacy. They are marketed like cooked crabmeat, fresh or frozen, in metal containers. They are packed tightly, and used in cocktails or as appetizers they serve 8 to 12.

Crab Luncheon Salad: Crab Claws and Citrus

1 large grapefruit
1 pound fresh cocktail crab claws
Salad greens
Special Dressing

Peel and section grapefruit. Drain. Wash and dry salad greens. Arrange a bed of greens on each plate and top with sections of grapefruit and crab claws or cooked crabmeat. Serve with Special Dressing:

SPECIAL DRESSING

1 cup mayonnaise
¼ cup chili sauce
2 tablespoons finely chopped onion

2 tablespoons chopped sweet pickle
1 tablespoon lemon juice
2 tablespoons finely chopped green pepper

Mix all ingredients and chill well before serving. Serves 6.

Quick Crabmeat Tangy

2 cups cooked crabmeat
¾ cup garlic French dressing
½ cup chopped celery
¼ cup chopped stuffed olives
Mayonnaise

Look over crabmeat and remove any shell particles or connective tissue. Put in a bowl and pour the French dressing over crabmeat. Allow to stand for 15 minutes or longer. When ready to serve toss with the celery and olives, using enough mayonnaise to bind. Serves 6.

Greek Crabmeat-Olive Salad

2 cups cooked crabmeat
⅓ cup olive oil
3 tablespoons tarragon vinegar
1 tablespoon lime juice
1 tablespoon chopped parsley
½ cup minced onion
1 teaspoon ground mustard
1 teaspoon salt
¼ teaspoon pepper

Place crabmeat in a shallow bowl, rubbed first with a cut clove of garlic. Mix other ingredients thoroughly and pour over the crabmeat. Chill and serve to 6.

Crab Flake Salad

2 cups cooked crabmeat
1 cup mayonnaise
1 cup chopped celery
1 cup chopped cucumbers
2 hard-boiled eggs, diced
2 tablespoons chopped sweet pickle
2 tablespoons lemon juice
½ teaspoon salt

Drain and flake crabmeat. Mix the mayonnaise with crab flakes, celery, cucumbers, eggs, sweet pickles, lemon juice and salt. Chill in refrigerator. Serve in large bowl lined with lettuce. Top with mayonnaise. Serve at once. Serves 8.

Marinated Crabmeat

1 pound cooked crabmeat
2 cups celery, sliced thinly
⅓ cup salad oil
¼ cup dry white wine
¼ teaspoon Tabasco sauce
¼ teaspoon salt
¼ teaspoon thyme
Hard crisp celery head
½ cup mayonnaise

Remove any shell particles from crabmeat. Mix with celery, in a bowl. Combine salad oil, wine, Tabasco, salt and thyme. Pour over crabmeat and celery and mix with two forks, so as not to shred crabmeat too finely. Just before serving cut up hard crisp celery head. Mix with crabmeat mixture and mayonnaise. Serves 6 to 8.

Hot Crab Salad

2 cups cooked crabmeat
5 tablespoons melted butter or
  margarine

½ teaspoon dry mustard
⅛ teaspoon salt
1 teaspoon paprika
½ teaspoon pepper
2 tablespoons tarragon vinegar

Melt butter in large skillet. Add all seasonings. When bubbly stir in the crabmeat. Toss until heated thoroughly. Delicious served with sesame seed crackers or rolls. Serves 6.

Black Cherry-Crabmeat Salad

½ pound cooked crabmeat
1 package cherry gelatine
2 cups cherry juice and water
2 cups cooked black cherries, drained
1 cup chopped pecan meats
8 stuffed olives, chopped

Heat cherry juice and water. Pour over gelatine, stir until dissolved. Chill until it begins to thicken. Stir in other ingredients and chill until firm in a mold.
   Unmold and serve on lettuce with mayonnaise. Serves 8.

Crabmeat and Stuffed Olive Mold

2 cups cooked de luxe crabmeat
1 tablespoon unflavored gelatine
¼ cup cold water
2 tablespoons lime juice
2 tablespoons water
1 teaspoon salt
⅛ teaspoon each paprika and pepper
¼ cup chopped stuffed olives
1 cup heavy cream
Cranberry sauce
Hard-cooked eggs
Salad greens

Mix gelatine in cold water. Place over hot water until dissolved. Stir into combined lime juice-water and add seasonings. Chill until partly set.

Pick over crabmeat for any shell or bony tissue. Mix chopped olives with crabmeat and blend in when gelatine is partly set. Whip cream and fold into crab mixture. Pour into oiled mold and chill until firm. Serve garnished with whole cranberry sauce and hard-cooked halved eggs on crisp salad greens. Serves 6.

Holiday Crabmeat Mold

2 cups cooked crabmeat (white)
1 envelope or 1 tablespoon unflavored
   gelatine
½ cup cold water
½ teaspoon salt
¼ teaspoon white pepper
¼ teaspoon paprika
1 teaspoon prepared mustard
2 eggs, beaten
1 cup coffee cream
¼ cup lime juice
½ cup chopped celery
¼ cup ripe, seeded olives, sliced

Look over crabmeat and remove any shell particles and connective tissue. Soften gelatine in cold water. In top of double boiler over hot, but not boiling water, combine seasonings, eggs and cream. Cook, stirring constantly, until mixture thickens.

Remove from heat and add gelatine, stirring until dissolved. Let mixture partially set, then sprinkle 1 tablespoon of lime juice over crabmeat. Mix. Fold crabmeat, celery, olives and remaining lime juice into gelatine mixture. Pour into mold. Chill. When set, unmold on salad greens and garnish with jellied cranberry sauce cut into cubes. Pass crisp saltines. Serves 8.

Crabmeat Mousse

2 cups cooked flaked crabmeat
1 tablespoon gelatine
¼ cup cold water
½ cup boiling water
½ cup chopped celery
2 tablespoons stuffed olives
1 tablespoon grated onion
1 teaspoon prepared mustard
½ teaspoon salt
Dash paprika
1 hard-cooked egg, chopped
½ cup whipping cream
¼ cup mayonnaise

Soften gelatine in cold water for 5 minutes. Add boiling water and stir until dissolved. Add next 6 ingredients. Chill until almost congealed. Add chopped egg and crabmeat. Whip cream; combine with mayonnaise and fold into gelatine mixture. Place in a 1-quart mold. Chill until firm. Unmold on platter. Garnish with salad greens. Serves 6.

Crab Salad with Aspic

1 pound cooked crabmeat
¼ cup lemon juice
1 cup chopped celery
½ cup chopped sweet pickles
½ cup mayonnaise
Salt and pepper to taste
Paprika

Look over crabmeat and remove any shell particles or connective tissue. Pour lemon juice over crabmeat. Mix with celery and pickles. Then stir in mayonnaise. Salt and pepper to taste and sprinkle with paprika. Serve on tomato aspic slices placed on green lettuce leaves. Serves 6 to 8.

LOBSTER MEAT FOR SALADS

Lobster meat is marketed the same as crabmeat in many places. Otherwise purchase lobsters alive or pre-cooked and follow instructions given under the section on lobster. The meat is used in all recipes for crabmeat and is good in some shrimp and flaked fish recipes, too. Lobster salad is easy to prepare, as are all other seafoods. It is delicious simply with chopped celery and mayonnaise or salad dressing, or in more elaborate recipes in combination with fruits, vegetables and aspics. When you serve lobster salad, you'll hear many compliments from guests and family.

Lobster Salad

2 cups cooked lobster, diced
2 cups finely minced celery
Mayonnaise
1 teaspoon lemon juice
Salt and paprika to taste
Lettuce

Chop the lobster. Mix with celery, mayonnaise, lemon juice and seasonings. Arrange lettuce in 6 nests. Use a small cup as mold and fill with mixture. Press firm. Invert the molded contents into each lettuce nest. Add 1 teaspoon mayonnaise and paprika or crossed strips of pimento. Serves 6.

Lobster-Paprika

4 lobster tails or 1½ pounds lobster
   meat
1 cup finely chopped celery
1 tablespoon minced onion
2 tablespoons lemon juice
1 cup mayonnaise
2 teaspoons paprika
Salt and pepper to taste

Cut lobster meat into bite-size pieces. Combine other ingredients and toss with lobster. Serve on individual plates lined with lettuce leaf and garnished with green asparagus tips, onion slices and tomato wedges. Serves 6.

Curried Lobster-Rice Salad

1 cup cooked lobster meat
3 cups cold cooked rice
1 cup chopped celery
1 cup unpeeled red apple, chopped
1 teaspoon grated onion
1 teaspoon curry powder
½ teaspoon dry mustard
¾ teaspoon salt
⅛ teaspoon white pepper
¾ cup mayonnaise
2 tablespoons lemon juice
Ripe olives
Raisins or nuts

Mix the lobster meat, rice, celery, apple and onion. In a small bowl blend curry powder, mustard, salt, pepper, mayonnaise and lemon juice. Toss the lobster mixture with mayonnaise mixture. Serve on lettuce with ripe olives. Sprinkle over salad ¼ cup soft raisins or chopped salted nuts. Serves 6.

Lobster-Potato Salad

1 cup cooked lobster meat
3 cups cooked, cubed potatoes
1 cup chopped celery
¼ cup chopped dill pickles
2 hard-cooked eggs, sliced
1 teaspoon salt
½ cup sour cream
2 tablespoons mayonnaise

Mix all ingredients, except lobster. Mix sour cream with mayonnaise. Combine cream dressing with potato mixture. Stir in lobster meat last. Serve in a large salad bowl, lined with lettuce and garnished with tomato halves. Serves 6. Cooked fish flakes, shrimp or crabmeat may be used instead of lobster, as in many of these recipes.

Tangy Lobster Salad

2 cups cooked lobster meat
⅓ cup olive oil
2 tablespoons wine vinegar
½ teaspoon salt
6 drops hot pepper sauce
¼ teaspoon ground mustard
½ cup salad dressing
2 cups thinly sliced celery
1 small onion, minced
Grapefruit sections

Cut the lobster meat about ½ inch thick and arrange on dish with shredded lettuce. Mix all the other ingredients and pour over lobster. Let chill in refrigerator and serve garnished with grapefruit sections. Serves 6.

Lobster Salad in Green Peppers

2 cups cooked lobster meat
2 hard-cooked eggs, chopped
1 cup chopped celery
½ cup mayonnaise
½ cup chili sauce
¼ teaspoon Worcestershire sauce
⅛ teaspoon Tabasco sauce
3 green peppers, halved
Paprika

Cut lobster into small pieces. Add other ingredients, except green peppers. Chill. When ready to serve, spoon salad into halved, seeded peppers. Top with a spoonful of mayonnaise. Sprinkle generously with paprika. Serves 6.

Lobster Salad Waldorf

2 cups cooked lobster meat
2 unpeeled red apples, chopped
2 tablespoons lemon juice
½ cup chopped nuts: pecans,
  walnuts or others
½ cup mayonnaise
Salt to taste

Mix lobster meat and apples. Pour lemon juice over and toss together. Add other ingredients, tasting to determine amount of salt needed, if any. Serve on crisp lettuce garnished with slivers of unpared apple sprinkled with lemon juice, to prevent their turning dark. Serves 6.

TIP: For a change, substitute 2 tablespoons drained capers or ripe olives, seeded and sliced, for the nuts.

Lobster-Chicken Salad

1 pound cooked lobster meat, cubed
    (2 cups)
2 tablespoons gelatine
½ cup cold water
1 quart chicken stock
½ teaspoon salt
⅛ teaspoon pepper
½ pound cooked chicken, cubed
    (1 cup)
2 tablespoons chopped parsley
½ cup chopped celery

Soak the gelatine for 5 minutes in cold water. Pour chicken stock into saucepan and bring to boiling. Add the soft gelatine and stir until completely dissolved. Set aside until cold. Add seasonings and parsley. Arrange lobster and chicken in bottom of an oiled mold and pour in the gelatine mixture. Chill in refrigerator several hours. To serve, unmold by placing a cloth wrung out in hot water over bottom of mold. Serve with mayonnaise. Serves 6.

Lobster Mousse

½ pound cooked lobster meat
1 tablespoon unflavored gelatine
¼ cup cold water
½ cup boiling water
½ cup chopped celery
2 tablespoons sliced stuffed olives
1 tablespoon grated onion
1 teaspoon prepared mustard
½ teaspoon salt
½ cup whipping cream
¼ cup mayonnaise or salad dressing
Salad greens

Cut lobster meat into ½-inch pieces. Soften gelatine in cold water for 5

minutes. Add boiling water and stir until dissolved. Add the next 5 ingredients. Chill until almost congealed. Add lobster meat. Whip cream. Combine mayonnaise and whipped cream; fold into gelatine mixture. Place in a 1-quart mold; chill until firm. Unmold on salad greens. Serves 6.

Frozen Lobster Salad

½ pound cooked lobster meat
1 3-ounce package cream cheese
½ cup mayonnaise or salad dressing
2 tablespoons chopped pimento
½ cup chopped nuts
½ teaspoon salt
5 drops Tabasco sauce
½ cup whipping cream
Lettuce

Cut lobster meat into ½-inch pieces. Cream cheese and mayonnaise. Add the next 4 ingredients and the lobster meat. Whip cream. Fold in whipped cream. Place in a 1-quart ice cube tray; freeze. Remove from freezer and let stand at room temperature for 15 minutes before serving. Cut into 6 slices and serve on lettuce. Serves 6.

Lobster Salad

1 pound cooked lobster meat
⅓ cup mayonnaise or salad dressing
1 tablespoon lemon or lime juice
¼ teaspoon salt
Lettuce
2 or 3 tomatoes

Cut lobster meat into ½-inch pieces. Add mayonnaise, lemon juice and salt. Serve on lettuce and garnish with tomato wedges. Serves 6.

There are not many ways of using oysters in salads but they may be used in recipes for other shellfish such as scallops. Always cook the oysters in their own liquid until they begin to curl around the edges, then drain, cool, and add to other salad ingredients.

Oyster Salad

1 pint oysters
¼ teaspoon celery salt
1 tablespoon butter
½ cup lettuce, chopped
2 hard-cooked eggs, diced
½ cup celery, diced
1 pimento, chopped
1 teaspoon onion, grated
1 teaspoon lemon juice
½ cup mayonnaise or salad dressing
½ teaspoon salt
⅛ teaspoon pepper
Lettuce

Drain oysters. Add celery salt and cook oysters in butter until edges begin to curl. Chill and dice oysters. Combine all ingredients and serve on lettuce cups. Garnish with paprika. Serves 6.

French Oyster Salad

1 pint oysters
¼ cup oil-vinegar or French dressing
½ cup minced celery
¼ cup minced mixed sweet pickles
Lettuce

Cook oysters in own liquid until they curl around the edges. Drain and dry thoroughly. Place in a dish and pour the oil-vinegar salad dressing over them. Refrigerate for 30 minutes or until chilled. Toss with celery and pickles. Serve on lettuce. Serves 4 to 6.

OIL-VINEGAR OR FRENCH DRESSING

¼ cup salad oil
½ cup cider vinegar or lemon juice
2 teaspoons salt
¼ teaspoon pepper

Mix ingredients in a jar and shake until well blended.

Oyster-Olive Salad

1 pint oysters
1 cup tender celery, chopped
⅓ cup mayonnaise
3 tablespoons chili sauce
2 tablespoons chopped stuffed olives
½ teaspoon salt
⅛ teaspoon cayenne pepper

Cook the oysters in own liquid until they curl. Drain and refrigerate until cool. Mix with other ingredients and serve on lettuce. Serves 4 to 6.

Oyster-Potato Salad

3 cups oysters
3 cups cold diced cooked potatoes
1 tablespoon minced onion
3 slices bacon, fried crisp and crumbled
Salt and pepper to taste
2 tablespoons vinegar
4 tablespoons olive or salad oil
½ teaspoon salt
¼ teaspoon cayenne pepper

Prepare potatoes. Heat oysters in their own liquid until they are plump and curl around the edges. Allow to cool. Mix potatoes and oysters with other ingredients—onion, bacon and salt and pepper.

Mix dressing ingredients together and shake vigorously in a jar. Use immediately on salad. Toss. Serves 6.

Scallop Salad

1 pint scallops
1 cup water
1 tablespoon vinegar
2 tablespoons salt
½ cup mayonnaise or salad dressing
1 cup diced celery
¼ cup chopped sweet pickles
2 tablespoons chopped pimento
Paprika

Cook scallops in boiling water to which vinegar and salt have been added. Cook about 10 minutes. Drain and let scallops cool at room temperature. Cut into small pieces and chill.

Mix mayonnaise, celery, pickles and pimento lightly. Stir in scallops. Chill. Sprinkle with paprika. Serve on lettuce. Serves 6.

Marinated Scallops

2 cups (about 1 pound or pint)
*   cooked scallops*
3 hard-cooked egg yolks
3 tablespoons hot water
3 tablespoons vinegar
3 tablespoons pepper sauce
1½ tablespoons olive oil
1 tablespoon horseradish
1 teaspoon salt
½ teaspoon creole mustard
¼ teaspoon celery seed

Mash egg yolks and stir in the water. Add vinegar and pepper sauce. Stir well. Add other ingredients and stir. Pour dressing over scallops and marinate in refrigerator for several hours. Serve with sliced tomatoes on lettuce. Top with ripe olives, if desired. Serves 6.

Scallop-Potato Zippy Salad

1 pound scallops
2 cups cooked, peeled, thinly sliced
*   potatoes*
2 tablespoons finely minced onion
2 tablespoons chopped parsley
*   (optional)*
1 tablespoon chopped pimento
2 tablespoons salad oil
2 tablespoons vinegar
¾ teaspoon salt
⅛ teaspoon pepper
½ teaspoon paprika

Simmer scallops in enough salted, boiling water to cover, for about 8 minutes. Drain and cool at room temperature. Cut into bite-size pieces. Combine scallops with potatoes, onion, chopped parsley (optional), and chopped pimento. Mix remaining ingredients into dressing and mix with salad.

Place in refrigerator until serving time, then serve on lettuce with bread-butter pickles as garnish. Serves 6.

Scallop Saffron Salad

2 cups cooked scallops, cut crosswise
*   into small pieces*
1 cup cooked, cubed potatoes
1 cup cooked peas
1 cup mayonnaise
3 tablespoons lemon or lime juice
⅛ teaspoon powdered saffron, mixed
*   well with 1 tablespoon water*

¼ teaspoon pepper
Dash Tabasco
2 tablespoons minced onion
1 teaspoon prepared mustard
1½ cups salad greens (lettuce,
   romaine or others)
Ripe olives and tomatoes

Combine scallops, potatoes and peas. Chill.
  Mix mayonnaise and lemon juice. Stir in saffron and water mixture. Add next 4 ingredients, mixing well. Cut up salad greens and add scallops, potatoes and peas. Toss lightly with the dressing. Chill and serve garnished with ripe olives and tomato quarters. Serves 6.

TIP: With this salad we suggest you serve first a bowl of hot, clear soup with thin crackers. Then the *Scallop-Saffron Salad* with a bowl of crisp, raw vegetables and slices of French bread. For dessert, strawberry tarts or peach shortcake.

Scallop Vegetable Salad

2 cups cooked scallops, cut crosswise
   into small pieces
1 cup cooked, cubed potatoes
1 cup cooked green beans, chopped
1 cup mayonnaise
3 tablespoons lemon juice
⅛ teaspoon powdered saffron, mixed
   thoroughly with 1 tablespoon water
¼ teaspoon pepper
1 teaspoon tarragon vinegar
2 tablespoons minced onion
1 teaspoon prepared mustard
Salad greens

Combine scallops, potatoes and beans.
  Mix mayonnaise and lemon juice. Stir in saffron and water mixture. Add all other ingredients, except greens, mixing well. Cut up salad greens and add scallop mixture. Toss lightly with the dressing. Chill. Serves 6.

COMBINATION SEAFOOD SALADS

*

Shrimp-Crab-Tomato Salad

1½ cups cooked shrimp
½ pound cooked crabmeat
½ cup thin French dressing
1 cup chopped celery
1 medium tomato, peeled and
   chopped
3 hard-cooked eggs, chopped
Salt and white pepper to taste
½ cup mayonnaise
2 tablespoons lemon juice
Lettuce

Shell, devein and cut shrimp into pieces. While still warm, pour over shrimp ¼ cup thin French dressing and let stand in refrigerator until ready to use. Look over crabmeat and remove any pieces of shell and connective tissue. Sprinkle remaining French dressing over crabmeat and refrigerate. Just before serving time combine all other ingredients with crabmeat and shrimp. Mix mayonnaise and lemon juice. Toss with mayonnaise-lemon juice. Serve on crisp lettuce garnished with more tomato wedges and slices of hard-cooked egg. Serves 6 to 8.

Deep Sea Pineapple Salad

3 cups cooked chopped shrimp, crab-meat or flaked fish
1 cup thinly sliced celery
½ teaspoon onion salt
1 minced seeded green pepper
1 No. 2 can pineapple chunks, drained (about 2 cups)
½ cup sour cream or ¼ cup may-onnaise thinned with 2 tablespoons evaporated milk

Mix all ingredients. Chill. Serve in lettuce cups. Garnish with whole shrimp and pieces of pineapple. Serves 6.

Seafood Stuffed Avocados

½ pound cooked crabmeat
½ pound cooked, peeled, deveined shrimp
3 avocados
3 tablespoons lime juice
Lettuce
Mayonnaise
Sour cream
Paprika

Remove any shell and cartilage from the crabmeat, being careful not to break the meat into small pieces. Cut avocados in half, lengthwise; remove seeds. Peel and immediately sprinkle the lime juice over the avocados to prevent discoloring. Place them on lettuce leaves. Pile centers of avocados with crabmeat and shrimp. Serve with dressing made of equal amounts of mayonnaise and sour cream. Sprinkle lightly with paprika.

Seafood and Vegetable Salad

1 can flaked fish or 2 cups fresh fish, cooked and flaked
1 can shrimp or 1 cup fresh cooked shrimp
1 cup diced chicken or white tuna
2 cups cubed ham
½ cup chopped sweet pickles
1 cup mixed chopped salad vegetables
2 tablespoons chopped onion
2 hard-cooked eggs, chopped

Mix all ingredients and toss with sauce made of ½ cup mayonnaise, 3 table-spoons catsup and ⅛ teaspoon garlic powder. Serves 6 to 8.

SEAFOOD SANDWICHES

SEAFOOD SANDWICH FILLINGS

For delicious sandwich fillings other than those given here, try the recipes for snacks, spreads and salads. Some are surprisingly good in sandwiches and all are easy. For the lunchbox, home luncheon or party fare, seafood sandwiches are liked by almost everyone.

Hot Fish-Flake Sandwiches

1 cup cooked flaked fish
1 can condensed cream of celery soup
1 tablespoon chopped onion
1 tablespoon chopped green pepper
1 tablespoon chopped pimento

Mix all ingredients and heat thoroughly. Spoon over toasted buns, with carraway seeds or plain. Serves 6 to 8.

TIP: For a change substitute condensed cream of mushroom soup instead of celery; substitute Tabasco for the pimento, and serve as above.

Hot Seafood Sandwiches with Mushroom Sauce

1 pound fish fillets
Seasoned cornmeal
Hot corn bread

Cut fish fillets into serving pieces. Roll in seasoned cornmeal. Fry crisply brown, having fat hot but not smoking. Drain and serve on sliced hot cornbread with *Mushroom Sauce.*

MUSHROOM SAUCE

2 tablespoons butter or other fat
1/3 cup sliced onions
1 can mushroom soup
1/2 cup milk
1/4 teaspoon dried thyme (optional)
1/4 teaspoon salt

Melt butter and sauté onions until soft. Gradually stir in soup and milk. Add seasonings. Heat, stirring. Makes 1½ cups sauce.

Tuna Luncheon Sandwiches

1 7-ounce can tuna
1/4 cup butter or margarine
1 teaspoon prepared mustard
6 slices trimmed bread
2 tablespoons minced onion
1/2 cup minced celery
2 chopped whole sweet pickles
   (about 2 tablespoons)
1/4 cup mayonnaise or salad dressing
6 slices cheese

Drain tuna and flake. Cream butter, blend in mustard, and spread on bread. Combine all other ingredients except cheese. Spread tuna mixture on bread. Place a slice of cheese on top of each. Place on a baking sheet and bake in a hot oven, 450 F, for 10 minutes, or until cheese melts and bread toasts around the edges. Serves 6.

TIP: For a change, use a small loaf of French bread instead of bread slices. Cut bread in half lengthwise and spread the mustard butter on both sides. Fill bread with tuna mixture and re-form. Cut loaf into 12 crosswise slices and wrap in aluminum foil. Bake in a hot oven, 450 F, for 30 minutes. Serves 6.

Shopping Day Shrimp Sandwiches

1 cup cooked shrimp, shelled and
   deveined
2 tablespoons sweet mixed pickles
2 tablespoons chopped celery
2 tablespoons mayonnaise
1/2 teaspoon salt
Dash cayenne pepper

Cut shrimp into very small pieces. Add chopped pickles, celery, mayonnaise, salt and cayenne pepper. Serve on thin buttered bread with a sprig of parsley or serve in a bowl, with crackers. Serves 2.

TIP: A bowl of hot clear soup starts the meal well and a slice of apple pie finishes it happily.

Shrimp-Pecan Sandwiches

1/2 pound cooked shrimp, finely
   chopped
1/4 cup chopped celery
1/4 cup chopped pecans
1 tablespoon lime juice
1/2 teaspoon salt
1/4 teaspoon pepper
1/4 cup mayonnaise

Mix all ingredients. Spread on buttered bread. Top with crisp lettuce. Serves 6.

Little Crabmeat Sandwiches

1 cup flaked crabmeat
1/2 cup chopped pecans
2 tablespoons chopped sweet gerkins
1 tablespoon chopped pimento
1 tablespoon chopped parsley
1/2 teaspoon salt
1/4 cup mayonnaise

Combine all ingredients. Chill. Cut off ends of bread. Spread with soft butter and crabmeat mixture. Cut sandwiches into fourths. Enough for 8 sandwiches before cutting.

Sandwiches for Two

½ cup cooked crabmeat
1 teaspoon lemon juice
½ apple, chopped
½ cup chopped celery
¼ teaspoon salt
⅛ teaspoon pepper
3 tablespoons mayonnaise

Pour lemon juice over crabmeat, add other ingredients, moistening with mayonnaise or salad dressing. Spread on buttered bread. Trim edges of sandwich and serve with seedless raisins.

Crabmeat Club Sandwich

2 cups cooked crabmeat (white or claw)
¼ cup chopped celery
4 tablespoons chopped sweet pickle
3 tablespoons chopped onion
⅓ cup mayonnaise or salad dressing
Salt
Pepper
18 slices buttered toast
4 tomatoes, sliced
6 pieces lettuce

Flake crabmeat, removing any bone or connective tissue. Combine celery, pickle, onion and mayonnaise. Spread on 6 slices of toast. Cover with second slice of toast. Fasten each with toothpicks. Cut in half. Serves 6.

Oyster Sandwiches

1 pint oysters
12 slices bacon
½ cup flour
½ teaspoon salt
⅛ teaspoon pepper
Lettuce
Tomatoes
Mayonnaise

Drain oysters. Fry bacon and drain on absorbent paper. Roll oysters in flour seasoned with salt and pepper. Fry in bacon fat, browning on both sides. Drain on paper. Arrange lettuce, oysters, bacon, tomato, and mayonnaise on toasted bread. Fasten with toothpicks and cut in half. Serves 6.

Seafood Crispies with Tangy Sauce

Fry fish and oysters (pre-cooked packaged products are fine)

TANGY SAUCE

⅓ cup mayonnaise
⅓ cup sour cream
1½ teaspoons grated lemon rind
1 teaspoon drained capers (optional)

Mix all sauce ingredients. Place fried fish and oysters on half of hamburger buns. Spoon sauce over top. Run under broiler heat until sauce is lightly browned. Serve with other half of bun spread lightly with mustard. Enough sauce for 4.

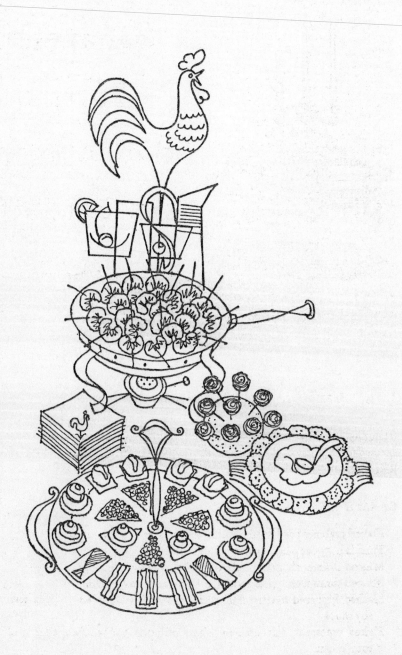

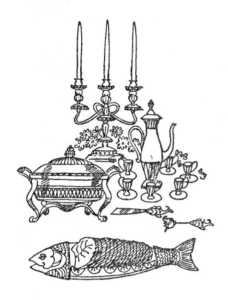

Canapés, Hors d'Oeuvres, Appetizers and Dips

Canapés, Hors d'Oeuvres and Appetizers

SEAFOODS *listed in these recipes are interchangeable and substitutions may be made. Flake fish and be sure to chop shellfish when using in canapés and dips.*

CANAPÉ SPREADS

  Flaked crabmeat or lobster, horseradish, chopped chives and sour cream
  Tuna fish, sweet pickle relish and sour cream
  Minced shrimp, chopped fresh dill and thin French dressing
  Minced shrimp, chopped pecans, coconut and mayonnaise
  Mashed kippered herring and dash each of Tabasco, lemon juice and
    soy sauce
  Flaked crabmeat, minced cucumber, chopped hard-cooked eggs and
    sour cream

Fish Canapés

2 cups flaked cooked fish
  (See that section)
1 cup sandwich spread
Salt and pepper to taste
4 hard-cooked eggs, chopped
½ cup chopped sweet pickles
Paprika
Parsley
18 slices buttered toast

Combine all ingredients except paprika and parsley. Cut toast in desired
shapes and sizes. Spread with this fish
salad. Sprinkle with paprika and top
each canapé with a sprig of parsley.
Serve open-face, with carrot curls and
potato chips. Serves about 8.

Zippy Tuna Canapés

1 7-ounce can tuna
1 tablespoon finely chopped celery
3 tablespoons mayonnaise
½ cup butter or margarine
3 tablespoons horseradish
32 toast points
Chopped parsley

Drain tuna. Flake. Add celery and
mayonnaise; blend into a paste. Combine butter and horseradish. Spread
horseradish-butter on toast points.
Top with tuna mixture. Garnish with
parsley sprinkled over the top. Makes
32 canapés.

Smoked-Salmon Canapés

1 7-ounce can smoked salmon
1 3-ounce package cream cheese
2 tablespoons mayonnaise or salad
  dressing

¼ cup finely diced celery
¼ teaspoon salt
¼ teaspoon prepared mustard
16 slices bread

Drain fish and grind twice. Cream
the cheese and mayonnaise. Blend in
fish, celery and seasonings. Remove
crusts from bread. Cut each slice into
3 strips and toast. Spread salmon on
toast strips and garnish. Makes 48
canapés.

Hot Tuna-Mushroom Canapés

1 7-ounce can tuna
½ cup condensed mushroom soup
1 tablespoon finely chopped pimento
1 tablespoon finely chopped green
  pepper
¼ teaspoon salt
Dash paprika
32 round crackers
½ cup grated cheese

Drain tuna. Flake. Add other ingredients except crackers and cheese.
Mix all well and spread on crackers.
Sprinkle with cheese. Place on a cooky
sheet. Broil 3 inches from source of
heat for 5 minutes until cheese browns.
Makes 32 canapés.

Hot Crabmeat Canapés

Spread rounds of pumpernickel bread
with mustard butter, below. Place on
top of each buttered slice of bread
a slice of tomato, and on that spoon
flaked crabmeat moistened with salad
dressing seasoned with salt and a dash
of curry powder. Cover the rounds
with stiffly beaten egg whites, seasoned with salt and white pepper.

Place the rounds on a cooky sheet and brown in a slow oven, 300 F. Serve immediately.

Mustard Butter: Cream 1 scant teaspoon prepared mustard in 1 tablespoon of sweet butter. Chill.

Crab Canapés

1 cup cooked crabmeat
1 teaspoon lime or lemon juice
Dash pepper sauce
¼ teaspoon seasoned salt
2 hard-cooked eggs
3 tablespoons mayonnaise
½ teaspoon Worcestershire sauce
⅓ cup cream cheese
2 tablespoons cream

Flake crabmeat and mix with chopped eggs and seasonings. Trim bread and cut into fourths. Spread with the crab mixture. Top with cream cheese softened with 2 tablespoons cream, and sliced stuffed olives or whole ripe olives. Makes 2 cups or enough for 24 canapés.

Shrimp Canapés

½ pound cooked shrimp
1 3-ounce package cream cheese
1 tablespoon chili sauce
¼ teaspoon Worcestershire sauce
1 teaspoon salt
Dash cayenne
Crackers, toast or bread

Grind shrimp. Soften cheese at room temperature. Combine all ingredients, except crackers, and blend into a paste. Spread on crackers, toast, or bread; garnish. Makes approximately 48 canapés.

Shrimp-Sour-Cream-Chive Canapés

½ pint sour cream
3 tablespoons chopped chives
1 cup small cooked shrimp, chopped
¼ teaspoon celery salt
Dash Tabasco sauce
Melba toast

Mix all ingredients. Crisp Melba toast in a slow oven. Spread toast with shrimp-sour cream mixture. Makes about 1½ pints, or enough for 12 pieces of toast.

Scallop Aspic Canapés

½ pound cooked scallops
2 tablespoons unflavored gelatine
½ cup cold water
1¾ cups tomato juice
1 teaspoon sugar
½ teaspoon salt
½ teaspoon Worcestershire sauce
½ teaspoon onion salt
2 tablespoons lemon juice
36 1-inch paper baking cups
36 Melba toast rounds

Cut scallops into 36 pieces. Soften gelatine in cold water for 5 minutes. Heat tomato juice to the boiling point; add gelatine and stir until dissolved. Add seasonings and lemon juice. Place a scallop piece in each baking cup; fill cups ¾ full with gelatine mixture. Chill until set. Unmold on Melba toast rounds. Makes 36 canapés.

Scallop Canapé Pockets

½ *pound cooked scallops*
2 *cloves garlic, finely chopped*
2 *tablespoons butter or margarine,*
  melted
½ *cup grated cheese*
¼ *teaspoon Worcestershire sauce*
Dash salt
Dash pepper
2 *cups pastry mix*

Chop scallops. Cook garlic in butter for 2 to 3 minutes. Add cheese, seasonings and scallops. Blend well. Prepare pastry mix as directed. Roll very thin and cut into 90 circles, 2 inches each. Place about 1 teaspoon of scallop filling in the center of 45 circles. Cover with remaining 45 circles; press edges together with a fork and vent top. Place on a baking pan, 18 x 14 inches. Bake in a very hot oven, 450 F, for 10 to 15 minutes, or until brown. Makes about 45 canapés.

Scallop Canapés with Bacon

½ *pound cooked scallops*
16 *slices bacon*
8 *slices white bread*
1 *8-ounce package sliced cheese*
Paprika

Cut large scallops in half. Fry bacon until crisp; drain on absorbent paper. Save bacon drippings. Trim crusts from bread. Place a slice of cheese and two slices of bacon on each piece of bread. Cut into quarters. Place scallops on top of bacon. Brush with bacon drippings. Sprinkle with paprika. Place on a greased broiler pan about 3 inches from source of heat. Broil 4 minutes. Makes 32 canapés.

Sardine Canapé Spread I

1 *can sardines, 3¼ ounces*
⅛ *teaspoon Worcestershire sauce*
1 *tablespoon tomato catsup*
Mayonnaise or sour cream
  (*both may be used*)
Paprika

Mash sardines. Add Worcestershire sauce and catsup. Moisten mixture with sour cream or mayonnaise, or half and half. Sprinkle with paprika. Serve on bread rectangles or crackers. Makes about 1¾ cups spread.

SARDINE CANAPÉ SPREAD II

Double above recipe and add 1 cup cottage cheese, ¼ teaspoon celery seeds, 6 drops Tabasco sauce and 2 tablespoons lemon juice. Serve with crackers or potato chips. Makes 2½ cups spread.

Lobster and Cheese Hors d'Oeuvres

½ *pound cooked lobster meat*
1 *tablespoon grated cheese*
2 *tablespoons butter or margarine*
1 *egg yolk, beaten*
1 *teaspoon lemon juice*
Paprika

Grind lobster meat. Cream the cheese and butter; add egg yolk, lemon juice and lobster meat. Shape by pressing into a teaspoon, and place on a well-greased cooky sheet. Sprinkle with paprika. Bake in a hot oven, 400 F, for 5 minutes. Serve hot. Makes about 48 hors d'oeuvres.

Lobster-Stuffed Eggs

1 pound cooked lobster meat
1 teaspoon grated onion
1 teaspoon chopped green pepper
1 teaspoon pimento
1 tablespoon chili sauce
⅔ cup mayonnaise or salad dressing
1½ dozen hard-cooked eggs
Parsley

Chop lobster meat. Add onion, green pepper, pimento, chili sauce, and mayonnaise. Chill. Cut eggs in half lengthwise and remove yolks. Place lobster mixture in egg whites. Garnish with parsley. Makes 36 canapes.

Broiled Spiny-Lobster Chunks

½ pound cooked spiny-lobster meat
¼ cup butter or margarine, melted
Paprika
2 tablespoons chopped parsley

Cut lobster meat into 1-inch pieces. Dip in butter; sprinkle with paprika. Place in a baking pan, 10 x 6 x 1½ inches, about 3 inches from source of heat. Broil for 2 to 3 minutes or until lightly browned. Sprinkle with parsley. Serve on toothpicks. Makes approximately 24 hors d'oeuvres.

Clam Appetizers

1 7-ounce can minced clams
1 3-ounce package cream cheese with chives
½ teaspoon salt
1 tablespoon lemon juice
4 drops Tabasco sauce
1 egg white
2 tablespoons chopped pimento

Drain clams. Soften the cream cheese at room temperature. Stir in clams. Combine with the other ingredients except egg white and pimento. Beat egg white until stiff and fold into cheese mixture. Sprinkle the chopped pimento over the top. Serve in a small bowl, with crackers. Makes 1½ cups.

Zippy Shrimp Appetizer

1 pound cooked shrimp (about 20 medium or 15 large)
1 cup Italian salad dressing
2 tablespoons instant minced onion or 1 large onion, chopped
1 clove garlic, minced
½ cup finely chopped parsley
1½ teaspoon salt
¼ teaspoon pepper

Shell and devein cooked shrimp. Combine dressing with other ingredients. Pour over shrimp and refrigerate several hours before serving. Serve with mixed crackers. Pass toothpicks to spear shrimp.

Shrimp Turnovers

½ pound cooked shrimp
1 teaspoon horseradish
2 tablespoons lemon juice
1 teaspoon prepared mustard
1 tablespoon chopped sweet pickle
1 teaspoon salt
3 tablespoons mayonnaise or salad dressing
1 cup pastry mix
Cream

Grind shrimp. Combine all ingredients, except pastry mix and cream; blend into a paste. Prepare pastry as directed. Roll very thin and cut into

2-inch circles. Place 1 teaspoon of filling in center of each circle. Moisten edges with cold water; fold over and press edges together with a fork. Prick tops and brush with cream. Bake in a hot oven, 475 F, for 12 to 15 minutes or until golden brown. Makes approximately 48 turnovers.

Deviled Fish Snacks

2 packages fish sticks
½ teaspoon lime juice
1½ teaspoons Worcestershire sauce
2 teaspoons grated onion
¼ cup soft margarine
¼ teaspoon powdered mustard
Dash hot pepper sauce
¼ cup chopped parsley

Place fish sticks close together in broiler pan. Combine all other ingredients and spread mixture over fish. Broil 9 to 10 minutes or until brown. Cut each stick into three pieces and serve on seafood platter. Pass a bowl of *Louis Dressing*.

Brown Salmon-Potato Balls

1 16-ounce can salmon
½ cup mashed potatoes
1 tablespoon minced celery
1 tablespoon minced onion
1 tablespoon butter or margarine, melted
¼ teaspoon salt
⅛ teaspoon pepper
1½ teaspoons Worcestershire sauce
1 egg, beaten
½ pound American cheese
½ cup dry bread crumbs

Drain salmon and flake. Combine first 9 ingredients and mix well. Cut cheese into 48 cubes, approximately ⅜-inch each. Portion salmon mixture with a tablespoons. Shape into small balls around cheese cubes. Roll in crumbs. Fry in a basket in deep fat, 375 F, for 3 minutes or until golden brown. Drain on absorbent paper. Serve on toothpicks. Makes approximately 48 balls.

Smoked-Salmon Rolls

1 7-ounce can smoked salmon
1 teaspoon horseradish
2 tablespoons lemon juice
1 teaspoon onion, grated
¼ cup mayonnaise or salad dressing
1 cup pastry mix
Paprika

Drain and flake salmon. Add seasoning and mayonnaise; blend into a paste. Prepare pastry according to directions. Divide in half; roll very thin in circle about 9 inches in diameter. Spread with salmon mixture. Cut into wedge-shaped pieces, and roll in jelly-roll fashion beginning at the round edge. Score top of rolls with a fork and sprinkle with paprika. Bake in a hot oven, 425 F, for 15 minutes or until brown. Serve hot or cold. Makes approximately 32 rolls.

Crabmeat Crunchies

1 cup cooked crabmeat
2 tablespoons mayonnaise
2 tablespoons sweet pickle relish
2 tablespoons tomato paste

Remove any shell particles or connective tissue from cocktail or white crabmeat. Blend other ingredients, add crab and spread on large potato chips or sesame seed crackers. Pass crunchies on a tray with other snacks or by themselves.

Dips

Party Fish Dip

1 cup fish flakes
2 packages cream cheese with chives
¼ teaspoon salt
1 teaspoon onion juice
1 teaspoon Worcestershire sauce
3 drops Tabasco sauce
2 teaspoons lemon juice

Soften cream cheese and blend in other ingredients. Add fish last. Serve with potato chips.

Fish Sour Cream Dip

1 cup fish flakes
1 teaspoon prepared mustard
1½ teaspoons onion salt
1 tablespoon Worcestershire sauce
1 cup commercial sour cream
2 teaspoons chopped parsley

Mix together mustard, onion salt, and Worcestershire sauce. Blend in sour cream lightly, then fish flakes. Chill. Garnish with parsley. Makes 1½ cups dip. Serve with crackers, potato chips and pretzels.

Shrimp-Swiss Dip

1 can frozen shrimp soup
1 small can shrimp or 1 cup cooked shrimp
1½ cups grated Swiss cheese
2½ tablespoons cooking sherry
Cubes of Italian or homestyle bread

Heat the shrimp soup in top of double boiler over boiling water. Drain canned shrimp, or cut cooked shrimp into small pieces. Set aside. Add cheese to soup and stir occasionally. When cheese is melted add the sherry and drained or chopped shrimp. Serve hot as a fondue with bread cubes. These are dipped into it on a fork. Serves 4.

Lobster meat may be substituted for crabmeat in all of these recipes.

Crab-Creamy Dip

1 cup cooked crabmeat
2 3-ounce packages cream cheese
¼ cup light cream
2 teaspoons lime juice
1½ teaspoons Worcestershire sauce
1 clove garlic, minced
6 drops Tabasco sauce
½ teaspoon salt

Shred crabmeat. Let cream cheese soften at room temperature. Blend cream and cheese. Mix in other ingredients, and stir in crabmeat last. Chill and serve in bowl, accompanied with crisp crackers or potato chips. Makes 1½ cups.

Crab-Avocado Dip

1 cup cooked de luxe crabmeat
1 ripe avocado
½ cup sour cream
2 teaspoons prepared horseradish
1 teaspoon salt

¼ teaspoon hot pepper sauce
Few grains cayenne pepper

Peel and mash avocado (1½ cups).
Combine with other ingredients. Chill
and serve in a bowl with de luxe
crabmeat around sides. Pass sesame
seed crackers or pretzels. Makes 2
cups dip.

Clam-Cheese Dip or Spread

1 7-ounce can minced clams
2 3-ounce packages cream cheese or
   1 large package

¼ teaspoon salt
2 teaspoons grated onion
1 teaspoon Worcestershire sauce
3 drops Tabasco sauce
2 teaspoons lemon juice
1 teaspoon chopped parsley
Potato chips

Drain clams. Save liquor. Soften
cheese at room temperature, mix with
mayonnaise and combine all ingredients, except potato chips. Blend
well. Gradually add ¼ cup clam
liquor, if thinner dip is desired. Omit
liquor for a spread. Chill. Serve with
potato chips. Makes 2 cups of dip.

These recipes are also good using canned minced clams, drained.

Tuna-Cream Dip

1 7-ounce can tuna
1 tablespoon horseradish
1½ teaspoons onion salt
1 teaspoon Worcestershire sauce
1 cup sour cream
2 teaspoons chopped parsley
Potato chips

Drain tuna. Flake. Blend in horseradish, onion salt, and Worcestershire
sauce. Fold in sour cream. Chill. Garnish with parsley and serve with potato chips. Makes 1½ cups of dip.

Tuna-Pineapple Dip

1 7-ounce can tuna
1 8-ounce can crushed pineapple
1 8-ounce package cream cheese
3 tablespoons pineapple juice
Dash salt

Dash nutmeg
Potato chips or crackers

Drain tuna and flake. Drain pineapple; save liquid. Soften cheese at
room temperature. Combine all ingredients except potato chips or crackers; blend into a paste. Chill. Serve
in a bowl surrounded by the chips or
crackers. Makes 1 pint of dip.

Deep Sea Dip

½ cup catsup
3 tablespoons lime juice
2 tablespoons salad oil
1 teaspoon grated lemon peel
½ teaspoon horseradish
Dash hot pepper sauce

Mix all ingredients, stirring well. Chill
and serve with fried seafood. Yields
¾ cup dip, or enough for 2 pounds
of fish.

Sauces

HERE ARE *a few good sauces for seafood. You will find many more throughout the book.*

SAUCES IN OTHER SECTIONS

French Lemon Dressing
Mild Barbecue Sauce
Soy-Tomato Sauce
Olive-Oregano Sauce
Almond Sauce
Anchovy Butter
Ripe Olive Butter
Lemon Butter Sauce
Tarragon Sauce
Madeira Sauce
Orange Sauce
Shrimp Sauce
Creamy Sauce
Mustard Sauce for
   Fried Crispies
Louis Dressing
Tartare Dill Sauce
Lemon Cream Sauce

Plain Sauce for
   Poached Fillets
Cream Sauce for
   Poached Fillets
Creole Sauce
Golden Sauce
Tomato Sauce
Lemon-Butter Sauce
Barbecue Sauce for Eel
Butter Sauce
Chinese Sauce
Guava Sauce
White Sauce
Marinade Sauce for Shrimp
Remoulade Sauce
Saucy Sauce
Red Devil Sauce
Tartare Sauce with Capers

Crab Louis Dressing
Easy Tartare Sauce
Barbecue Sauce for Stone Crab
Cocktail Sauce for Lobster
Shrimp Newburg Sauce
Cocktail Sauce for
 Oysters I
Cocktail Sauce for
 Oysters II
Oyster Sauce for Chicken
Cocktail Sauce for Clams
Sunshine Sauce
Cocktail Sauce for Scallops
Quick Seafood Sauce
Mustard Sauce
Cucumber Sauce
Mushroom Sauce
Louis Dressing
Barbecue Sauce

Spanish Sauce
Mustard Butter Sauce
Cucumber-Sour Cream Sauce

LARGE-QUANTITY SAUCES

Shellfish Cocktail Sauce
White-Cap Cocktail Sauce

SALAD DRESSINGS

Vinaigrette Sauce
Curry French Dressing
Sour Cream Dressing
Tarragon-Ginger Dressing
Special Salad Dressing
Special Dressing

Piquant Sauces for Breaded Frozen Fish Sticks

Fry the frozen fish sticks in small amount of butter, margarine, or other fat, or heat in oven, following package instructions. Serve with one of the following sauces:

Chili Lemon Sauce

½ cup chili catsup
3 tablespoons lemon juice
2 tablespoons grated lemon peel
½ teaspoon prepared horseradish

Blend ingredients and chill. Makes ¾ cup sauce.

Quick Tomato Sauce

1 8-ounce can tomato sauce
2 teaspoons lemon juice
½ teaspoon salt
¼ teaspoon pepper
¼ teaspoon Worcestershire sauce, or
 soy sauce

Mix ingredients and simmer on top burner over low heat for 4 to 5 minutes. About ¾ cup sauce.

Pink Sauce

1 cup mayonnaise or salad dressing
4 tablespoons tomato catsup
2 tablespoons chopped sweet mixed
 pickles
⅛ teaspoon salt

Combine ingredients and chill until ready to serve. Makes 1¼ cup.

You will find several variations of tartare sauce in this book—not surprisingly, since it is a classic with most seafood.

Blue Sea Tartare Sauce

1 cup mayonnaise
1 tablespoon lime or lemon juice
1 tablespoon minced onion
½ teaspoon Tabasco sauce
1 tablespoon chopped parsley
2 tablespoons chopped stuffed olives
2 tablespoons chopped pickle

Stir lime or lemon juice and Tabasco into mayonnaise. Mix in other ingredients. Makes 1¼ cups.

Lime Dressing for Fish

½ cup mayonnaise
¼ cup sweet pickles, chopped fine
½ cup sour cream
1 tablespoon lime juice
1 teaspoon grated onion
2 tablespoons chopped ripe olives
Dash cayenne pepper
Salt and pepper to taste

Mix all ingredients and chill. Serve on any seafood. Makes about 1½ cups.

Hot Diggity Sauce

½ cup catsup
½ cup chili sauce
2 tablespoons horseradish
1 tablespoon lemon juice
6 drops Tabasco sauce

Mix all ingredients. Serve with fried seafood.

Easy Home Mayonnaise

1 egg
¼ teaspoon ground mustard
1 tablespoon white vinegar
1 teaspoon salt
¼ teaspoon pepper
½ cup salad oil
½ cup olive oil
2 tablespoons lemon juice

Use a small deep mixing bowl. Put into it the egg, mustard, vinegar, salt and pepper. Beat with rotary beater or mixer for 1 minute. Combine the oils. Pour in ⅓ cup of oil and beat for a minute. Repeat twice, beating after each addition. If mayonnaise is a little too stiff, add just a little more oil. After the last beating, add lemon juice. Be sure to use at least ½ cup *olive oil* to give it needed flavor.

Celery-Mustard Sauce for Grilled Fish

2 pounds fish fillets, fresh or frozen
4 stalks celery, chopped
1 small onion, chopped
¼ cup butter or margarine, melted
1½ teaspoons salt
1 teaspoon celery seeds
1 teaspoon mustard seeds
2 tablespoons tarragon vinegar

Thaw fish if frozen. Wash and dry fish and place in greased broiler pan. Broil 3 inches from heat for 5 minutes. Remove pan. Make the sauce by cooking the celery and onion in the butter until soft, and adding the other ingredients. Cover fish and return to oven for 3 minutes' more cooking time. Serves 6.

Cucumber Sauce

1 cucumber, peeled and sliced thin
1 large sweet onion, sliced thin
½ cup thin garlic French dressing
1 tablespoon chopped parsley
1 tablespoon light cream

Peel and thinly slice onion. Pour French dressing over it and let stand several hours. When ready to serve stir in the cream and parsley and pour over the thinly sliced cucumber. This is good over baked fish fillets. Makes about 1 cup sauce.

Shrimp Sauce for Fish

½ pound cooked shrimp
2 tablespoons butter or other fat, melted
2 tablespoons flour
1 cup half cream, half milk
¼ teaspoon salt
⅛ teaspoon white pepper
3 hard-cooked eggs, chopped

Chop shrimp finely and brown in butter 4 minutes. Blend in flour and add milk gradually, stirring. Add salt and pepper to season. Stir and cook until thick. Add chopped egg and heat again. Serve over cooked fish. Serves 6.

Foolproof Hollandaise Sauce

5 egg yolks
2 tablespoons water
½ pound melted butter
Juice of 1 lemon
Dash of Tabasco sauce

Mix egg yolks with water. Whip thoroughly. Heat in top of double boiler over simmering water (do not let top of boiler touch the water). Whip constantly until creamy and thick. Remove and cool slightly. Add the ½ pound melted butter, a small amount at a time, beating well. Pour in the lemon juice and add a dash of Tabasco sauce. Makes 2 cups.

Mock Hollandaise Sauce

1 cup medium white sauce
2 egg yolks
2 tablespoons butter
1 tablespoon lemon juice

Make the white sauce in the top of a double boiler. Beat the egg yolks slightly; stir into them about ¼ cup of the hot sauce. Stir the mixture into the remainder of the sauce. Add the butter, stir in the lemon juice and stir for about 1 minute. Remove from the stove. Keep tightly covered until serving time. Makes 1¼ cups.

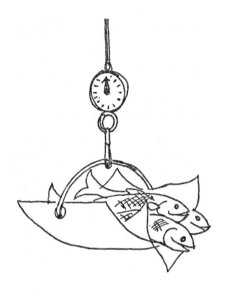

Hints to Fishermen

How to Care for Your Catch

WHAT TO TAKE:

FIRST OF ALL we remind you that it is, of course, important to go prepared when you start on that fishing trip. You *will* catch fish, so take with you the following minimum equipment besides your fishing tackle and accessories:

1. A sharp knife
2. Salt, pepper and bottled lemon or lime juice
3. Fresh citrus fruits, if available
4. A portable ice chest filled with coarsely cracked ice
5. A roll of paper toweling

If you plan to camp overnight don't forget:

1. Heavy-duty aluminum foil
2. A frying pan with folding or detachable handle
3. Paper plates
4. Plastic forks, spoons, and coffee cups

You will also need a large kettle for boiling water and, incidentally, an easy way to warm canned foods is to drop them unopened into boiling water for about 5 minutes. Remove, open and serve from the can.

Another hint is to prepare at home several cartons of water frozen in empty milk containers. Pack these around perishable foods and later you can use the water for drinking or other purposes.

CLEANING AND STORING AS YOU FISH

Make it a rule always, except when the fishing action is at its peak, to immediately clean and store your fish on ice, or take other precautions to preserve its freshness. This way you are assured firm, wholesome fish at the end of the day. When fish are placed on a stringer or in a bag for a long period of time they die slowly and the flesh is flabby and deteriorates fast. It's easy to cut quickly around the collar and down the underside, remove the head and viscera, rinse and place on ice. If icing must be delayed an hour or more, clean the fish and rub the stomach cavity with a mixture of table salt and 1 tablespoon pepper a cup. Use about 1 tablespoon of salt per pound of fish. Sprinkle a little on skin, too. Store fish temporarily in a box lined with damp burlap. Place fresh green leaves between the fish and top cover of burlap, which should be kept moist with water and laid just lightly over the fish.

If you do not plan to cook your fish in camp but will transport them home, here is how to clean and dress them:

After scaling (which is best done with fish wet), turn fish underside-up and cut from vent to throat. Remove viscera and scrape blood stripe loose with thumbnail. Rinse fish in cold water. Cut around and remove the pelvic fins on the underside near the head. Remove the head, including pectoral fins at the ears by cutting above the collarbone. Cut down to the backbone on each side of the fish if it is large, and then snap the backbone by bending it over the edge of a table or board. Cut off the tail.

Remove the dorsal (large back) fin by cutting along both sides of it. Give a pull toward the head of the fish and remove the fin with the root bones attached. Cut out other fins in the same way. To skin a fish, make a deep cut around the body at head and back to tail. Pull skin loose with pliers working toward tail. Remove head and tail. Slit along both sides at dorsal fin and lift it out. For splitting or filleting, place fish on its side, cut in at the tail and follow backbone with knife held flat, toward the head. Cut down through back at ribs, working knife over them. Lift off the cut side in one piece. Turn and repeat on the other side.

If the fish is large you might want to cut it crosswise, into steaks, after cleaning. If you wish, sprinkle cleaned fish with salt, pepper and a little lemon juice, wrap in wax paper and store in ice chest.

Fishermen's Tips for Dressing Fish

TO SCALE A FISH

Place the fish on a large sheet of paper, remove the scales with a fish scaler or a knife. Start at the tail and work toward the head. If fish is slippery, hold it with a cloth.

TO CLEAN FISH

Make a slit down body cavity from gills to vent, remove insides and wash away any blood. Scrape backbone with knife tip and remove any black membrane by rubbing with salt. Remove fins, gills and eyes. If you wish the head and tail removed, cut off gill with head. Wash fish thoroughly and dry.

TO FILLET A LARGE FISH

Remove the fins. Scale the fish and clean it. Split open from the vent to the head. Cut down the backbone just above the collarbone. Turn the knife flat and cut the flesh along the backbone to the tail allowing the knife to run over the rib bones. Lift off the entire side of the fish in one piece. Turn the fish over and repeat the procedure on the other side.

TO SKIN A FISH

Do not scale. Cut around the back fins and pull them off or grasp the rear part of a fin and give it a sudden pull toward the fish's head. Both the fin and its bony structure will come away. Or cut off the fins with scissors, allowing a small part to remain visible so the bones may be located easily after the fish is cooked.

Place fish on flat surface, run a knife point down the entire length of the backbone. Loosen the skin near the head of the fish and around the gills, then strip it off toward the tail. Reverse the fish and repeat the process on the other side.

Feel the fish all over with the fingers to find small bones that may have remained in the flesh, and remove them with tweezers or a short-bladed knife and the thumb.

TO SCALE A FISH

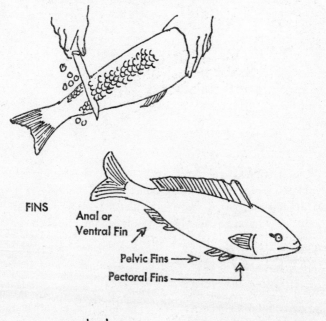

FINS

Anal or
Ventral Fin

Pelvic Fins

Pectoral Fins

CUTTING TO REMOVE DORSAL OR TOP FIN   REMOVING FIN

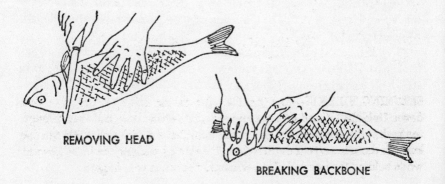

REMOVING HEAD

BREAKING BACKBONE

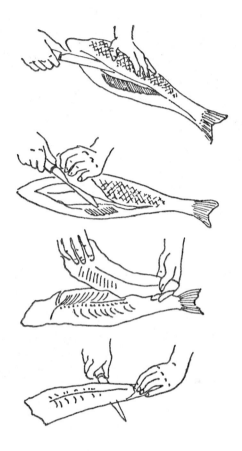

TO FILLET A LARGE FISH

SKINNING FILLETS—Lay the fillets flat on the cutting board, skin side down. Hold the tail end with your fingers, and with a sharp knife cut through the flesh to the skin about one-half inch from the end of the fillet. Flatten the knife on the skin and cut the flesh from the skin by pushing the knife forward while holding the free end of the skin firmly between your fingers.

FRESH-WATER FISH

Although in some states the fresh-water varieties are not caught and marketed commercially, there are many enthusiastic fishermen and fisherwomen who bring home creels full of delicious food fish. More often than not lucky neighbors and relatives get to share this bounty. Old-timers know how to prepare them, but there are many persons who do not know much about this type of food. Again, there is little or no trick to any fish cookery. Any recipes for salt-water species apply to the fresh-water varieties. Just remember the number one rule: do not overcook. In oven cooking or barbecuing add more fat if the fish seems dry.

Campfire Cookery—Fish

When you get ready to cook your fresh, delicious fish, there are numerous convenient recipes for variety. In pan frying, remember to have the fat *hot* but not smoking. Roll fillets or small whole dressed fish in cornmeal and fry in the fat, turning to brown other side.

Do not overcook. It's done when the flesh flakes easily when tested with a fork.

For something different, tear pieces of aluminum foil large enough to completely wrap fish fillets or steaks. Wash and dry each piece. Place in center of foil and top with 1 small onion, sliced, 1 teaspoon salt, dash pepper, 1 teaspoon paprika, 2 tablespoons bottled lemon juice and ¼ cup butter or margarine, melted. Wrap fish tightly in foil, pressing down so no air remains in the package. Put on grill or at edge of campfire for 1 hour, turning packages occasionally.

For quick broiled fish on the grill, place a piece of foil under fish and brush with melted butter. Broil over heat for 10 to 15 minutes. Sprinkle with salt, pepper, paprika, and serve with lemon-garlic sauce made by blending 4 tablespoons melted butter with 1 teaspoon lemon juice, ⅛ teaspoon pepper, 1 clove garlic, minced. This makes ⅓ cup of sauce.

To avoid breaking fish when turning it, cut a piece of foil a bit larger than the fish. Place directly under the fish. To turn, slip a pancake turner under foil and turn fish and foil. Pull off the foil; brush fish with butter and finish broiling the second side.

Campfire Cookery—Shellfish

In season and if available, have an oyster and shrimp roast. The oysters are washed thoroughly and placed in a single layer on a solid plate or grid placed over a wood fire for 12 to 15 minutes. The larger half of the oyster shell is placed downward. When shells pop open, remove meats from shell, dip in hot melted seasoned butter. *Good!*

Shrimp can be placed on aluminum foil, brushed with melted butter, and roasted for 10 to 12 minutes. They turn pink when cooked. They can be roasted either in the shells or after being shelled and deveined. If shelled, they require much shorter roasting period (not over 5 minutes). Punch some holes in the foil with an icepick or knife point for quicker heat.

Boiled crabs are easy to fix and delicious. Season enough water to cover crabs completely, with ¼ cup vinegar, 2 tablespoons salt and 1 tablespoon red pepper for each 2 quarts of water. Drop live crabs in water when it comes to a boil. Then let simmer 15 to 20 minutes. Drain and cool crabs. Break off claws and break body apart with hands, remove meat and serve with melted butter and lime or lemon wedges.

Seafoods are good out of doors in so many ways—pan fried, deep-fat fried, pan broiled, barbecued, campfire-roasted or baked in foil, boiled, in stews and soups and cold in sandwiches. Just be sure to bring your catch to camp in good condition; you'll find it pays in good food and nutrition. Don't forget to freeze the surplus.

Lobsters, clams, and turtle steaks also take well to campfire cookery. There is little difference in outdoor and indoor cookery. Just remember, it's the heat that cooks and not the stove. Gauge your fire accordingly.

Outdoor Cookery Hints

Think of your grill and fire first. If you have one of the efficient permanent gas grills in your own yard, you are ready for business as soon as you regulate the gas. The permanent ceramic briquets are soon hot. They do not get red in color when hot, but do provide an intense, even distribution of the heat. The briquets last for years and will not burn to ashes. You can control the gas flame and never have to bother with charcoal. What about charcoal flavor? There is really no such thing, as charcoal is flavorless and odorless; using it is just a method of providing heat that is intense enough to sear and cook food. The outdoor "barbecue" flavor is a result of the charring and searing. Flavor and aroma come from the smoke of natural juices dripping on hot briquets.

If you don't have a grill there are many innovations. You can make a grill using a charcoal bucket, flanked on either side by bricks or concrete blocks to hold up a grill (the metal rack from your oven will answer the purpose). It should be 4 or 5 inches from the coals. In a charcoal bucket use hickory, apple, or baywood chips, which you will find at grocery and tackle shops. There are many barbecue grills now available so you have a fine selection.

If you plan a spot away from home, get together in a large basket your implements and accessories, such as foil, tongs, spatula, iron skillet, pot holders and a hinged grill for broiling fish, paper dishes, plastic forks and towels.

In another basket put your food supplies. Look over your recipes. Keep them simple for each trip, but do change recipes often for variety. Sauces can be mixed in advance and carried to the picnic or outdoor cooking location.

Outdoor Cookery

A SEAFOOD BARBECUE is lots of fun for the whole family. It's easy and offers out-of-door recreation in which everyone can join in the preparation and fun. First, get everything ready in advance to save steps. You will need:

Heavy duty aluminum foil
A hinged grill (for fish)
An iron skillet (for fish-fry)
Tongs for turning
Pastry brush for melted butter

Swab for barbecue sauce. You can make a swab by tying several folds of cheese cloth on the handle of a wooden spoon
Heavy mitts or pot holders
Paper dishes

Now, you are ready to get down to work—or should we say "play"? Because the whole idea of outdoor cooking and eating is to put on a smile and relax.

Your dealer (or husband, in case he's a fisherman) will dress the fish for you. Rinse off in cool water, dry on paper towel and wrap in waxed paper. If recipe calls for marinating seafood this can be done the night before the outing. Then take fish to barbecue pit or picnic spot (or out to the yard) in the same dish or pan with foil over top.

Starting the Fire

1 Line the bottom of the fire bowl with heavy-duty aluminum foil. This gives additional fuel economy by reflecting the heat and makes cleaning easier.

2 If the bottom of the fire bowl is not perforated, a gravel base will permit the fire to "breathe" and give an even-heat distribution. Use enough gravel to make the bed level out to the edge of the bowl. Gravel or crushed stones ¼ to ⅜ inch in diameter will give best results.

3 Start the fire far enough in advance to get a good bed of coals before beginning to barbecue. One method, which takes about 45 minutes, is to stack briquets in a pyramid and soak lightly with a recommended lighting fluid. Let stand 1 minute, then light. Take necessary precautions when lighting the fire. **Never use gasoline!**
4 When the briquet surface is covered with a gray ash, spread the coals evenly and the fire is ready.
5 Make the charcoal layer slightly wider than the food to be cooked on the grill.
6 Wood chips give a pleasant smoky flavor to fish. Soak the chips in water at least an hour before using, so they will produce maximum smoke and not burn too rapidly. Add a few chips at a time while cooking. If chips flame up, add more wet chips.
Remember: Never overcook your fish; they contain no tough connective tissue and cook very quickly. Fish should be cooked only until they flake easily when tested with a fork.

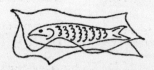

Barbecue Sauce

1 stick butter or margarine
1 clove garlic, minced
½ cup tomato catsup
¼ cup wine vinegar
2 tablespoons Worcestershire sauce
¼ cup water
1 teaspoon chili powder
1 teaspoon salt
½ teaspoon pepper
6 drops Tabasco or hot pepper sauce

Melt butter and sauté minced garlic a few minutes. Add all other ingredients and bring to a boil. Dissolve 1 teaspoon cornstarch in a little water and add to sauce. Stir until slightly thickened. Remove from heat and use to baste fish, shrimp or other seafood.

Hickory Fish Fry

Have fire high under grill with hickory in the coals. Heat lard in frying pan on grill. Salt and pepper fish and sprinkle with small amount of lemon juice. Roll in white cornmeal and fry until crisply browned on both sides. Remove to sheet of foil with paper towels on it to drain fish. If your outdoor grill has a hood, keep closed to retain hickory flavor. Serve with *Hush Puppies*.

Fish Fries Crispy

*2 pounds fish fillets or whole small
   fish, dressed*
1 cup buttermilk
1 cup white cornmeal
Bacon fat

Sprinkle fish with salt and pepper. Dip in buttermilk, then in cornmeal. Pat meal on thoroughly. Place fish in flat pan or on cooky sheet over waxed paper. Cover and take to grill or barbecue pit.

Heat bacon fat (saved from breakfast) or other fat in iron skillet on grill over light fire or turn gas grill regulator to low. Fry fish until brown on both sides. Serve with *Hush Puppies,* crisp salad and fruit-filled cookies. Serves 6.

Barbecued Halibut Steaks

*2 pounds halibut or other fish steaks,
   fresh or frozen*
¼ cup chopped onion
2 tablespoons chopped green pepper
1 clove garlic, finely chopped
2 tablespoons melted fat or oil
1 8-ounce can tomato sauce
2 tablespoons lemon juice
1 tablespoon Worcestershire sauce
1 tablespoon sugar
2 teaspoons salt
¼ teaspoon pepper

Thaw frozen steaks. Cook onion, green pepper, and garlic in fat until tender. Add remaining ingredients and simmer for 5 minutes, stirring occasionally. Cool. Cut steaks into serving-size portions and place in a single layer in a shallow baking dish. Pour sauce over fish and let stand for 30 minutes, turning once. Remove fish, reserving sauce for basting. Place fish in well-greased, hinged wire grills. Cook about 4 inches from moderately hot coals for 8 minutes. Baste with sauce. Turn and cook for 7 to 10 minutes longer or until fish flakes easily when tested with a fork. Serves 6.

Fisherman's Barbecued Mullet

2 large mullet or other fish
½ teaspoon salt

BARBECUE SAUCE

1 cup vinegar
1 cup catsup
2 tablespoons Worcestershire sauce
¼ cup butter or other fat, melted
1 small clove garlic, minced
Dash of hot pepper sauce

Remove head and backbone of fish (large size better for this way of barbecuing). Spread fish open and sprinkle with salt. Place scale side down on grill over moderately hot gas briquets or coals. Baste frequently on open sides of fish with the barbecue sauce. Grill until flesh flakes easily when tested with a fork. Allow 1 fish for each person, as this is a delicious way of preparing fish on an outdoor grill.

Barbecued Fish Smoky

2 pounds fish fillets
⅓ cup salad oil or bacon fat
Paprika to cover fish
1 large onion, sliced thin
½ small bottle catsup
½ cup pickle vinegar or vinegar and
*   water*
½ teaspoon oregano
½ teaspoon black pepper
1 teaspoon Old Hickory Smoked Salt

Grease shallow pan with part of fat and place fish in it. Mix remainder of fat with catsup and seasoning. Sprinkle paprika over fish, cover with sliced onion. Spread catsup mixture over all. Cook on lower rack of a very hot oven, 450 F, for about 10 minutes, basting often and adding water if fish becomes dry. Brown under broiler for a few minutes just before serving. This dish requires careful watching so as not to be overcooked. Serves 6.

Fish in Foil on Grill

2 pounds fish fillets, fresh or frozen
2 medium onions, sliced
2 green peppers, sliced
¼ cup butter or margarine, melted
2 tablespoons lemon or lime juice
2 teaspoons salt
1 teaspoon paprika
⅛ teaspoon pepper

Thaw frozen fillets. Cut into serving-size portions. Cut six pieces of heavy-duty aluminum foil, 12 x 12 inches each. Grease lightly. Place a portion of fish, skin side down, on foil. Top with green pepper and onion.

Combine remaining ingredients. Pour this sauce over fish. Bring the foil up over the food and close all edges with tight double folds. Make 6 packages. Place packages on a grill about 5 inches from hot coals or briquets. Cook for 45 to 60 minutes or until fish flakes easily when tested with a fork. Serves 6.

Quick Broiled Fish Steaks

4 pounds fish steaks (snapper,
*   grouper, salmon)*
¼ cup lime or lemon juice
Salt
Black pepper, freshly ground

Wash and dry fish steaks. Several hours before cooking sprinkle the fish steaks with salt and pepper. Pour over them the lime or lemon juice and set aside. When ready to grill place on hot, greased solid grill over charcoal and broil until lightly browned. Turn and broil other side. Serve with *Spanish Sauce.*

SPANISH SAUCE

¾ cup chili sauce
¼ cup tomato catsup
2 tablespoons salad oil
2 teaspoons lime or lemon juice
1 large green pepper, chopped
2 tablespoons celery seed
½ teaspoon salt
6 drops Tabasco sauce

Heat all ingredients together but do not boil. Serve with broiled fish steaks.

Grilled Red Snapper Steaks

2 pounds red snapper steaks or other
*   fish steaks, fresh or frozen*
½ cup melted fat or oil
¼ cup lemon or lime juice

2 teaspoons salt
½ teaspoon Worcestershire sauce
¼ teaspoon white pepper
6 drops Tabasco sauce
Paprika

Thaw frozen steaks. Cut into serving-size portions and place in well-greased, hinged wire grills. Combine remaining ingredients except paprika. Baste fish with sauce and sprinkle with paprika. Cook about 4 inches from moderately hot briquets or coals for 8 minutes. Baste with sauce and sprinkle with paprika. Turn and cook for 7 to 10 minutes longer or until fish flakes easily when tested with a fork. Serves 6.

Oriental Swordfish Steaks

2 pounds swordfish steaks or other
    fish steaks, fresh or frozen
¼ cup orange juice
¼ cup soy sauce
2 tablespoons catsup
2 tablespoons melted fat or oil
2 tablespoons chopped parsley
1 tablespoon lemon juice
1 clove garlic, finely chopped
½ teaspoon oregano
½ teaspoon pepper

Thaw frozen steaks. Cut into serving-size portions and place in a single layer in a shallow baking dish. Combine remaining ingredients. Pour sauce over fish and let stand for 30 minutes, turning once. Remove fish, reserving sauce for basting. Place fish in well-greased, hinged wire grills. Cook about 4 inches from moderately hot gas briquets or coals for 8 minutes. Baste with sauce. Turn and cook for 7 to 10 minutes longer or until fish flakes easily when tested with a fork. Serves 6.

Grill-Cooked Yellow Perch

2 pounds pan-dressed yellow perch
    or other fish, fresh or frozen
2 tablespoons lemon juice
2 teaspoons salt
¼ teaspoon pepper
1 pound sliced bacon

Thaw frozen fish. Clean, wash, and dry fish. Brush inside of fish with lemon juice and sprinkle with salt and pepper. Wrap each fish in a slice of bacon. Place fish in well-greased, hinged wire grills. Cook about 5 inches from moderately hot gas briquets or coals for 10 minutes. Turn and cook for 10 to 14 minutes longer or until bacon is crisp and fish flakes easily when tested with a fork. Serves 6.

Hickory-Smoked Fish

2 pounds sablefish steaks or other fish
    steaks, fresh or frozen
⅓ cup soy sauce
2 tablespoons melted fat or oil
1 tablespoon liquid smoke
1 clove garlic, finely chopped
½ teaspoon ginger

Thaw frozen steaks. Cut into serving-size portions and place in a single layer in a shallow baking dish. Combine remaining ingredients. Pour sauce over fish and let stand for 30 minutes, turning once. Remove fish, reserving sauce for basting. Place fish in well-greased, hinged wire grills. Cook about 4 inches from moderately hot gas briquets or coals for 8 minutes. Baste with sauce. Turn and cook for 7 to 10 minutes longer or until fish flakes easily when tested with a fork. Serves 6.

Grilled Fish
with Mustard Butter

2 pounds fish fillets or steaks
Salt
Paprika
⅓ cup melted butter
¼ teaspoon Tabasco sauce

Cut fillets into serving-size pieces or leave whole. Sprinkle fish with salt and paprika. Place whole fillets or serving pieces and steaks on individual pieces of aluminum foil; bring up sides of foil. Combine butter and Tabasco. Pour over fish. Secure foil tightly. Place on grill 4 inches from heat. Grill 8–10 minutes, or until moist and easily flaked with a fork. Serve with lime or lemon wedges.

FOR PAN-FRIED FISH: Dip fillets, steaks or small whole fish into milk, evaporated milk or 1 egg beaten with 2 tablespoons water. Sprinkle with salt; roll in flour or fine dry bread crumbs. Place in hot (not smoking) fat in skillet. Cook quickly about 2 to 3 minutes on each side or until moist and easily flaked with a fork. Serve with *Mustard Butter sauce.*

MUSTARD BUTTER SAUCE

1 cup sour cream
2 tablespoons prepared mustard
1 tablespoon lemon juice
1 tablespoon minced onion
1 teaspoon salt
1 teaspoon Worcestershire sauce
4 drops Tabasco sauce
Dash pepper

Combine all ingredients, blending well. Serve over hot grilled fish. Makes 1¼ cups.

Grilled Packaged Seafoods

Heat on grill the convenient cooked seafoods, such as frozen fish sticks, crab and clam sticks, fish balls, scallops, fillets, butterfly or fan-tail shrimp. Use a sheet of lightly greased aluminum foil over grill unless it is solid. Baste the seafood with melted butter or margarine to prevent drying out. Serve with *Cucumber-Sour Cream Sauce:*

CUCUMBER-SOUR CREAM SAUCE

½ cup finely diced cucumber
½ cup sour cream
¼ teaspoon salt
1 teaspoon mustard

Combine above ingredients. Chill. Serve over browned fish sticks and other cooked seafood. Sprinkle chopped green onions over top or parsley flakes or capers.

TIP: Serve with tomato and lettuce salad, a big buttered potato and a citrus dessert. Or for a quickie sauce combine ½ cup mayonnaise with 2 tablespoons catsup and 2 teaspoons lemon juice.

Broiled Panfish
with Tarragon Butter

2 whole panfish per person
Salt and pepper
Lime juice
Melted butter
Dried crushed tarragon

Dress fish but leave head and tails on. Wash and dry. Season with salt,

thoroughly. Baste kabobs with seasoned fat. Cook about 4 inches from moderately hot gas briquets or coals for 4 to 6 minutes. Baste with sauce. Turn and cook for 4 to 6 minutes longer or until fish flakes easily when tested with a fork. Serves 6.

pepper, and a squeeze or two of lime juice. Brush with a mixture of melted butter and dried crushed tarragon leaves. For 8 fish use 1 cup butter and 1 tablespoon crushed tarragon leaves.

Grease grill or use greased hinged broiler and cook fish over direct coals or gas briquets about 4–5 inches away for 3 minutes. Turn and slash skin in several places. Brush with tarragon-butter and broil 3 minutes more. Serve with more butter and lime quarters.

Grilled Fish Kabobs

2 pounds fish fillets
⅓ cup French dressing
3 large firm tomatoes
1 1-pound can whole potatoes, drained
1½ teaspoons salt
Dash pepper
⅓ cup melted fat or oil

Thaw frozen fillets. Skin fillets and cut into strips about 1 inch wide by 4 inches long. Place fish in a shallow baking dish. Pour dressing over fish and let stand for 30 minutes. Wash tomatoes. Remove stem ends and cut into sixths. Remove fish, reserving dressing for basting. Roll fillets and place on skewers alternately with tomato pieces and potatoes until skewers are filled.

Place kabobs in well-greased, hinged wire grills. Add salt, pepper, and remaining dressing to fat; mix

Wine Sauce for Grilled Fish

(Marinade and basting)
1 cup dry vermouth
¾ cup melted fat or oil
⅓ cup lemon juice
2 tablespoons chopped chives
2 teaspoons salt
1 clove garlic, finely chopped
¼ teaspoon marjoram
¼ teaspoon pepper
¼ teaspoon thyme
⅛ teaspoon sage
⅛ teaspoon Tabasco or hot pepper sauce

Combine all ingredients and pour over fish. Let stand for 4 or more hours, turning occasionally. Remove fish, reserving sauce for basting. Enough for 2 pounds fish steaks or fillets.

Tuna Barbecue

2 cans (6½ or 7 ounces each) tuna
½ cup chopped onion
2 tablespoons tuna oil
½ cup chopped celery
½ cup chopped green pepper
1 cup catsup
1 cup water
2 tablespoons brown sugar
2 tablespoons vinegar
2 tablespoons Worcestershire sauce
1 teaspoon prepared mustard
½ teaspoon salt
Dash pepper
6 hamburger rolls

Drain tuna, reserving oil. Break tuna into large pieces. Cook onion in oil until tender in a large kettle over hot briquets or coals. Add remaining ingredients except tuna and rolls. Simmer uncovered for 20 minutes, stirring frequently. Add tuna and simmer 10 minutes longer, stirring frequently. Split rolls and toast. Place approximately ½ cup tuna mixture on bottom half of roll. Cover with top half of roll. Serves 6.

Salmonburgers

1 1-pound can salmon
½ cup chopped onion
¼ cup melted fat or oil
⅓ cup salmon liquid or milk
⅓ cup dry bread crumbs
2 eggs, beaten
¼ cup chopped parsley
1 teaspoon powdered mustard
½ teaspoon salt
½ cup dry bread crumbs
⅓ cup mayonnaise or salad dressing
1 tablespoon chopped sweet pickle
6 hamburger rolls, buttered

Drain salmon, reserving liquid. Flake salmon. Cook onion in fat until tender. Add salmon liquid, crumbs, egg, parsley, mustard, salt, and salmon; mix well. Shape into 6 burgers. Roll in crumbs. Fry in hot fat in a heavy fry pan about 4 inches from hot gas briquets or coals for 3 minutes. Turn carefully and fry for 3 to 4 minutes longer or until brown. Drain on paper towel. Combine mayonnaise and pickle. Place burgers on bottom half of each roll. Top with about 1 tablespoon mayonnaise mixture and top half of roll. Serves 6.

Shrimp and Bacon on Skewer

Shrimp
Bacon
Salt
Freshly ground pepper
Worcestershire sauce

Slip the end of a strip of breakfast bacon on skewer, next impale raw shelled shrimp, then pierce the bacon again, followed by another shrimp until skewer is full. Grill until bacon is browned and shrimp are cooked. Season during cooking with salt, freshly ground pepper and Worcestershire sauce.

Shrimp-Ham Skewered

12 large cooked shrimp
12 medium mushrooms (or large pieces of pineapple)
12 pieces of boiled or baked ham, cut into cubes

SAUCE

⅔ cup tomato catsup
⅔ cup prepared mustard
½ cup soy sauce
½ teaspoon salt
¼ teaspoon freshly crushed black pepper
1 cup cracker crumbs
4 tablespoons butter for covering

Boil, shell, and devein shrimp (or use ready-to-cook frozen product, slightly defrosted and placed in boiling water for 1 minute and drained.)

For 4 persons, fill 4 skewers in this order: shrimp, pineapple or mushrooms (both may be used if desired) and ham. Start with shrimp again, etc.

Blend well all the sauce ingredients. Brush surface thickly with sauce, then coat with cracker crumbs and brush with melted butter or margarine. Cook over outdoor grill 4 inches from moderately hot gas briquets or coals. Turn and baste as needed with melted fat. Broil 5 minutes on each side.

Roasted Shrimp in Shells

Shrimp are delicious roasted. Place a sheet of aluminum foil over the grill about 3 to 4 inches from moderately hot gas briquets or coals. Spoon over foil enough melted butter or other fat to prevent scorching. Wash and dry shrimp in the shells. Place on foil and toss lightly until they turn pink and are tender. Serve with small cups of melted butter and lime quarters. Allow ½ pound shrimp for each person if they are large.

Scallops Over the Campfire

2 pounds sea scallops
½ cup butter
1 cup chopped mushrooms or 1 can
*   button mushrooms*
Lime juice
Salt, pepper, paprika

Wash and dry scallops. Place 6 scallops on each of several heavy aluminum foil squares. Top with mushrooms. Sprinkle with salt, pepper, paprika and 2 teaspoons lime juice. Wrap well, pushing out any air from packages. Place packages in hot coals at edge of fire. Bake 30 minutes. To

serve, slash foil in a cross at top with sharp knife.

TIP: Have a baked potato, green salad and dunking sauce to go with scallops.

Scallops Hawaiian

2 pounds sea scallops
½ cup butter
1 cup drained pineapple chunks
Salt, pepper, paprika
Lemon juice

Wash and dry scallops. Place 6 scallops on each of several aluminum foil squares. Top with pineapple. Sprinkle with salt, pepper, paprika, and 2 teaspoons lemon juice. Wrap well, pushing out any air from packages. Place in hot coals at edge of fire. Bake 30 minutes. To serve, slash foil in a cross at top with sharp knife.

Scallop Kabobs

1 pound scallops
1 13½-ounce can pineapple chunks,
*   drained*
1 4-ounce can button mushrooms,
*   drained*
1 green pepper, cut into 1-inch
*   squares*
¼ cup melted fat or oil
¼ cup lemon juice
¼ cup chopped parsley
¼ cup soy sauce
½ teaspoon salt
Dash pepper
12 slices bacon

Thaw frozen scallops. Rinse with cold water to remove any shell particles. Place pineapple, mushrooms, green pepper and scallops in a bowl. Combine fat, lemon juice, parsley, soy sauce, salt and pepper. Pour sauce over scallop mixture and let stand for 30 minutes, stirring occasionally. Fry bacon until partly cooked but not crisp. Cut each slice in half. Using long skewers, alternate scallops, pineapple, mushrooms, green pepper and bacon until skewers are filled. Cook about 4 inches from moderately hot gas briquets or coals for 5 minutes. Baste with sauce. Turn and cook for 5 to 7 minutes longer or until bacon is crisp. Serves 6.

Tasty Grilled Soft-Shell Crabs

12 dressed soft-shell blue crabs, fresh or frozen
¾ cup chopped parsley
½ cup melted fat or oil
1 teaspoon lemon or lime juice
¼ teaspoon nutmeg
¼ teaspoon soy sauce
Dash liquid hot pepper sauce
Lemon wedges

Thaw frozen crabs. Clean, wash, and dry crabs. Place crabs in well-greased, hinged wire grills. Combine remaining ingredients except lemon wedges. Heat. Baste crabs with sauce. Cook about 4 inches from moderately hot coals for 8 minutes. Baste with sauce. Turn and cook 7 to 10 minutes longer or until lightly browned. Serve with lemon wedges. Serves 6.

Grilled King-Crab Legs

3 12-ounce packages precooked, frozen king-crab legs
½ cup butter or margarine, melted
2 tablespoons lemon or lime juice
½ teaspoon paprika
Melted butter or margarine

Thaw frozen crab legs. Combine butter, lemon juice, and paprika. Baste crab meat with sauce. Place crab legs on a grill, flesh side down, about 4 inches from moderately hot gas briquets or coals. Heat for 5 minutes. Turn and baste with sauce. Heat 5 to 7 minutes longer. Serve with melted butter. Serves 6.

Stuffed King-Crab Legs

3 12-ounce packages precooked, frozen king-crab legs
1 4-ounce can mushroom stems and pieces, drained
2 tablespoons melted fat or oil
2 tablespoons flour
½ teaspoon salt
1 cup milk
½ cup grated cheese
Paprika

Thaw frozen crab legs. Remove meat from shells. Remove any cartilage and cut meat into ½-inch pieces. Cook mushrooms in fat for 5 minutes. Blend in flour and salt. Add milk gradually and cook until thick, stirring constantly. Add cheese and crabmeat; heat. Fill shells with crab mixture. Sprinkle with paprika. Place stuffed crab legs on a grill, shell side down, about 4 inches from moderately hot coals. Heat for 10 to 12 minutes. Serves 6.

Oyster Roast

36 shell oysters
Melted butter or margarine

Wash oyster shells thoroughly. Place oysters on a grill about 4 inches from hot gas briquets or coals. Roast for 10 to 15 minutes or until shells begin to open. Serve in shells with melted butter. Serves 6.

Grilled Spiny-Lobster Tails

6 spiny-lobster tails (8 ounces each),
fresh or frozen
¼ cup butter or margarine, melted
2 tablespoons lemon or lime juice
½ teaspoon salt
Melted butter or margarine

Thaw frozen lobster tails. Cut in half lengthwise. Remove swimmerettes and sharp edges. Cut 6 pieces of heavy duty aluminum foil, 12 × 12 inches each. Place each lobster tail on foil. Combine butter, lemon or lime juice, and salt. Baste lobster meat with sauce. Bring the foil up over the lobster and close all edges with tight double folds. Make 6 packages. Place on a grill, shell side down, about 5 inches from briquets or hot coals. Cook for 20 minutes. Remove lobster tails from the foil. Place lobster tails on grill, flesh side down, and cook for 2 to 3 minutes longer or until lightly browned. Serve with more melted butter. Serves 6.

Steamed Clams Outdoor Style

6 clams per person (small hard-shell
clams, in the shell)
melted butter
Lemon or lime wedges

Scrub clams well under cold running water. Soak in cold salted water to remove the sand. Place unopened clams on aluminum foil on a grill. Low to medium setting or medium-hot coals is best for clams. Shells pop open when clams are ready for eating. Serve with melted butter and lemon or lime wedges.

New England Clambake

6 dozen steamer clams
12 small onions
6 medium baking potatoes
6 ears of corn in the husks
6 live lobsters (1 pound each)
Rockweed (optional)
Lemon or lime wedges
Melted butter

Wash clam shells thoroughly. Peel onions and wash potatoes. Parboil onions and potatoes for 15 minutes; drain. Turn back husks, remove corn silk, and replace husks.

Cut 12 pieces of cheesecloth and 12 pieces of heavy-duty aluminum foil, 18 × 36 inches each. Place 2 pieces of cheesecloth on top of 2 pieces of foil. Place 2 onions, a potato, an ear of corn, a lobster, 1 dozen clams and rockweed on cheesecloth. Tie opposite corners of cheesecloth together. Pour 1 cup of water over the package. Bring foil up over the food and close all edges with tight double folds. Make 6 packages.

Place packages on a grill about 4 inches from hot gas briquets or coals. Cover with hood or aluminum foil. Cook for 45 to 60 minutes, or until onions and potatoes are tender. Open packages and crack lobster claws. Serve with lemon or lime wedges and melted butter. Serves 6.

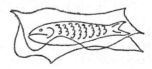

Good Things to Fix with Seafood on the Grill

*

BARBECUED FRUITS AND VEGETABLES

Foil-Roasted Potatoes/Onions

Scrub required number of potatoes and brush with salad oil. Wrap each in double thickness of heavy aluminum foil, overlapping ends. Cook potatoes on hot grill until tender (about 1 hour). Turn potatoes about every 10 minutes.

NOTE: If desired, cut potatoes lengthwise into 3 slices, brush slices with butter and sprinkle with seasonings before wrapping in foil.

Toppings for roasted potatoes:

Sour cream, chopped parsley and
   desired seasonings
Cream cheese, sour cream and desired
   seasonings
Chopped olives and sour cream
Crumbled, crisp bacon
Sautéed sliced mushrooms
Grated cheddar cheese
Chopped chives
Sautéed chopped onion

Onions are also delicious when foil roasted. Cook the same as potatoes except use butter instead of cooking oil. Cook about 45 minutes.

Foil-Roasted Shoestring Potatoes

2 pieces (48 inches each)
  heavy aluminum foil

4 potatoes (about 6 ounces each),
  pared
3 tablespoons butter
1½ teaspoons salt
¼ teaspoon pepper
2 tablespoons chopped onion
  (optional)
½ cup grated, sharp, processed
  American cheese
3 tablespoons chopped parsley
½ teaspoon paprika
½ cup light cream

Fold aluminum foil, crosswise, for a double thickness. Cut potatoes in lengthwise strips as for French fried potatoes, and place on one piece of foil. Dot with butter; sprinkle with salt, pepper, onion, cheese, parsley and paprika. Pull edges of foil upward and pour cream over mixture. Put remaining folded piece of foil over food; seal all 4 sides tightly with double folds. Cook on hot grill until done (1 to 1¼ hours); turn package about every 10 minutes. Serves 4.

Roast Corn, Indian Style

Turn back husks and strip off silk. Lay husks back in position. Soak ears in cold water for 5 minutes. Line ears up on grill over hot coals. Keep turning ears frequently. Cook 15 to 20 minutes, or till husks are dry and browned. Corn will look sun-tanned. For browner, sweeter corn, continue roasting it to suit your own taste. Dunking ears in a pail of water occasionally will keep the kernels moist and tender. To serve, break off husks. Now, on with plenty of butter, salt, and pepper.

Corn in Foil

If desired, corn may be husked, brushed with melted butter and sprinkled with salt and pepper. Wrap each ear securely in heavy aluminum foil. Roast on hot grill 20 to 40 minutes; turn about every 10 minutes.

Green Beans

Use 1 can (about 16 ounces) cut or whole green beans. Add 1 cup almond slivers, salt and freshly ground pepper. Mix well in a mixing bowl. Put individual servings in double thickness of aluminum foil. Add a teaspoon of butter to each serving, wrap foil completely around and seal edges. 20 minutes cooking time. Turn often.

Campfire Frozen Vegetables

Place a block of frozen vegetables on a double thickness of heavy aluminum foil. Season with salt, pepper and butter. Bring edges of foil together; wrap to provide space for steam expansion and seal with double folds. Cook on hot grill until done (about 20 minutes); turn package after 10 minutes' cooking. Cooking in their own juices gives the vegetables a truly succulent flavor.

Candied Sweet Potatoes

Use 1 whole canned sweet potato per serving. Cut each potato lengthwise and lay 2 halves on double thickness of aluminum foil with flat side of potato up. Put 4 wedges of sliced orange on top of each potato. Do not remove orange peel. Add 1 tablespoon of brown sugar, a dash of cinnamon, and a few dabs of butter to each and fold foil completely around. Seal edges of foil by creasing and folding. 30 minutes cooking time.

Baked Apples in Foil

6 large apples
6 squares (double thickness) heavy aluminum foil
Orange marmalade
½ cup chopped nuts
Lemon juice

Core apples and pare upper halves. Place on foil squares. Fill centers with orange marmalade and walnuts. Sprinkle with lemon juice. Bring foil up loosely over apples and seal with double folds. Cook apples on hot grill (25 to 45 minutes); turn about every 10 minutes. Serves 6.

Barbecued Bananas

Buy firm ripe bananas and peel, 1 per person. Place 2 bananas on a double thickness of aluminum foil. Squirt lemon juice on top of bananas and sprinkle generously with brown sugar. A sprinkle of cinnamon or nutmeg will add a pleasant spicy flavor. Put on a few dabs of butter and fold foil over tops and seal edges. 8 minutes should be ample cooking time.

Recipes for a Crowd

SEAFOOD FOR A CROWD

QUANTITY TO PURCHASE

THE SAME GAUGE used in purchasing fish in smaller amounts applies when planning for a crowd. When serving steaks, fillets or sticks, use ⅓ pound per person or 30 pounds per 100 people; ½ pound of dressed fish per person or 45 pounds per 100 people. When purchased in the round or whole, allow 1 pound fish per person or 90 pounds per 100.

PURCHASING CANNED FISH

Servings of canned fish, such as salmon, are usually based on a 1-pound can to serve 6, or 16 to 24 cans per 100 people. However, much depends on how the fish is to be served, whether in a casserole, cakes or salad.

PURCHASING FROZEN FISH

Frozen fish should be delivered still frozen and should be kept frozen until time to thaw just before preparing. (When barely limp, fish is thawed enough to cook.) Once the fish thaws it should be used immediately. Never refreeze fish.

Dressed frozen fish, fillets, and steaks may be cooked as if they were in the unfrozen form; however, additional cooking time must be allowed. When fish are to be breaded and fried, or stuffed, it is more convenient to thaw them first to permit easier handling. Thawing is necessary for the cleaning and dressing of whole or drawn fish.

All other suggestions given throughout the book on handling and preparation of seafood apply when cooking for a crowd.

Here are some quantity recipes that will serve 25 to 100 people.

Shellfish Cocktail Sauce for a Crowd

1 quart catsup
1 cup vinegar or lemon juice
½ cup horseradish, grated
1 tablespoon salt
½ tablespoon Tabasco sauce
1 pint celery, finely chopped
or
2 tablespoons celery seeds

Mix all ingredients thoroughly. Chill. Serve with shellfish cocktails or *Seafood Tidbits*. Serves 50.

Seafood Tidbits for a Crowd

Number of fish sticks and scallops should be on the packages. If only sticks are used and each cut into 3 pieces, it will be easy to estimate amount needed. Allow 3 pieces and 1 or 2 scallops for each person. Serve on paper plates with muffin paper cups for sauce. Serves 50.

Arrange frozen precooked fish sticks and scallops in single layer on cooky sheets. Heat in hot oven, 425 F, 15 minutes. Cut each stick into 3 pieces. Squeeze lemon juice over all. Slide in broiler 3 to 5 minutes to crisp coating. Serve with a cocktail sauce.

Cottage Cheese-Olive Canapés for a Crowd

4 cups creamed cottage cheese
1 cup olive spread or chopped olives
2 teaspoons grated onion
Pimento (optional)
Thin sliced bread or crackers

Mix cottage cheese with chopped olives and onion. Toast bread triangles and spread with soft butter or margarine. Place a mound of cheese on toast. Garnish with pimento, or mix small amount of chopped pimento in with cheese mixture for color and serve on crackers.

Neptune Dip for a Crowd

4 7-ounce cans minced clams
4 6-ounce packages cream cheese
1 tablespoon Worcestershire sauce
2 tablespoons onion, grated
1 tablespoon salt
¼ cup lemon juice
2 tablespoons parsley, chopped
Potato chips

1. Drain clams. Save liquor.
2. Soften cheese at room temperature.
3. Combine all ingredients except potato chips and liquor and blend into a paste.
4. Gradually add some of the liquor and beat until consistency of whipped cream.
5. Chill. Serve in a bowl surrounded by potato chips.
6. Or for a school party, spread on crackers, reducing the amount of liquor added in recipe to allow easy spreading. Serves 50.

Pickled Herring

4 (1 pound) salt herring
1½ teaspoons allspice
4 bay leaves
1 teaspoon ginger
1 teaspoon mustard seed
2 teaspoons prepared horseradish
4 cups sliced sweet red onion
2 cups white vinegar
½ cup sugar

Cut off heads and clean herring. Refrigerate in cold water, covered, overnight. Drain and remove all bones; then cut herring crosswise into ½-inch slices.

Pour into a saucepan ⅔ cup water and add all ingredients except herring. Cook and stir over low heat until sugar is dissolved. Cover and boil 5 minutes. Let stand at room temperature until cool.

In two 1-quart jars, alternate layer of herring pieces and pickling mixture with onion slices until all are well distributed. Cover and refrigerate, several days. Serve herring in the pickling mixture. Makes 2 quarts.

Shrimp Relish for a Crowd

9 pounds shrimp, large, cleaned
    and cooked
4 cups onion, minced
4 cups parsley, snipped
3 cups salad oil
1⅓ cups vinegar
4 cloves garlic, minced
2 tablespoons salt
1 tablespoon pepper

1. Several hours before serving time, combine in a bowl the shrimp, onion and parsley.

2. In a bowl mix other ingredients. Pour over shrimp.

3. Refrigerate at least 1 hour or until ready to serve.

4. Place in serving dish and let guests spear with toothpicks. Serves 50.

Fish Flake Spread or Salad for a Crowd

10 7-ounce cans fish flakes
1 dozen apples, chopped
7 eggs, hard-cooked and diced
2 cups celery, chopped
2 cups sweet pickles, diced
1 pint mayonnaise or salad dressing

1. Drain fish flakes and separate with a fork.

2. Combine other ingredients with fish and serve on crackers. Or serve as a salad on lettuce. Serves 50.

Potato-Shrimp Salad for a Crowd

4 pounds potatoes
4 pounds shrimp, boiled
2 cups celery, cut fine
4 whole pimento, diced
6 green onions, sliced fine
1½ dozen eggs, hard-cooked
4 tablespoons olive oil
Dash monosodium glutenate
1 tablespoon salt
½ cup prepared mustard
1 quart mayonnaise

1. Boil potatoes and dice while hot. Cut shrimp and chop eggs, reserving 6 for garnish.

2. Add other ingredients at once.

3. Chill and garnish. Serves 25.

Scallop Salad for a Crowd

8 pounds bay scallops
1 tablespoon salt
1 pint onion, chopped
1 clove garlic
1 quart French-dressing
¾ quart celery, chopped
¾ quart pickles, chopped
1 pint mayonnaise
Lettuce

1. Drain and rinse scallops.
2. Drop into boiling water and add salt, onion and garlic.
3. Cook for 10 minutes.
4. Drain and chill.
5. Dice scallops and marinate in French dressing for one hour.
6. Combine with celery, pickles and mayonnaise and serve on crisp lettuce. Garnish with cucumber pickles. Serves 50.

Tuna-Chinese Noodle Salad

6 7-ounce cans solid-pack tuna
2 cups sliced celery
½ cup chopped green pepper
½ cup chopped pimento
½ cup minced onion
2 teaspoons salt
½ teaspoon white pepper
½ cup lemon juice
1 cup chow mein noodles

1. Drain tuna but reserve the liquid.
2. Combine tuna, celery, green pepper, pimento, onion, salt and pepper.
3. Refrigerate with tuna liquid. Before serving time combine 4 tablespoons reserved tuna liquid with lemon juice.

4. Pour over tuna mixture; then add chow mein noodles and toss. Mayonnaise to bind may be added if needed. Serves 25.

TIP: This is delicious served with a spoonful of cottage cheese on a ring of tomato aspic.

Oven-Fried Fillets for a Crowd

15 pounds fish fillets
¼ cup salt
1 quart milk
1 quart bread crumbs
1 pound margarine

1. Salt fish fillets.
2. Dip in milk.
3. Roll in bread crumbs.
4. Place in buttered baking pan and dot generously with butter.
5. Bake in moderate oven 350 F until golden brown. Serve with *Catsup Sauce.* Serves 50.

CATSUP SAUCE

1 quart catsup
½ pint lemon juice
1 pint celery, finely chopped
½ cup horseradish, grated
1 tablespoon salt
½ tablespoon Tabasco sauce

Mix all ingredients thoroughly and chill. Serves 50.

Rock and Rolls for a Crowd

15 pounds fish fillets
2 tablespoons salt
½ tablespoon pepper
¾ pound bacon, sliced (optional)
Bread stuffing for Rock and Rolls

1. Remove skin and cut fillets into serving size portions. Season.

2. Place a small roll of *Bread Stuffing for Rock and Rolls* on each piece of fish.

3. Roll fish around stuffing and fasten with toothpicks or skewers.

4. Place rolls in well-greased baking pans and lay one-third slice of bacon on the top of each.

5. Bake in moderate oven, 350 F for about 30 minutes.

6. Remove fastenings, garnish and serve immediately, plain or with a sauce. Serves 50.

Bread Stuffing for Rock and Rolls

1 pint onions, chopped
1 pint celery, chopped
1 pound butter or other fat, melted
4 pounds bread crumbs, soft
½ cup lemon juice
1¼ tablespoons salt
¼ tablespoon pepper
2 tablespoons poultry or fish seasoning
½ cup parsley, chopped

1. Fry onions and celery in fat until tender but not too brown.

2. Combine all ingredients and mix well. If too dry, a small amount of water or stock may be added. Enough for 50 *Rock and Rolls.*

Salmon Loaf for a Crowd

24 1-pound cans salmon
1 quart celery, diced
1 quart onions, diced
1 pound butter or other fat
2 quarts milk and salmon liquor
1 gallon bread crumbs, soft
2 tablespoons salt
½ tablespoon pepper
1 pint lemon juice
2 dozen eggs, beaten

1. Drain salmon, reserve liquor, remove bones and skin, flake.

2. Fry celery and onions in melted fat until tender but not brown.

3. Combine all ingredients and mix well.

4. Shape into loaves and place in well-greased baking pans.

5. Bake in a moderate oven, 350 F, for about 1 hour, or until slightly brown.

6. Serve with a rich, colorful sauce. Servings: 100—approximately 6 ounces each.

This recipe yields 100 servings of approximately 5 ounces each or 2 cakes. Claw meat, which is cheaper, may be used instead of white flake meat.

Crab Cakes for a Crowd

24 pounds crabmeat
1½ pounds butter or other fat
¾ quart onion, chopped
2 quarts bread crumbs
2 dozen eggs, well beaten
½ cup mustard, dry
4 tablespoons salt
2 tablespoons pepper
1 pound flour

1. Remove any shell or cartilage from the crabmeat.

2. Melt butter, add chopped onions and cook until tender and brown.

3. Mix crabmeat, onions, bread crumbs, beaten eggs and seasonings.

4. Form into small cakes and roll in flour.

5. Place one layer at a time in basket and fry in deep fat heated to 375 F 2 or 3 minutes until browned.

6. Drain on absorbent paper and serve immediately with a sauce.

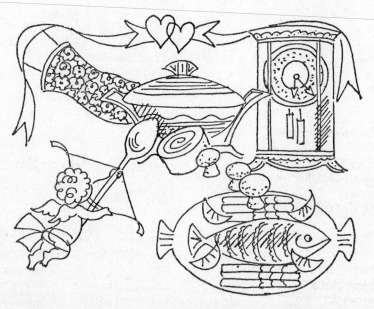

Brides—Just for You!

WHEN YOU GET SETTLED in your home and begin planning meals, remember that you have a most important job. It is something no one else can do as well as you. Be creative and happy. Remember a smile is the most important ingredient.

The following recipes have been prepared for your convenience. They are easy to cook and we know you will receive lots of compliments. When family and guests come for dinner, double or triple the amounts. You can use all the recipes in the other sections of the book, by cutting amounts in half or less.

Fish and shellfish have high nutritive value. An average portion of fish or shellfish provides nearly all the animal protein you need each day to help build and repair body tissue. In addition, fish are valuable sources of iodine, calcium, iron, copper, and phosphorus—and also supply essential vitamins. Since fish is easily digested, it is good for everyone.

Remember, to give your budget life, serve fish several times a week.

Use the convenient frozen and canned seafoods, when fresh are not available. Always read and follow package instructions. Experts have put them there, so when we follow their advice results are always satisfactory.

Good luck and good cooking!

Hints

- For 2 persons buy:

1 pound fish fillets or steaks
2 pounds whole fish (enough for 2
  meals)
1 pound of shrimp in the shell

½ pint oysters, clams, or scallops
1 lobster
1 pint or pound of cooked crabmeat
  (enough for 2 meals)

- Do not overcook fish, shrimp, scallops, clams or oysters, or other seafoods. All require short cooking periods, just until the flesh is opaque. Fish is done when it flakes easily when tested with a fork.
- Add a sliced lemon or lime to salted water in which fish and shrimp are boiled. Also, for a spicy flavor, add a tablespoon of vinegar and of pickling spices, either loose in the water, tied in a piece of cheesecloth, or placed in a tea ball.
- Use cooked rice mixed with plumped raisins for delicious whole fish stuffing. Needs no trussing. Chopped ripe olives (¼ cup) or canned mushrooms may be used instead of raisins for a change. (To plump the raisins put them in boiling water to cover until they plump up and are slightly softened.)
- Poach (just like eggs) any surplus fish you may have. Drain and flake from bones and skin and use in recipes calling for cooked, flaked fish. Fish flakes freeze well, too.
- Sprinkle the corn meal coating with a dash of cinnamon before frying panfish. Delicious!
- Mix a spoonful of grated American cheese in the flour when you roll scallops or oysters for frying.
- After shelling and deveining marinate shrimp in thin French dressing with a clove of minced gàrlic for an hour or longer before frying or broiling.
- Pan broiling shelled shrimp in a little melted butter is quick and easy. After shrimp are removed to platter, add salt, pepper and 2 tablespoons lemon juice to pan. Heat and pour over the little pinkies. Good!
- When using canned crabmeat, especially the big chunks of king crabmeat, be sure to drain off every bit of the liquid before adding meat to the dish you are preparing.

- For a quick delicious salad, open a can of white-meat chunk tuna and a can of white asparagus tips. Place some of both on lettuce leaf and top with finely chopped pecans or walnuts. Pass mayonnaise sprinkled lightly with paprika.
- Add to a crabmeat casserole some slivers of boiled or baked ham. It will stretch the casserole and is good, too.
- Slice a lemon into fresh tomatoes when you stew them. Pour stewed tomatoes over cooked seafoods, such as crabmeat, and serve with cooked rice.
- Make hush puppies very tiny. Use a teaspoon for measurement. Drop them into hot fat where fish was fried, or just fry in ½ inch of fat and serve with cooked vegetables.
- Make up hush-puppy batter. Dip fish fillets or steaks in it and fry as usual. Makes fish and hush puppies all in one.

Boiling is the basic way to cook shrimp. Peel before or after cooking, as you prefer. The only difference is more water and salt are needed if shrimp are boiled in the shell.

For two buy 1 pound, or get more to prepare for two meals.

Do NOT OVERCOOK: *boil shrimp 3 minutes (after placing in boiling, seasoned water) if shelled, 5 minutes if not shelled.*

Spicy Lemon Shrimp

1 pound fresh or frozen shrimp in
   shells
3 cups water
1 tablespon salt
2 tablespoons lemon juice (or 1
   lemon sliced)
1 teaspoon pickling spices

Combine water, salt, lemon juice (or sliced lemon) and pickling spices. When water boils add shrimp. Cover. At second boiling point turn heat down and simmer for 5 minutes. Drain.

When cool enough shell shrimp. Cut shrimp down the back and wash out the vein. Chill and serve in a salad or as a cocktail with easy *White Cap Cocktail Sauce.* Serves 2.

White Cap Cocktail Sauce

1 cup mayonnaise
⅓ cup whipped cream (or
   commercial sour cream)
1 teaspoon pepper sauce, such as
   Tabasco
3 or 4 drops garlic juice

Combine all ingredients. Chill and serve in a small bowl, with *Spicy Lemon Shrimp.* Serves 2.

Clam-Celery Crunch

2 stalks celery
4 tablespoons cottage cheese
2 tablespoons cream cheese
1 7-ounce can minced clams, drained
⅛ teaspoon salt
Dash white pepper
Paprika

Cream together the two cheeses. Add clams, salt and pepper. Stuff celery and cut into portions. Sprinkle top with paprika. Serves 2.

Bride's Bouquet Salad

¼ package prepared mixed salad
  greens
½ cucumber, sliced
½ tomato, cut into wedges
1 cup small cooked shrimp
1 hard-cooked egg, quartered
¼ cup chopped celery
2 tablespoons chopped green onion

Mix all ingredients and toss with 1 tablespoon wine vinegar and 1 tablespoon olive oil (or use bottled Italian Salad Dressing). Serves 2.

Home-for-Lunch Sandwiches

½ cup flaked cooked fish
1 teaspoon lemon juice
½ apple, chopped
¼ cup pecans, chopped
½ cup chopped celery
¼ teaspoon salt
⅛ teaspoon pepper
3 tablespoons mayonnaise

Pour lemon juice over fish flakes and add other ingredients. Moisten with mayonnaise or salad dressing. Spread on buttered bread. Trim edges of sandwich and serve with seedless raisins.

TIP: A bowl of hot canned or frozen clam chowder is good with these sandwiches. Iced tea or milk, and lemon cream cookies, will complete the luncheon menu.

EASY BAKED FISH

If you purchase a whole fish to bake, we suggest it weigh 2 or 3 pounds. When you bake the fish serve only half of it at one meal. Flake the flesh from bones and skin of the other half, and refrigerate or freeze for use later. (Use in any recipe calling for cooked flaked fish, fish flakes, or canned fish.)

Have the dealer dress a whole fish, removing head, fins and tail, if you wish. When you get home, rinse the fish in cool water. Drain and dry with a paper towel. Place in a shallow bakeproof dish or baking pan. Sprinkle generously with salt and pepper inside and out. Pour over the fish 3 tablespoons lemon juice or ¼ cup thin French dressing. Let it stand in the refrigerator until ready to bake.

Preheat oven to 425 F and bake fish 10 minutes per pound. If you have a 3-pound fish bake 30 minutes.

Serve piping hot in same utensil with canned or cooked vegetables around fish. Place a pat of butter on vegetables and sprinkle with salt and pepper.

Seafood-Ham-Asparagus on Toast

4 thin slices of boiled or baked ham
1 can condensed cream of asparagus soup
1 cup cooked fish flakes (canned are fine) or chopped shrimp, crab or lobster meat, drained
4 slices toast

Heat the ham in a hot oven, 400 F, for about 3 minutes. Don't let it get dry. Heat soup, undiluted, in a saucepan and add the fish flakes or other seafood. Place a slice of toast on each plate; top with a slice of ham, then spoon the sauce over the top. Serves 4.

TIP: With this quick luncheon dish, serve lettuce and tomato salad or a mixed citrus salad, with apple or cherry tarts for dessert.

Cheesy Clams and Eggs

½ cup minced clams (drain, if canned)
2 tablespoons butter or margarine
¼ cup cheese (cut into small pieces)
2 eggs
½ teaspoon salt
¼ teaspoon freshly cracked black pepper

Melt butter in small skillet. Stir in cheese and heat until melted. In small bowl break eggs. Add salt, pepper and drained clams. Pour into skillet over cheese and stir vigorously with a fork. When eggs are set, turn out onto a heated platter.

TIP: Serve with sliced tomatoes, little green peas and hot biscuits. Cherry pie would be good for dessert.

Scallops with Super Sauce

7–8 breaded scallops per person (can be bought frozen)
1 cup sour cream
½ cup mayonnaise
1 tablespoon horseradish
2 tablespoons chopped stuffed or ripe olives (sometimes use dill pickle)
¼ teaspoon salt
⅛ teaspoon pepper
Paprika

Fry scallops, drain and keep warm. Make sauce by combining all ingredients except paprika. Serve sauce with paprika sprinkled over top, either hot or cold. If you heat it, be sure not to let it boil—just heat thoroughly. It is good cold as a different kind of tartare sauce. Enough for 4.

TIP: This sauce is also good with fish sticks.

Bride's Quick Fish and Spaghetti

1 cup cooked fish flakes, fresh or canned
2 cups spaghetti
2 tablespoons butter
2 tablespoons chopped green pepper
1 can cream of tomato soup

Cook spaghetti according to directions on package. Drain. Melt butter in skillet and cook green pepper until tender. Add soup, fish flakes and spaghetti. Cook over low heat 7 minutes. Serves 4.

In this recipe you may use canned fish flakes, any kind of leftover cooked fish, or fish poached and flaked as described in the section of fish flakes.

TIP: With a crisp green salad, buttered pull bread and fresh fruit or gelatine dessert, you have a real "quickie" meal.

Special for Brides

*

RECIPE FOR HAPPINESS

Take one man, one woman and a number of children.

This last ingredient isn't absolutely necessary, but it adds greatly to the over-all flavor. Start with a strong determination for marriage success.

Add companionship, democracy, understanding. Mix well with uncountable measures of admiration, trust and courtesy. Blend in common interests and family fun.

Create a homy atmosphere with the aroma of newly baked apple pies and bread, requiring lots of time in the kitchen. Sprinkle with the smallest amount possible of tears and heartaches.

Cover with kind tenderness, a deep religious faith, and keep warm with a steady degree of love. Garnish with smiles and hearty laughter. Dash with kisses for the hurt places. Create happiness. Remember it can't be bought, found nor given to us. Served this way, there will be calls for second helpings.

Index